52 Texas Weekends

52 Texas Weekends

GREAT GETAWAYS AND ADVENTURES FOR EVERY SEASON

PATRICIA SCOTT

COUNTRY ROADS PRESS

NTC/Contemporary Publishing Group

Library of Congress Cataloging-in-Publication Data

Scott, Patricia.
    52 Texas weekends : great getaways and adventures for every season /
Patricia Scott.
        p.   cm. — (52 weekends)
    Includes index.
    ISBN 0-8442-4299-3
    1. Texas Guidebooks.   I. Title.   II. Title: Fifty-two Texas weekends.
III. Series.
F384.3.S36   1999
917.6'40463—dc21   99-26796
                                                          CIP

Cover and interior design by Nick Panos
Cover and interior illustrations copyright © Jill Banashek
Map by Mapping Specialists, Madison, Wisconsin
Picture research by Elizabeth Broadrup Lieberman and Jill Birschbach

Published by Country Roads Press
A division of NTC/Contemporary Publishing Group, Inc.
4255 West Touhy Avenue, Lincolnwood (Chicago), Illinois 60712-1975 U.S.A.
Copyright © 2000 by Patricia Scott
Printed in the United States of America
International Standard Book Number: 0-8442-4299-3
00 01 02 03 04 05 QV 18 17 16 15 14 13 12 11 10 9 8 7 6 5 4 3 2 1

For my family

Contents

Winter

Spring

Summer

Fall

Acknowledgments

A NOTE OF THANKS IS IN ORDER TO ALL THE PEOPLE WHO HAVE helped make this book possible. Thanks to all those at the Texas Parks and Wildlife, Texas Department of Transportation, Texas Tourism Division, and Texas state employees who maintain and operate parks, museums, and other attractions, plus answer questions. A special thanks to all the friendly Texans encountered along the way and to city employees running the local chamber or tourism bureau. Thanks to all those at NTC/Contemporary Books, who meticulously read and edited this book. Last but certainly not least, thanks to friends and family for all your support and suggestions.

Introduction

THIS BOOK BEGAN WITH MEMORIES OF MY PARENTS' OLD white station wagon, the interstate highways before they grew to four paved lanes crisscrossing the state, Astroworld when it first opened in the middle of farmland, a train ride through Texas, ball games in the Astrodome, days on Padre Island beach collecting shells, shopping for bargains in Mexican markets, and lunch at the top of the Tower of Americas during the '68 HemisFair. When I think about traveling, the adventures in the old station wagon with my five brothers and sisters, and occasionally the dog, come to mind. My parents instilled a sense of adventure in me. Today, I pack my children in the car when I can for our own journeys. But sometimes I leave the young ones at home.

Over the years I have become acquainted with Texas, having lived in Houston, Pasadena, San Antonio, Corpus Christi, Angleton, Alice, and Nacogdoches. Although I have lived in other states, my heart has always belonged to Texas. In Texas you can find beaches, mountains, deserts, plains, forests, swamps, islands, small towns, and a few of the largest cities in the country. In Texas you can go mountain climbing, camp at the top of a canyon, hike through forests, explore caves, surf, sail, fish, and scuba dive. In Texas you can taste authentic Mexican food in the southwest or Cajun cooking in the southeast, take a look at dinosaur tracks, see forts built during frontier days, and examine mysterious mounds left by ancient civilizations.

In Texas you can enjoy the best in opera, theater, and symphony. Shop the cities, Mexican markets, and some of the largest flea markets in the country. See where some of your favorite movies were filmed. Find a cure for what ails you. Golf some of the most scenic courses in the country. Search for the past left behind in ghost towns. See the real Southfork Ranch from the television series *Dallas*. Watch thousands of butterflies emerge from their chrysalis for their first flight south. Take a couple wild nights at a rodeo or Mardi Gras. Catch a rattlesnake, and then have it made into a belt to wear. Spend the night underneath the stars.

This book will introduce you to many wonders unique to Texas. Starting with the New Year, you can take 52 weekend adventures. Inside you will find adventures for every season and every part of the state. Some sections have a central theme and give you a choice of what area of the state you want to visit. Other sections are focused on a particular place. These weekend journeys can be enjoyed as a family, as a couple, or on your own. For people who like to drive, Texas provides a lot of highway. Considering the limited amount of time in a weekend, you can either choose a place close to where you live or combine flying and driving. For those who prefer to fly, Texas has several airports servicing all areas of the state. Trains also still serve many parts of Texas and can become an interesting part of your weekend.

So, pack your bags and start making memories of your own.

52 Texas Weekends

Winter

1

Start the New Year Off with Warmth

PADRE ISLAND

THE BEAUTIFUL BEACHES OF SOUTH PADRE ISLAND PROVIDE year-round warmth to visitors. Many northerners flock to Padre Island and the lower Rio Grande Valley every year to escape the cold weather. Padre Island, named for a Spanish priest, is said to be the longest barrier island in the world, 113 miles of sand.

The island extends from Corpus Christi to the Mexican border with most of the island designated as the National Seashore. Swimming, camping, bird-watching, surfing, shelling, and fishing are what attracts visitors. An 80-mile stretch of the National Seashore is accessible only to four-wheel-drive vehicles, three-wheel dune motorcycles, hikers, or charter boats from Port Mansfield, Port Isabel, and Port Aransas. The beaches in this area may not be as clean as they are in more developed areas, and trash washing up on the shore isn't cleaned up as often. While surfers enjoy the Gulf of Mexico, it doesn't have the huge breakers of the Pacific Ocean or the North Atlantic.

The towns of Port Isabel and South Padre Island are good places to look for accommodations. Port Isabel, which used to be a small fishing village, has turned into a seaside resort community. The towns of Port Isabel and South Padre are joined by a causeway built in the 1950s. High school and college students flock to the island during spring break. January would be a good time to visit the island without running into spring breakers. With the right accommodations, a cool January day can be an ideal time to sit in front of the fireplace with the crashing waves of the Gulf Coast in view outside your window.

Besides the round of spring breakers in March, each February is the Border Surf and Citrus 100, an organized bike ride that combines the roads on South Padre Island with some of the roads on the mainland between Port Isabel and Los Fresnos. Of course, not everyone will want to bike 100 miles. Experienced or inexperienced cyclists will find South Padre Island a nice place to cruise. The terrain is flat, and the roads are wide enough to allow room for bikes. The resort area of the southern end offers bikers many places to stop for food, drinks, or rest. Be prepared for sun exposure and constant wind during the ride. Further north on the island are unspoiled beaches where only dune buggies, horses, and bicycles travel.

Surfing is another activity for island visitors to indulge in. Most days the surf is ridable, but storms in the Gulf of Mexico increase the swells. The largest swells reported in South Padre Island cove were at 12 to 15 feet. Blue Liquid Surfer's Paradise is the stop for hardcore surfers. It is located on State Highway 100 in Los Fresnos. Laguna Surf Shop has new and used surfboards and surf accessories. It is located at 822 Michigan Avenue in Laguna Heights. Call 956-943-1562 for surf conditions and weather.

Another activity reportedly indulged in on South Padre Island is nude sunbathing. If you want to do this, the best way to prevent being hassled is to stay away from anyone who might be offended by nudity. North of South Padre Island town proper is a good place to start. Signs have been posted by anonymous individuals indicating the "official" nude beach location, about five miles north of the end of the road. Just keep driving north until there is a nice dune on an unpopulated stretch of beach. Due to drug dealing activity in that area, the local law enforcement does patrol on a regular basis. Texas obscenity laws are aimed at nudists who have the intent to arouse or gratify sexual attention.

A more common island activity is shell collecting. Many visitors walk along the beach with their heads down in search of a particular shell. Shell collecting is almost as popular as stamp collecting. The most sought after shell on the coast is the sand dollar. The best months to find sand dollars are January and February. After storms or during low tide are also good times to hunt. For more information on shell collecting, the Island Traders Bookstore at 104 W. Pompano Street on South Padre Island has a display and a selection of books on the subject.

Lodging suggestions include the Holiday Inn Sunspree Resort at 100 Padre Boulevard. Call 800-531-7405 to reach the Holiday Inn. The Sheraton Fiesta at 310 Padre Boulevard can be reached at 800-222-4010. At Pirates Crossing, four to six adults can fit in two-bedroom condominiums. They are fully equipped with refrigerators, microwaves, laundry facilities, silverware, and more. Bring dishwashing and laundry detergents. The nearest HEB supermarket is about a 10-minute drive. Call 512-949-7306 for more information.

South Padre Island attractions include the following places.

- Isla Blanca County Park features two beachfront pavilions, a 1,000-foot sea walk, a marina, restaurants, gift shops, and showers. Fish off a jetty, find a place to set up an RV, and try surfing at this county park. The park is located at the southern end of South Padre Island. Call 956-761-5493 for more information.

Start the New Year Off with Warmth

- The Coastal Studies Laboratory, a branch of the University of Texas Pan American, has aquarium displays of fish and other marine life indigenous to the area and an extensive shell collection. The laboratory is located in Isla Blanca County Park; call 956-761-2644 for information.

- Laguna Atascosa National Wildlife Refuge is a 45,000-acre federal preserve dedicated to the preservation of native plants and animals. You can see endangered species such as the ocelot, jaguarundi, brown pelican, and alligator. The refuge is open daily year-round from sunrise to sunset. It is popular with bird-watchers. The refuge is located 20 miles northwest of South Padre Island. Call 956-748-3608 for information.

Winter

- An internationally known environmental artist, Wyland picked South Padre Island to paint the 53rd Whaling Wall, and the only one in Texas. Wyland is planning to paint 100 walls during his career to educate people on the importance of marine conservation. The Whaling Wall is located on the South Padre Island Convention Centre. The wall is also next to the Nature Walk, a boardwalk overlooking wetlands where various species of birds live. The walk contains informative signs about dune systems and bird species in the area. Both are always open to the public and are at the Convention Centre on the north end of South Padre Island. Call 956-761-3000 for information.

- The Sabal Palm Grove Wildlife Sanctuary is a 172-acre wildlife sanctuary owned by the National Audubon Society. It is the largest and best preserved Texas Sabal Palm Forest in the United States. Self-guided tours are permitted and a visitors center is open year-round. It is located on Farm to Market 1419; call 956-541-8034.

- Turtle, Inc. is the home of the "Turtle Lady," Ila Loetscher, who has dedicated her life to saving and rehabilitating sea turtles, including the endangered Kemp's ridley sea turtle. Shows featuring the turtles are given at 5805 Gulf Boulevard on South Padre Island. Call 956-761-2544 first to see if they are open.

- The South Padre Island Aquarium, 2305 Laguna Boulevard, houses over 25 aquatic species indigenous to the Laguna Madre and the Gulf of Mexico. Inhabitants include five nurse sharks, red snapper, trout, pufferfish, sting rays, eels, and more. Divers can enter the tank, which will soon house more species of sharks.

- Get a bird's-eye view of the entire barrier island area from the top of the Port Isabel Lighthouse. Built in 1853, it is now a state historic site. The Port Isabel Lighthouse is one of the oldest lighthouses in the state. It was restored in 1951 and opened to the public in 1952. You can get a panoramic view of the Laguna Madre Bay and the Queen Isabella Causeway. The lighthouse is located near the end of the Queen Isabella Causeway in Port Isabel.

- Andy Bowie County Park on the north end of town, across from the South Padre Island Convention Centre, has two beachfront pavilions, concessions, boogie-board and umbrella rentals, barbecue areas, and a beach free of vehicles.

- Take a two-hour narrated tour of the Laguna Madre, the body of water that separates Padre Island from the Texas coast, aboard the *Isabella Queen*. Watch for the Lady

Start the New Year Off with Warmth

Bea, a shrimp-boat monument commemorating the local shrimping industry.

- Boats from Port Isabel's fleet can be seen docked all around the harbor area. Watch them head offshore every morning from South Padre Island. You can take a one-day gambling cruise on the casino ship *TSS Istral*.

- Places to see in nearby Brownsville include the Stillman House Museum, an 1850 brick Greek Revival–style building that was home to Brownsville's founder. The home is furnished with family artifacts. A teddy bear exhibit is featured at Christmas. The museum is located at 1305 E. Washington Street in Brownsville.

Winter

- The Historic Brownsville Museum is located in the renovated Southern Pacific Railroad Depot at 6th and Madison in Brownsville. The museum houses photographs, historic artifacts, and a walk-through display of historic Brownsville.

- The Gladys Porter Zoo is rated one of the nation's best zoos, with more than 1,800 mammals, reptiles, birds, and other animals. The zoo is located at Ringgold and Sixth streets in Brownsville. Call 956-546-7187 for information.

- The Confederate Air Force/Rio Grande Wing houses aviation memorabilia and 15 historic aircraft still in flying condition. The museum is located at the Brownsville/ South Padre Island Airport, 955 Minnesota in Brownsville, 956-541-8585.

- The Brownsville Fine Arts Museum and Historical Neale House include both the Fine Arts Gallery and the Old Neale House Studio. This is the oldest wood-frame house in town and contains original Neale family furnishings. Also featured are art exhibits and the original gazebo from Fort Brown. The museum is at 230 Neale Drive in Brownsville; call 956-542-0941 for information.

- Shopping across the border in Matamoros, Mexico, is a popular side trip for area visitors. South Padre Island is about 25 miles north of the Mexican border. Shoppers can find fine Mexican handicrafts, leather goods, jewelry, and souvenirs for sale in the huge markets. Matamoros is accessible by foot from Brownsville. Many tourists park cars on the American side of the border. If driving into Mexico, be sure to have Mexican insurance for your vehicle. For more information about other regulations regarding restrictions on merchandise you can purchase and bring back to the United States, ask the border patrol before crossing.

Start the New Year Off with Warmth

2

Time for Reflection

SAN ANTONIO MISSIONS

REMEMBER THE ALAMO? TUCKED SNUGLY IN DOWNTOWN San Antonio today, the Alamo was the scene of one of Texas' most notorious battles against Mexico in the 1830s. Hollywood directors cast John Wayne as Davy Crockett, and turned Texas men into national heroes. Every Texan learns in school how Davy Crockett, Jim Bowie, and less than 200 men struggled to hold the Alamo. These Texans held off 7,000 Mexican troops for 13 days. Mexican troops surrounded the outer stone walls. Today, the walls are gone, the battle is over, and the dead buried, but the monument stands with the Texas flag flying overhead. And the heroes live on with their story etched in bronze inside the Alamo. Almeron "Susannah" Dickinson, her baby, and two servants were the only survivors of the siege. Even on the hottest Texas day, the story of these brave souls who stood up for the state of Texas can send a chill down your spine.

The Alamo attracts more than 3,000,000 visitors every year. While most think of it as a fort, the Alamo was a mission established by Spain to convert Indians to Christianity. The Alamo, or San Antonio de Valero, was the first mission established on the San Antonio River. The Alamo was established as a way station between missions already existing in East Texas and Mexico. It moved several times and was destroyed by hurricane in 1724. In 1836, the Alamo was established in its permanent home. The mission was more than 100 years old when the Battle of the Alamo was fought March 6, 1836. There is a visitors center and museum of early Texas artifacts. It has been under the care of the Daughters of the Republic of Texas since 1905. Four other missions were established along the San Antonio River in the 1700s. The Alamo is located at Alamo and Houston streets in Alamo Plaza. There is no admission charged and it only closes for Christmas. Call 210-225-1391 for information. To avoid the crowds, don't go during the summer or holidays. You can combine other San Antonio attractions with a visit to the Alamo or take the mission trail through the city before traveling to other missions near San Antonio.

Sitting in the courtyard on a sunny afternoon at most Texas missions seems a tranquil, even peaceful experience. Many find the missions a great place to meditate and reflect. In the 1600s and 1700s these same grounds were hosts to Indian fights, a war with Mexico, and commerce. The Spanish missions were established to give Spain a claim to more real estate, but that claim was made by the hands that held the ground. The missions introduced natives to the Spanish culture as well as Catholicism. Many missions relocated a few times. Some were taken over and used as forts during the 1800s as the new United States battled Mexico to keep Texas.

Four of the missions in San Antonio—San Jose, San Juan, Concepcion, and Espada—were originally founded in East Texas. These continue to operate as active parishes of the Catholic church and all are open to the public. Through a cooperative agreement with the Archdiocese of San Antonio, the San Antonio Missions National Historical Park of

Winter

the National Park Service administers and maintains these missions today. Drought, malaria, and French invasions forced the missions to relocate to San Antonio. The missions flourished during the mid-1700s, but the lack of military support to fend off Apaches and Comanches, coupled with disease, hastened their decline.

San Jose, established in 1720, came after the Alamo and about five miles downstream. It was established by Fray Antonio Margil de Jesus, who had previously left a failed mission in East Texas. A model among the Texas missions, San Jose gained a reputation as a major social and cultural center. Among the San Antonio missions, it also provided the strongest garrison against raids from Indians. Mission San Jose is in the 3200 block of Roosevelt at Napier. Call 210-229-4770 for information.

San Juan Capistrano, 1731, became a regional supplier of agricultural and other products including iron, wood, cloth, and leather goods produced by the Indians in its workshops. Orchards and gardens outside the walls provided melons, pumpkins, grapes, and peppers. Beyond the mission complex, Indian farmers cultivated maize (corn), beans, squash, sweet potatoes, and sugarcane in irrigated fields. A few miles southeast of the mission was Rancho Pataguilla, which in 1762 reported 3,500 sheep and nearly as many cattle. In 1756, the stone church, a friary, and a granary were completed. A larger church was begun, but was abandoned when half complete due to the decline in population. The National Park Service has plans to re-create the role of this mission by establishing for it a source of water from the San Juan Acequia, an irrigation ditch. The water will irrigate a Spanish Colonial demonstration farm. Water was brought to the settlement by using a system that was used by the ancient Middle East, Rome, and the Indian civilizations in Mesoamerica. This means of irrigation was adopted by Anglo-American, German, and Italian settlers in South

Time for Reflection

Texas. San Juan is located on the 9100 block of Graf at Ashley Road.

Concepcion, 1731, the most attractive of the San Antonio missions, looks as it did more than 200 years ago when it stood at the center of local religious activity. The mission was well known for its religious celebrations. Not visible today are the colorful geometric designs that covered the exterior surface of the mission. Inside, however, are original paintings of religious symbols and architectural designs. Concepcion is located at 807 Mission Road at Felisa.

Mission San Francisco de la Espada was originally named San Francisco de los Tejas. Espada was renamed and relocated to San Antonio in 1731. It is the southernmost of the chain of missions in San Antonio. It features a very attractive chapel, along with an unusual door and stone entrance archway. Mission Espada is at 10040 Espada Road. Call 210-627-2021 for information.

While the mission trail of San Antonio allows you to see five missions in one place, there are two missions in Goliad, Espiritu Santo and Presidio La Bahia, which could be seen along with the San Antonio missions in one weekend. The Goliad missions are a half mile apart on State Highway 183 by Goliad.

The Mission Espiritu Santo started in 1722 on the coast of Texas and then relocated to Goliad in 1749. Espiritu at one time had the largest ranch in the area with 40,000 head of cattle. The area Indians, Aranama, liked the mission life, and at one time 300 lived there. Today the mission is located in the Goliad State Historical Park with a museum, hiking trails, and camping facilities. Given these facilities, the park makes a nice place for families to stop overnight. A variety of activities can keep everyone happy. Much of the restoration work on the mission buildings was done in the 1930s. There are remnants of the original structure in partial walls, which look like piles of rocks. Park guides can explain the

Winter

significance of the area's features to you. Over the years the mission grounds were home to the Hilyer Female Institute and the Presbyterian Aranama College for men. Today the restored mission is surrounded by trees and can be seen from State Highway 183. The church has been colorfully decorated inside, but is no longer used as a chapel. The park is open every day but Christmas.

Also in Goliad is the Presidio La Bahia, established in 1749 to protect the missions around La Bahia, as Goliad was known until 1829. The Presidio has been restored and is still an active church. The Presidio La Bahia Museum contains artifacts from nine different civilizations.

The Alamo wasn't the only mission at that time to be the site of mass killings. During the struggle over Texas between Mexico and America, more than 300 men under Colonel James Fannin were imprisoned within the walls of Presidio. On Palm Sunday in 1836 the prisoners were executed, making this the largest mass execution of the battle. A statue of Fannin is on the grounds of Presidio. An amphitheater built of stone also is on the grounds.

Today a peaceful Presidio La Bahia is set apart from the world by stone walls. Presidio La Bahia is three-quarters of a mile south of Goliad on State Highway 183, just one half mile south of Mission Espiritu Santo. For information, call 512-645-3752.

Time for Reflection

3

Fruit of the Vine

EASTERN FORESTS—WESTERN PLAINS

THERE ARE 27 WINERIES IN TEXAS, EACH WITH ITS OWN method of production and distinctive flavor. The wine industry has grown rapidly across the state. Some say Texas will take over California's lead in the wine industry. For those interested in touring a winery, there are many choices to peruse, from the forests of the east to the plains of the west. Some wineries include accommodations for guests, tours, tastings, museums, and other attractions.

Grapes for west Texas wineries are grown around Lubbock. The Hill Country has several wineries of note and three federally recognized grape growing areas. These are the Bell Mountain, Fredericksburg, and Texas Hill Country Appellations. The moderate climate of Texas is similar to that of California and France, and the soils are high in minerals. Many wineries have bottling, fermenting, and distribution operations in the Hill Country, which is situated in the center of Dallas, Houston, Austin, and San Antonio.

Near Houston in Old Town Spring you will find two wineries. Red River Winery at 421 Gentry Street #204 was established in 1995. At Red River Winery proprietors blend, cellar, and bottle their own wines, as well as carry other Texas wines. Red River is just 20 miles north of Houston and can be reached by calling 281-288-WINE. Also in the historic town of Old Spring you can see Wimberley Valley Winery at 2825 Loneman Mountain Road. For information, call 281-350-8801.

In West Texas you can see several wineries as you enjoy the hilly scene. Cordier Estates, Inc., in Fort Stockton is open to tours and tastings. Call 915-395-2417 for an appointment. Fairly near Fort Stockton, you can visit Blue Mountain Vineyards on Route 1 in Fort Davis, 915-426-3763. Pheasant Ridge Winery on Route 3 in Lubbock can be reached at 806-746-6033 to arrange winery tours and tastings.

Another Lubbock stop is Cap-Rock Winery, a modern winery with state-of-the-art equipment from around the world. On Route 6, Cap-Rock is open to tours and tastings by calling 806-863-2704. A caprock, the geologic feature that inspired the winery founders, is an impervious stratum of resistant rock usually at the summit of a mesa. Cap-Rock Winery sits on such a geologic formation. The Texas High Plains with semiarid and mild climate and soils suited to grape vines has become a major growing area for grapes. Vineyards in the Lubbock area use the trellis system along with hand harvesting and traditional farming methods. There are American oak barrels and stainless steel tanks, German stemmer/crusher and presses, and an Italian bottling line. The winery has the capacity to store 139,000 gallons of wine.

Also in Lubbock, don't miss Llano Estacado. Call 806-745-2258 for tours and tastings. Llano Estacado began as a casual project on the patio of a Texas Tech horticulturist. Bob Reed's patio in Lubbock became the home for discarded grape vines, uprooted in the late '50s to make room for a highway. They were to be planted as a decorative trellis. However, when the trellis began producing stunning yields, Reed's interest turned from landscaping to wine.

In the 1970s, Reed, along with Clint McPherson, a Texas Tech chemistry professor with an interest in winemaking as a teaching tool, began working together. They planted more than 100 grape varieties on 10 acres as a test to see which types fit the climate and soil and were best suited for wine making. In 1976, Llano Estacado Winery was founded. Llano Estacado Winery produces nearly 80,000 cases of wine annually, which are sold in more than 30 states and Europe.

Not to be outdone by the West, the Hill Country region of Texas also has some wineries worth visiting. Bell Mountain Vineyards in Fredericksburg is open to tours and tastings. Call 830-685-3297 for information. Also in Fredericksburg is the Fredericksburg Winery located at 247 W. Main. You can call for tours or tastings at 830-990-8747.

Becker Vineyards and winery, 10 miles east of Fredericksburg, off Highway 290 on Jenschle Lane in Stonewall, was completed in 1995 prior to the first harvest. The vineyard was planted during 1992 in Stonewall Valley on the site of an ancient stand of native mustang grapes prized by German ancestors in the Hill Country. There are 36 acres of French vinifera grapes planted in the vineyard and surrounded by peach orchards and fields of native wildflowers. The winery is a replica of the original 19th-century German stone barn next to a 1880s log cabin, well, and milk house to re-create the appearance of the original farmstead. Wine is aged in French oak barrels in an underground wine cellar. Tourists can taste wines on the porch during the spring and summer, or by the hearth of an open fire during the winter. Call 830-644-2681 for information.

While in Austin, you can visit the Cana Cellars Winery at 11217 Fitzhugh Road, off Highway 290 just past Oak Hill. For information call 512-288-6027. Or you can see Slaughter-Leftwich Vineyards at 4301 James Lane. Call 512-266-3331 for tour and tasting times.

Fruit of the Vine

A Hill Country gem is Fall Creek Vineyards, established by Ed and Susan Auler in Tow in 1975. The winery's beginnings can be linked to when the couple noted the similarity between climate and terrain in France to their Hill Country ranch while overseas purchasing cattle. With a few grapes from their first plantings, the Aulers borrowed a wine press in 1979 and produced their first commercial wine in a renovated garage. Now Fall Creek wines include Sauvignon Blanc, Chardonnay, Johannisberg, Riesling, Muscat Canelli, and Chenin Blanc, Cabernet Sauvignon, Merlot, and a blush White Zinfandel. The proprietary wines are Granite Blush and Granite Reserve. The winery has grown up from its humble beginnings.

The winery is a combination of new and old, from the fermentation room with modern winemaking equipment to the oak casks residing in a room secured by antique stable doors from the Louis Pasteur Laboratory outside of Paris. The upstairs of the winery serves as guest quarters and the decor combines early Texas with antique French and English furnishings. Over the fireplace hangs a triptych in pastels by artist Sheila Lichacz of "The Miracle at Cana," where Jesus turned the three vessels of water into wine at the wedding feast. In 1985, James Michener, author of *Space*, *Centennial*, and *Tales of the South Pacific*, stayed at Fall Creek while researching his book, *Texas*.

The 65-acre vineyard and winery are located on the northwest shores of Lake Buchanan. Warm to hot days mixed with cool nights and low average relative humidity provide the perfect weather for growing grapes. Harvest occurs between July and September. Grapes are hand-picked and pressed in a Bucher membrane press. In 1995, Fall Creek produced 21,000 cases.

For more information about Fall Creek, call the winery and vineyard office at 915-379-5361. Tasting and tours are available with a visitors center on the grounds.

Other wineries in Texas you can visit include:

Grape Creek Vineyards, P.O. Box 102, Stonewall. Call 830-644-2710 for information about winery tours.

Hidden Springs Winery, 256 North Highway 377, Pilot Point; 940-686-2782.

Hill Country Cellars, 1700 N. Bell Boulevard, U.S. Highway 183 North, Cedar Park; 512-259-2000 or 800-264-7273. Call for tours and tastings.

Messina-Hof Wine Cellars, 4545 Old Reliance Road, Bryan. Call 409-778-9463 for winery tours.

Piney Woods Country Wines, 3408 Willow Drive, Orange; 409-883-5408. Call for tasting times; tours are by appointment.

Sister Creek Vineyards, Farm to Market 1376, Sisterdale, 830-324-6704. Call for hours.

Spicewood Vineyards, P.O. Box 248, Spicewood, 830-693-5328. Tours and tastings may be scheduled.

Fruit of the Vine

4

On the Border

EL PASO TO BROWNSVILLE

TRAVELING FROM EL PASO TO BROWNSVILLE ALONG THE RIO Grande River towns bordering Mexico give North Americans an opportunity to visit another country and culture without difficulty. Good food and margaritas, shopping for bargains, unusual entertainment like bullfights . . . whatever the reason, Texas border towns make a good place to stay while experiencing Mexico. Border towns range from larger cities like Laredo, where an average of 12,000 people cross daily, to smaller communities like Los Ebanos, where a three-car ferry takes visitors across the river.

Los Ebanos Ferry is the only existing hand-operated ferry on the border. The ferry, recognized with a state historical marker in 1975, crosses the Rio Grande from an area of ebony trees, hence the name *Los Ebanos*. The ferry, which operates daily, is off U.S. Highway 83 near Mission.

Laredo is much farther north of Los Ebanos where U.S. Highway 83 meets U.S. Highway 59 and Interstate 35. Laredo and Nuevo Laredo residents share business, family, and culture. The sister cities are often called Los Dos Laredos. Visitors can cross the border from Laredo to Nuevo Laredo at two bridges by car or on foot. Mexican insurance is required on any vehicle taken into Mexico. Be sure to obtain insurance before crossing, as motorists involved in accidents are required to settle the claim before returning to the States. International Bridge #1 is the recommended crossing point for visitors because it empties directly into Guerrero Street, location of the main strip. International Bridge #2 runs directly off Interstate 35 into a neighborhood eight blocks east of the shopping center. It is used mostly by locals or truck drivers not headed for the markets.

There are lots of typical Mexican shops on Guerrero Street and in the Market Plaza, which is just off Guerrero, two blocks from International Bridge #1. The market is located between Bravo Street to the north and Victoria Street to the south. Shops are filled with baskets, hand-dyed cloth, serapes, clothing, leatherwork, silver goods, fruits, vegetables, and other foods. Food cannot be transported back across the border, but many vendors sell fresh fruit in cups or frozen on a popcicle stick, which makes a nice treat on a hot day. Fruit pops can vary from blueberry and strawberry to fresh watermelon and pineapple.

Another shopping area is Soriana, a commercial shopping center at Gigante and Blanco Streets. Soriana may have good prices on items typically used in the American home. A primary shopping venue in Nuevo Laredo is the Nuevo Mercado de la Reforma, an entire city block of stalls that feature Mexican handicrafts.

Besides a variety of fresh fruit, Nuevo Laredo is also known for its seafood, fresh from the Gulf and at reasonable prices. Try the cabrito, a slightly stringy meat that tastes good barbecued. A margarita and plate full of panchos, a special nacho, could hit the spot after a day of shopping in the markets. For dining out try Arturo's, El Dorado Bar, Nuevo Leon, or El Rincon del Viejo. For entertainment of a sort not seen in the United States, the bullring is six miles from the bridge. The Plaza de Toros, "La Fiesta" bullfighting ring is off Guerrero Street. The Handcraft Museum, filled with displays to show how Mexican handcrafts are made, is near the bullring.

Don't miss the archeological park, the only such park on the northern border. It features replicas of important art objects from seven principal pre-Hispanic cultures. These include the Mayan, Aztec, Olmeca, Huasteca, Totonaca, Tolteca, and Teothihuacan. The park is located one block south and two blocks east from International Bridge #1 on Bravo Street.

On the U.S. side, visit Fort McIntosh, the Nuevo Santander Museum, Republic of the Rio Grande Building, and St. Augustine Church, built in 1872. Tourists can ride on the Texas-Mexican Railroad. Take the "Tex-Mex Express," a 1940s-vintage train that runs across south Texas from Laredo every afternoon to Corpus Christi and returns the next morning.

Laredo is the only city in Texas to have flown seven flags. For years, Mexico and the United States were involved in a border dispute that rendered Laredo a no-man's-land. The frustrated citizens of the area proclaimed their city to be the Republic of the Rio Grande and designated Laredo as its capital. The republic lived for 283 days. Read all about it at the Museum of the Republic of the Rio Grande.

Whether in Nuevo Laredo or other border towns, don't bring weapons of any kind or illegal drugs into Mexico. The sentence for possession of marijuana is 10 years. Be aware that while liquor and drinks are freely sold, it is against the law to be publicly intoxicated. Drink bottled water, as local water may cause digestive problems. Exchange money at the border, where you will get the best rate. Many shops take American money in Nuevo Laredo and sometimes will mark down the price for American dollars. There are cash machines in the market areas and most banks will cash a check with proper identification.

Visitors can stay in Mexico for 72 hours with no paperwork as long as they are within 26 miles of the border. Shoppers can bring back up to $400 worth of merchandise without paying duty. For more information about Laredo, call the Convention and Visitors Bureau at 800-292-2122.

Also along the border is the town of Mission, established in 1824 by the Oblate Fathers on a site three miles south of the present town. The first experiments with citrus in the lower Rio Grande Valley occurred here when a priest planted an orange grove. Mission calls itself the home of the grapefruit, especially the Texas ruby red grapefruit. Mission is also known for its poinsettia displays at Christmas time.

Nearby, Anzalduas Park in Hidalgo County at the Anzalduas Dam on the Rio Grande has a covered bird-observation pier, pavilion, and boat dock. You can picnic in a shady wooded area equipped with barbecue grills. The park is located about three miles south, near La Lomita Chapel.

La Lomita Chapel is hidden in Texas mesquite on Farm to Market 1016. La Lomita, "Little Hill," was built in 1865 as an adobe overnight way station for the Oblate Fathers, who regularly traveled on horseback between Brownsville and Roma. Only 12 by 25 feet in size, the original structure was rebuilt of sandstone in 1889. The chapel still has its original brick floors, and its rough, heavy-beamed ceilings were cut from native trees. An outdoor beehive-style oven and the original water well are still there. The chapel is used for weddings. It is surrounded by a park with picnic facilities, brick walkways, and historical site signs.

Bentsen Rio Grande Valley State Park is a 600-acre area set aside to preserve the natural environment of the lower Rio Grande Valley. Visitors can canoe on the Rio Grande, fish, bird-watch, and study nature in the park. Some 200 species of birds have been sighted, including such rare specimens as Audubon's oriole, hooded oriole, zone tailed hawk, and red-eye cowbird. The Old Military Road route of the U.S. Army from Fort Ringgold to Brownsville was near the present day park entrance. Evidence of the thoroughfare is visible. The park is off U.S. Highway 83, six miles from Mission.

Also close to Mission is Shary Estate, the former home of John H. Shary. He was the first in Texas to grow fruit commercially and is known as the father of the Texas citrus industry. Across from the house is Shary Memorial Chapel and park maintained as a memorial to Shary. There are no public tours, but the grounds are worth seeing when passing through. It is located four miles north of Mission on Shary Road or Farm to Market 494.

On the Border

5

Do It in the Big "D"

DALLAS

DALLAS HAS SEVERAL PLACES OF INTEREST IF YOU WANT TO learn something new or old, experience culture from around the world, or shop. Dallas culture can be traced back to immigrants from mostly European countries. Taking a chance on settling in the rough western prairie, the founders of Dallas held their community to higher standards than their next-door neighbor, Fort Worth. While Butch Cassidy and the Sundance Kid were frequenting Hell's Half Acre in Fort Worth's town square, the people of Dallas were a bit more sophisticated. Highly educated and diverse, the community placed a priority on the arts. Many immigrants settling in Dallas were professionals in science and other fields in their former countries.

Starting in the center of Dallas in Deep Ellum, you will find one of the city's most happening places. Traditionally, Deep Ellum has entertained and enlightened with its offerings of new music or new art, everything avant garde or alternative. Blues legends Blind Lemon Jefferson, Huddie "Leadbelly" Ledbetter, and Lightnin' Hopkins came from Deep Ellum. It's an urban neighborhood where once abandoned warehouses and historic buildings have been transformed into shops, bars, restaurants, galleries, and lofts. The area is home to live theater and poetry readings. Murals and graffiti add to the atmosphere. Deep Ellum was a jazz, blues, and speakeasy neighborhood during Prohibition.

West End Market Place in the West End Historic District is a good place to shop or have a good time at nightclubs, bars, restaurants, and a seasonal outdoor ice rink. Admission is charged for Dallas Alley nightclubs.

For more refined taste in music, experience the Dallas Symphony Orchestra, which will celebrate its centennial in the year 2000. Located in the Morton H. Meyerson Symphony Center in Dallas, the orchestra's beginnings can be traced to a 40-member ensemble that performed under the direction of German-born Conductor Hans Kreissig. Kreissig conducted the orchestra for five seasons while trying to finance the organization.

The Dallas Wind Symphony, also located in the Morton H. Meyerson Concert Center, has an annual concert subscription series. The symphony is the leading professional wind band in America. Comprised of 50 woodwind, brass, and percussion players, the band performs a blend of musical styles ranging from Bach to Bernstein and Sousa to Strauss.

Another organization dedicated to the arts is the Dallas Opera, a 42-year-old company with an international reputation. The opera began with a community effort as several people worked to found an opera company in 1957.

The Afterimage Gallery, established in 1971, is an art gallery devoted to photography. Over the years, the gallery has held one-person shows for many of the greatest photographers, as well as unknown and regional photographers. Along with original prints, the gallery also handles in-print photography books. Owner Ben Breard, a native of Dallas, became interested in photography while studying journalism at Northwestern University. The gallery is located in the Quadrangle, a complex north of downtown Dallas.

The Science Place helps people of all ages understand how things work. From the solar system to honeybees, it is a place where patrons can use their senses of touch, sight, hearing, and smell, as well as imagination to understand the wonders of science and mathematics.

The African-American Cultural Heritage Center in the Nolan Estes Educational Plaza displays items reflecting the contributions of African Americans, including wood carvings from Mali, fertility dolls from Ghana, a Bamum chief's stool from Cameroon, and a Mingani dancer from Pende. Decorative quilts, baskets, textiles, pottery, jewelry, and paintings are also on exhibit. There is a collection of documents and photographs to piece together the black experience in Texas.

The Asian-American Cultural Heritage Center in the Tom Gooch Early Childhood Center fosters understanding of the Asian arts, philosophy, and customs. Dolls, carved temple figures, musical instruments, porcelain tea sets, jewelry, and an exhibit of children's school supplies from the People's Republic of China can be viewed. Paintings on cloth, silk screens, wood block prints, temple rubbings, and shell paintings are included.

The construction of the Biblical Arts Center is reflective of early Christian-era architecture. The limestone entrance was modeled after Paul's Gate in Damascus. The Atrium features a life-size replica of Christ's garden tomb at Calvary. The Biblical Arts Center is a nondenominational museum that uses art to help people visualize the places, events, and people of the Bible. From the masters to contemporaries, in both permanent and changing galleries, exhibits display artifacts and paintings. The center is the site of a 124-by-20-foot mural depicting more than 200 biblical characters.

The Sixth Floor Museum depicts one of America's most tragic events: the assassination of John F. Kennedy on

Do It in the Big "D"

November 22, 1963. The county purchased and renovated the Texas School Book Depository 14 years after the assassination. The sixth floor remained virtually untouched since Lee Harvey Oswald allegedly perched with a rifle in the southeast corner window. It became an educational museum examining the event. About 435,000 visitors trek through annually, almost assuredly taking time to look through the sixth floor windows to view Dealey Plaza and the route of the presidential motorcade as it passed in front.

When in Dallas it is hard to ignore the fact that the city is Cowboys country. Texas Stadium, home of the Dallas Cowboys of Super Bowl fame, regularly has Dallas Cowboys tours. The tour includes a visit to the locker room, a behind-the-scenes look at the stadium, and a look at the playing field.

Many people do not realize that the roots of professional hockey in Dallas date back 55 years to the fall of 1941. It was a strange sight for Southerners when the Fair Park Ice Arena brought the northern sport to Dallas residents for the first time. Advertised in the papers as "murder on ice," the lights came up on a debut unlike any other. Before the Stars arrived in Dallas in 1993, the Central Hockey League operated a team in Dallas from 1967 to 1982 called the Dallas Blackhawks, a minor league affiliate of the Chicago Blackhawks.

The ultramodern Dallas City Hall was controversial when it opened in 1978, a time when city fathers were trying to cultivate an international reputation for the city. City Hall was designed by renowned architect I. M. Pei, who also designed the Morton H. Meyerson Symphony Center in the Arts District. Outdoor festivals and special events are held in City Hall Plaza.

Old City Park, a 13-acre park where restored historic homes and businesses have been gathered, allows you to see the humble origins of this megacity.

The Wilson Block Historic District is a group of circa 1898–1902 homes. It is just east of downtown in the 2900 block of Swiss Avenue.

Reunion Tower, alongside the huge, reflective-glass Hyatt Regency, affords the best view of Dallas. The tower has a revolving cocktail lounge and restaurant on top.

The Dallas Arts District, starting at Ross and Harwood Streets, is the largest centralized arts development area in the nation. The Dallas Museum of Art houses a permanent collection spanning several periods from pre-Columbian to modern, and also hosts major touring exhibitions. You can view works by Church, Oldenburg, Monet, Van Gogh, Matisse, Rodin, Henry Moore, and others. The museum is located at 1717 N. Harwood. Looking across Harwood Street from the museum is the sculpture garden of the Trammell Crow Center. The 22 French bronzes include works by Rodin. Two blocks east on Flora Street is the Morton H. Meyerson Symphony Center.

The Meadows Museum, on the campus of Southern Methodist University, provides a handsome setting for a permanent collection of paintings, drawings, and prints from five centuries of Spanish art.

Fair Park, a 277-acre park southeast of downtown Dallas off Interstate 30, has been the site of the annual State Fair of Texas since 1887. Attracting more than 3.5 million visitors annually, the State Fair is one of the largest in the United States. This National Historic Landmark is also the locale of several major permanent attractions, such as the Museum of Natural History, Dallas Horticultural Center, Hall of State, and the Age of Steam Railroad Museum. Fair Park has the nation's largest collection of Art Deco buildings. You will find Fair Park at First Street and Grand Avenue.

At the Dallas Zoo and the Wilds of Africa, you can see many of the 1,400 animals from a monorail train. The newest exhibit is Lemur Lookout. Look for the gigantic giraffe marking the entrance at 621 E. Clarendon in the Oak Cliff section of Dallas.

The Dallas Arboretum and Botanical Garden is a 66-acre arboretum and botanical garden with rolling lawns and blooming gardens on the shore of White Rock Lake. It does not yet reflect the indigenous plants of the Texas Xeriscape movement, but it does have impressive azaleas. See this at 8525 Garland Road. Call 214-327-8263 for more information.

The city's newest park is Pioneer Plaza downtown at Young and Griffin streets, near the Dallas Convention Center. The park commemorates the Old West cattle drives with 20 large bronze longhorn steers and cowboys on horseback. Fifty more steers will eventually be added to this impressive herd.

The Dallas Aquarium is one of the largest inland aquariums in the nation. Don't miss the scheduled shark and piranha feedings at the aquarium, located in Fair Park. The Dallas World Aquarium is a converted warehouse in the West End Historic District that houses living reef tanks and a walk-through shark tank. The aquarium is located at 1801 N. Griffin Street.

Dallas Surrey Services offers daily horse-drawn carriage rides through downtown's West End. In Dallas, the McKinney Avenue Trolley is an authentic early 20th-century trolley-car line running from downtown to the McKinney Avenue entertainment district. The Dallas Convention and Visitors Bureau offers maps of downtown Dallas skybridges and underground walkways open weekdays during business hours.

Take a look at two cities planted in the center of Dallas. Highland Park and University Park are incorporated cities surrounded by Dallas with large estates and beautifully landscaped neighborhoods. Both warrant a leisurely drive through. In University Park you will find Southern Methodist University with its handsome red brick buildings. Retail and service businesses within the Park Cities include Highland Park Shopping Center, one of the nation's earliest shopping centers, and Snider Plaza, near Southern Methodist University.

At South Fork Ranch you can see the ranch where the famous soap opera *Dallas* was filmed. At the "Texas Legends—Fact to Fantasy" exhibit, you can see the gun that shot J.R., Lucy's wedding dress, and other Ewing memorabilia. The ranch is also available for private parties and catered events, ranging from elegant five-course, seated dinners in the mansion to casual barbecue and Tex-Mex meals.

Board the *Texas Queen* for lunch and enjoy the charm of a double-deck paddlewheeler. Dinner cruises will give you a chance to enjoy the sunset on a leisurely cruise. The *Texas Queen* is 105 feet long and 24 feet wide and can accommodate 200 passengers. There is a covered observation deck where you can feel the breeze off the water as you watch the world go by. All cruises depart from Elgin B. Robertson Park, I-30 east to Dalrock Exit. Turn south into park and left at the "T" in the road. It is the first parking lot on the left.

For more information about any of the attractions in Dallas, contact the Dallas Convention and Visitors Bureau at 1201 Elm Street, Suite 2000, 800-232-5527.

Do It in the Big "D"

6

Rocking in the Rodeo

FORT WORTH–HOUSTON–PASADENA

IF YOU'RE READY FOR A WILD, ROCKING TIME, THEN HEAD TO any Texas rodeo. Rodeo action can be found at almost every county fair or livestock show. Big cities like Houston, Dallas, and Fort Worth have ongoing rodeo action. Some rodeos are connected to educational pursuits and others are purely for entertainment.

The Fort Worth Stock Show and Rodeo is an annual event that runs for 17 days in January and February. The stock show is a showcase for the best livestock and an auction gives youth a chance to sell the products of their hard work. Educational scholarships are awarded to many youth. People come from all over to visit the stock show, officially known as the Southwestern Exposition and Livestock Show. In the 1990s, nearly a million visitors came to the livestock show each year.

The event began in 1896 when a small group of ranchers gathered along Marine Creek in North Fort Worth to exhibit stock and trade breeding tips. In 1918, the world's first indoor rodeo was added. In 1944 the stock show moved to the Will Rogers Memorial Center to accommodate its growth. Barns were built just south of the Coliseum and Auditorium. Buildings to house horse shows, auction sales, free Western shows, petting zoos, as well as beef and dairy cattle, horses, mules, donkeys, swine, sheep, goats, llamas, pigeons, poultry, and rabbits were added.

Wandering around barns to see livestock is a good way to excite the future ranchers in your family, but it isn't what most family members want to see. The real action is in the rodeo arena each night. At the Fort Worth Stock Show and Rodeo you can choose from 30 exciting rodeo performances with prize money awarded to the world's best cowboys and cowgirls. There are chuck wagon races, feature performers, and clowns. But while you're wandering around the exhibits, be sure to try some of the food available. Usually barbecue, turkey legs, and even fried alligator or shrimp are good treats. Leather goods are abundant, and Western art from paintings to sculpted bronze can be purchased.

If you are just looking for the excitement of bull-riding contests, there are other events in Texas which don't include a stock show or exhibits for shoppers. The X-Treme Bull Riding Tour was created for top-notch bull riders and bull-riding fans. X-Treme matches top riders with top-rank bucking bulls. Every performance has 35 of the top-ranked bull riders challenge 35 of the baddest bulls around. The top eight bull riders of the night are matched against eight of the roughest and toughest bulls for a showdown. For information about the X-Treme Bull Riding Tour dates and locations, call 888-226-3881.

Just what are bull riders facing? Southern Rodeos, Inc., provides bulls for riders and here are just a few bulls they have had on the circuit. Okie Skar at age five bucked 21 riders in one year. Only three riders successfully stayed on Okie Skar for eight seconds. Hawkeye only bucked 20 in a year with four riders lasting eight seconds. Six-year-old Sugar Bear, owned by Wilson/Robertson Rodeo Co., bucked 41 in a year with three riders making eight seconds of rock-

ing and jerking. Sugar Bear was the son of a famous rodeo bull named Wrangler Rivots. Sugar Bear likes to take out riders by spinning extremely fast.

Grab your boots, hat, and best Western wear and join more than a million others who will head for the Houston Livestock and Rodeo Show, the largest rodeo show in the country. Black Heritage Day and Go Tejano Day are two of the more popular days. The show also has one of the best chili cook-offs you can find anywhere. In February and March all the cowboys and cowgirls are in Houston. The Future Farmers of America and 4-H groups also camp out in Houston to show the products of their labor and compete for scholarships.

On the average, youth who show animals go home with at least $1,600. Money earned at the livestock show will help pay for college. Cattle, pigs, chickens, llamas, sheep, rabbits, and goats are among the entries, with a grand champion picked for each category. A llama sold for $80,000, a turkey for $70,000, a Grand Champion Broiler for $100,000, and the Grand Champion Lamb went for $140,000 at the auction one year. The person who raises the Grand Champion Steer gets $60,000, while the steer sells for more than $500,000. With all that money exchanging hands, the auction is an exciting place to be during the show. The Houston Livestock Show and Rodeo is mainly a charitable event. It has awarded about $50 million in scholarships, graduate assistantships, endowments, and grant contributions since 1957.

In 1974 the Houston Livestock and Rodeo Show held a poster contest for the first time. That event has turned into an art contest with 16,000 entrants from 15 Texas school districts. Those entrants were chosen from an even greater number of students who were taking advantage of their

Rocking in the Rodeo

chance to participate in the show. The winning pieces of Western artwork were auctioned off in the Astrohall Sales Pavilion. One year the grand champion artwork sold for $100,000. Thirty-nine judges selected the winners for the auction from the 16,000 entries. Sales in the Junior Market and School Art auctions have reached more than $5.5 million.

The real excitement is the rodeo action happening nightly. In 1998, Houston's world championship rodeo competition drew more than 500 contestants hoping to win some of more than $700,000 in prize money. A $25,000 bonus goes to the rodeo's All Around Cowboy. In 1998 four Houston rodeo records were broken. Cody Ohl from Orchard, Texas, broke the calf roping record with a time of 7.6 seconds; Vic Morrison from Bowie, Texas, and Shot Branham of Midland, Texas, broke the team roping record with a time of 4.5 seconds; Tom Duvall from Henrietta, Oklahoma, broke the steer wrestling record with a time of 3.3 seconds; and Ty Murray of Stephenville, Texas, broke the bull-riding record with a score of 90 points.

Some entertainers who have performed at the Houston show include Alan Jackson, Clint Black, LeAnn Rimes, Lynyrd Skynyrd, Alabama, Tanya Tucker, Brooks and Dunn, La Mafia, Selena, Lorrie Morgan, Reba McEntire, Vince Gill, and Mark Chesnutt. For information call the Houston Convention and Visitors Bureau at 800-231-7799 or 713-227-3100.

In Pasadena, a rodeo is a nightly event in the September Pasadena Livestock Show. A trail ride involving many participants and horse owners starts before the event and ends at the event kickoff. A parade and auction are scheduled for the show. Every year Pasadena has added to the livestock location. Plans call for a new press box and announcer stand with six company suites, a mayor's box, and a president's box. Plans for work on the arena include a permanent sound stage. Pasadena's annual event includes arts and crafts booths. See the up-and-coming talent perform on the Campbell Hall Stage, and cool your heels in the Silver Spur Club. For information, call the Pasadena Chamber of Commerce at 281-487-7871.

7

Fat Tuesday or Mardi Gras

GALVESTON

PLAN AHEAD FOR A WEEKEND IN FEBRUARY FOR GALVESTON'S Mardi Gras celebration. Galveston has two or more parades on two different weekends. The city spends all year preparing for the event. The whole city participates and unlike the New Orleans version, you can find a place to stand. Children enjoy catching strings of beads thrown from splashy floats in the parade. The parade route travels down the Strand and Seawall in front of hotels and restaurants where the less rambunctious sit and watch. Mardi Gras begins with Fat Tuesday, the day before Ash Wednesday, which usually is at the beginning of February.

Mardi Gras may be a reason to come to Galveston, but it doesn't have to be the only one. Galveston is filled with history, city fun, and beaches. The seawall stretches along 32 miles of beach and one side of the city, which seems to be built around it. Roller-blading, bicycling, swimming, shopping, and fine dining can be had along the seawall.

Karankawas lived on Galveston Island before Cabeza de Vaca came to take it for Spain. France and Mexico also had their turns at ruling the island. Pirate Jean La Fitte made his home on the island between 1817 and 1821; he was forced to leave after his buccaneers attacked a U.S. Revenue Cutter. Galveston also played an important role in the Texas War for Independence and the Civil War. It was the country's third largest port in the late 1800s, and one of the South's most affluent communities.

You could spend months looking at Galveston's 1,500 historic places with 550 listed on the National Register of Historic Places. An exceptional number of buildings along the Strand display Victorian iron-front architecture. The Strand with its collection of shops, galleries, and restaurants is home to one of the best places to stay, the Tremont House Hotel, and the Strand Street Theatre. Every December, Dickens on the Strand, a Victorian Christmas celebration, brings a bit of 19th-century London to Galveston's historic district. Trolley tracks connect the Strand to downtown.

Winter

You can take a carriage tour of the East End and the Silk Stocking historic districts. Elaborate 19th-century homes, such as Ashton Villa, the Williams Home, the Grand 1894 Opera House, Port Bolivar Lighthouse, Powhatan House, and the Bishop's Palace, in which 61 artisans spent seven years carving the oak stairway by hand, are a few of the places you should see. The grand Victorian Moody Mansion built in 1892 with 42 rooms has been restored. The Moody family has played a significant role in forming today's Galveston. Take a look at the 1890 Trube House, 1627 Sealy Avenue. It is a 39-room Danish castle, a copy of one in Keil, Germany. The Bishop's Place, 1402 Broadway, built in 1886, is a four-story Victorian structure made of granite, limestone, and red sandstone. In 1920, the house was purchased by the Catholic Diocese and used by the church as a bishop's residence until 1950. For a quick tour of a lot of ground, take the trolley from the Railroad Museum, located at 25th Street in the Strand. Also, take some time to stop in the museum and see more than 20,000 pieces of railroad history.

Stop at the *Elissa*, which is a restored three-masted square-rigger built in 1877 and rescued from the scrapyard. It is typical of the cargo ships calling on the port of Galveston. *Elissa* sailed to Galveston in 1883 and 1886. A film on *Elissa*'s restoration can be viewed at the Strand's Visitor Center, 2016 Strand. Next to the *Elissa* you'll find the Texas Seaport Museum, which has extensive documentation of local maritime history. A computer there may help you trace your roots. It has records of thousands of immigrants who entered America through Galveston's port.

Don't miss Seawolf Park on Pelican Island, an old immigrant station in the Galveston Harbor area. You can reach Pelican Island via 51st Street. It is across the harbor from the Port of Galveston. The island is the result of dredging and serves as an industrial complex and home to Texas A&M University at Galveston. Also in the harbor area, you'll find the WWII submarine *Cavalla* and the destroyer escort USS *Stewart* on display and open for tours. The Galveston Harbor area is a good place to view ships up close. Take the Boliver Ferry, with or without a car, for a view of Galveston's Harbor and Seawolf Park. While on Bolivar Peninsula take a mile drive to Bolivar Lighthouse, built in 1872.

The Port of Galveston added an area for visitors from Pier 19 to 25. Pier 25 is maintained for cruise ships headed for foreign destinations. Around Pier 19 are restaurants and the *Elissa*. For those looking for a short cruise or charter boat, you'll find some available for fishing and partying. The pier area is also home to Galveston's Mosquito Fleet, more than 100 shrimp trawlers. Each boat brings in a thousand or more pounds of shrimp daily. You can also find sailboat or windsurfing equipment rentals on Offatts Bayou. Rentals are available on 61st Street and on Bayou Drive beside Offatts

Bayou, or for some fun try Bumper Boats at Stewart Beach, a seawall park.

If the water isn't your interest, but flying is, don't miss the Lone Star Flight Museum, which has a collection of classic 1930s and 1940s aircraft in operating condition. Some are the last of their kind. Take your own flight at the Galv-Aero Flight Center at Scholes Field Executive Terminal. It's a good way to see the entire island. Call 409-740-1223 for information.

At Moody Gardens, you have the option of staying dry or getting wet. Moody Gardens is a collection of attractions so finely landscaped that it is enjoyable just to walk around its garden pathways. Set on Offatts Bayou, Moody Gardens has three large pyramids that look much like the ancient pyramids of Egypt or Mexico, only these glass structures shine in the sun.

There is a tropical rain forest exhibit with more than 1,700 plants and butterflies from Asia, Africa, and South America inside one pyramid. You can tour the rain forest as many times as you want in one day. With a full acre of scenery including waterfalls, deep caverns, fish, and a Mayan colonnade, you may have to take a second look. Be sure to look inside the bat cave for a glimpse of the Moody Gardens resident colony of fruit bats. The Butterfly Hatching Hut lets you see butterflies emerge from their chrysalises and fly into the pyramid. Daily launchings are scheduled.

The Discovery Pyramid houses three dozen NASA-inspired exhibits. Try the X-38 space station lifeboat or create your own alien inside the Discovery Museum. Go inside a space habitat, walk on the moon, and experience life in space. Also, for some fun without strain, Moody Gardens has a 3-D IMAX theater.

A third pyramid, which opened in 1999, is a 200-million-gallon aquarium with marine life from around the world. Also, next door to the pyramids and in the Moody Gardens complex, a 304-room luxury hotel opened in 1999. For information or to make reservations at Moody Gardens Hotel, call 888-388-8484.

Palm Beach at Moody Gardens is a white-sand beach with freshwater lagoons and a waterfall. It is just outside the pyramids on the shores of Offatts Bayou. The white sand around the lagoons came from Florida. It is a great place to take small children for a beach atmosphere without the mess, but those older than 9 or 10 may be bored.

Docked by Moody Gardens is *The Colonel*, a replica of an 1800s paddle wheeler. You can take an hour-long cruise during the day or a dinner cruise in the evening. Board at 7 P.M. for three hours of live music and an all-you-can-eat buffet. You can easily find a secluded corner on deck to watch the moon rise for a unforgettably romantic experience. Children will love to explore the paddle wheeler and can learn about how it operates while taking a good look at the bay during the afternoon cruise. For more information about *The Colonel*, call 409-740-7797. Evening cruises are usually on the weekend, but not during the week. For more information about Moody Gardens, call 800-582-4673. For more information about Galveston, call the Galveston Island Convention and Visitors Bureau, 2106 Seawall Boulevard, toll-free in Texas, 800-351-4236, or toll-free in the United States, 800-351-4237.

Fat Tuesday or Mardi Gras

8

The Hunt for Healthy Solutions

MINERAL WELLS–COOPER CLINIC

RETHINKING HABITS, REDEFINING YOUR LIFESTYLE, AND REVI-
talizing yourself after a stressful week on the job may be
the best vacation you can take. It also may be the one to
change your life. In Texas, remedies for what ails you have
been sold from the back of wagons in the frontier days to
health food store shelves of modern-day malls. But a cure
aimed at your whole body and mind isn't boxed, bottled, or
shelved. The cure for what ails the mind and body can be
found in a place.

Many health-related businesses claim that they have the
answer to all your ailments. Some provide weights and other
exercise equipment along with trainers to show you how to
use them. Hot showers or saunas provide some comfort to
strained and tired muscles. Other health-related businesses
are marketing cures in the form of super vitamins to give
you energy during long days of work. The search for a cure
isn't a new phenomena; it has been going on for centuries.
Today you can still visit Lake Mineral Wells State Park and
Trailway where a health resort was located, or you can visit
a modern health resort like Cooper Clinic by Dallas.

Lake Mineral Wells State Park is located along Rock Creek, a large tributary of the Brazos River. Like many parts of Texas, this area was home to several Native American tribes including the Comanche. Settlers arrived in the early 1850s and fought with Indians for the land. The area was considered to be good ranch land with its rugged terrain and lush native grasses, so settlers moved in to establish ranches. You will find plenty of ranchers working the land around the park today. Ranching is a great part of the economy in the area.

Texans flocked to Mineral Wells for "the cure" in the 1880s. Proponents of the cure began their campaign to bring in business in 1885. Mineral Wells quickly became a world renowned health resort. People from everywhere came around to try the water. The reported curative effects of the local well water prompted many to bathe in it. Traffic was heavy as many headed for the town of Mineral Wells.

Business reached its height in 1899 when more than 33,000 passengers were railed into Mineral Wells. Most were there for the cure, although not all. The railroad was geared up for expansion as the popularity of the place had grown to such a great magnitude, but the financial panic of 1903 stopped the railroad's plans. The number of people heading to Mineral Wells to take advantage of the towns "healing water" dropped sharply. Mineral baths and resorts faded as luxuries no longer affordable. By the time the panic ended, people had forgotten about Mineral Wells.

You can still head to Mineral Wells State Park and enjoy the water. Maybe a bit of fresh air and exercise is just as much a cure as taking a dip in the magical waters of Mineral Wells. Taking a hike or indulging in some rock climbing is sure to revitalize your mind and body. As the ranchers discovered, and so will you, the terrain is hilly. The elevation varies between just over 700 feet to 950 feet above sea level.

The Brazos and Trinity tributaries break up the landscape. The environment is ideal for wildlife, including white-tailed deer, turkeys, raccoons, ducks, birds, and squirrels. The weather is hot in the summer with an average high of 98 degrees and mild in the winter with an average low of 32 degrees. The spring and fall are ideal times to go to Minerals Wells, but April and May are rainy. Excessive rain can make trails muddy and campsites too wet to enjoy.

For those who are ready for the benefits of walking, the park expanded to add the Lake Mineral Wells State Trailway. The trail begins northwest of Weatherford in central Parker County, and travels 20 miles westward to the downtown district of Mineral Wells in eastern Palo Pinto County. You may not want to walk all 20 miles, but it is possible to take shorter hikes. The Trailway is connected to Lake Mineral Wells State Park and has four trailheads located near Weatherford, in Garner, in the state park, and in downtown Mineral Wells.

The Trailway follows an old railroad track path through farm and ranch land and into a typical West Texas town. This same path was the way people from all over came to take a chance on the cure. The railroad was purchased by the tycoon Jay Gould after the panic of 1903. Gould owned other railroads at the time, but shortly after, the Texas & Pacific Railway Company took control.

The railroad continued to change hands up until 1989 when the city of Mineral Wells purchased the line and renamed it the Mineral Wells and Eastern Railroad. The city used it for hauling freight commercially until it became too costly to operate. The line was closed permanently in 1992 and converted into the trailway.

Lake Mineral Wells State Park and Trailway is located four miles east of Mineral Wells on U.S. Highway 180. For park reservations, call 512-

The Hunt for Healthy Solutions

389-8900. For more details, call the Park Information line at 800-792-1112.

If you are looking for something more comprehensive and medically sound to revitalize or realign your lifestyle to improve your health, then you should check into the Cooper Clinic. The clinic was founded in 1970 by Kenneth H. Cooper, M.D., M.P.H., who first gained attention after the publication of his first book, *Aerobics*, in 1968. Cooper's message about aerobics is credited with creating the jogging boom of the 1970s.

At the Cooper Clinic you will find a 30-acre gated Cooper Aerobics Center estate as the perfect place for rejuvenation. Its wooded land with trails passing duck ponds is located just minutes from Dallas. An attentive staff will make your retreat from the real world relaxing. A 62-room guest lodge, two restaurants, and fitness and recreational facilities at the Cooper Fitness Center health club make this a one-stop vacation to improve your mind and body. Medical spa retreats in the wellness program include lectures, workshops, cooking classes, and supervised fitness training.

For those who are looking for a complete health assessment, there is a six-hour medical exam conducted by a qualified professional team. You will be seen by physicians, dietitians, exercise test technologists, laboratory and X-ray technicians, a psychologist, cardiologists, radiologists, and laryngeal consultant if needed. Examination plans are based on individual needs, family history, age, and gender.

A thorough examination is a good place to start when you are ready to get serious about health. But nutrition is the key to a total health plan at the Cooper Clinic. Registered dietitians educate patients in healthful eating, cooking, and food shopping practices. While at Cooper, you can enjoy three gourmet, heart-healthy meals prepared daily. The fat and calorie content are carefully monitored. For

Winter

those looking to shed a few pounds, Cooper Clinic's dietitians will help you plan for a wise diet.

Along with nutrition, you will need to take at look at an exercise program to fit your needs. Cooper Fitness Center houses the latest cardiovascular or resistance weight training equipment, a steam room, sauna, whirlpool, indoor and outdoor tracks, lap pools, as well as tennis, racquetball, basketball, and volleyball courts. Optional services include private lessons with sports pros and massage therapy treatments.

When you are ready to relax, take a trip to the spa where licensed massage therapists and beauticians give Swedish, sports, or aromatherapy massage, deep cleansing facials, manicures, pedicures, seaweed masques, and other relaxing body treatments.

The Cooper Wellness Program is a minimum four-day program, so you will need to plan a long weekend to take advantage of the clinic. Special interest programs are also offered. Medical examination, accommodations at the Guest Lodge, spa services, and private lessons are optional and priced separately. Call 800-444-5192 to select your own program.

The Hunt for Healthy Solutions

9

A Search for the Past

GHOST TOWNS

HISTORY BUFFS MAY WANT TO TOUR TEXAS GHOST TOWNS. Some have visible remnants, museums, or markers showing tourists the keys to bygone days of cattle crossings, oil booms, and railroad expansion. Some towns lead travelers to religious, military, black, Indian, or German history. Settlers following gold left their mark on trails and towns. Those looking for good land to start a ranch or farm helped Texas grow. Speculators drilling for oil also produced towns overnight. In many cases, these overnight sensations died as quickly as they began.

To begin a journey to some Texas ghost towns, start with the state's most famous one, Luckenbach. While Waylon, Willie, and the boys may not be in Luckenbach, you will still find an old store, a post office, and the remains of a cotton gin. Tourists enjoy stopping in front of the post office to shoot a picture of the family. Some weekends, you may find a crowd in Luckenbach as it is a favorite gathering spot for many. Don't be surprised to find people camped along Grape Creek, the original homestead of German immigrant farmers who settled in the area during the 1850s. A reverend and his wife opened a store, which is still in operation sporadically. The reverend's brother-in-law, Albert Luckenbach, provided the name for the town, which slowly died. Hondo Crouch, an Austin area country music fan, and others purchased the town. Austin area musicians came to Luckenbach to play at the dance hall. The 1977 song "Luckenbach, Texas" made the town's name familiar. Luckenbach can be found on Farm to Market 1376, which is about six miles east of Fredericksburg. It is a scenic drive if you travel to Luckenbach from Blanco.

Morris Ranch is next on the ghost town trail—just twelve miles southwest of Fredericksburg. Take State Highway 16 west seven miles to Farm to Market 2093. Then you turn south on Morris-Tivydale Road, go two miles to a four-way intersection to find the center of the former Morris Ranch. You may see what looks like an old farm. Hidden among the trees and shrubs are old foundations. Structures are located on private property, but can be seen from the road. According to T. Lindsay Baker's book, *Ghost Towns of Texas*, the Morris Ranch post office and town store closed in 1954. Morris Ranch died due to legislative action that banned the town's livelihood. The town was built to breed and train racehorses. In 1856, Francis Morris purchased 23,000 acres, where he built a racetrack, barns, hotel, a stone store, a house for jockeys, a large home for the owners, and a school with a steeple that was used as a church on Sunday. In the 1890s, laws making horse racing illegal were enacted in many states. With no demand for horses, the owners were forced to sell off land and animals that remained. Horse racing came back to Texas later in the 1900s, and today you can enjoy the sport in a few Texas cities.

Peyton Colony has a unique history as it was founded by freed slaves after the Civil War. Some descendants of what was sometimes called "Freedmen's Colony" remain in the area. Robert Peyton was the founder of the town, which was located eight miles east of Blanco. While you can read about this in Baker's book, you can also find out about this town on many websites and in the Blanco area. If you pick up a local map in Blanco, the name is spelled "Payton," with an *a* replacing the *e*. To find Peyton Colony, at the junction of Farm to Markets 2325 and 165, turn north, and go a half mile on a dirt road. It is easy to miss since the church is still in use and not what you may expect to find in a ghost town. You should see the remains of an old schoolhouse, which was the first black school in Texas. If you get out of the car for a closer look, it would be wise to not try to enter the schoolhouse as it is deteriorating quickly. The old Peyton Colony graveyard, which is marked on some maps, is on private property. Gravestones from the Peyton Colony residents are kept in a cemetery off Farm to Market 165. You won't see the graveyard as you drive along 165. The old town site is said to be one of the most haunted spots in Texas, so be careful as you explore these grounds. A ghost may start a conversation with you. Visitors have taken photographs of unexplained apparitions. Those who have managed to spend a night in the area tell of loud parties going on when no living soul is awake.

For those visiting Luckenbach, Morris Ranch, and Peyton Colony, don't forget to stop by Fredericksburg for food and shopping. Fredericksburg, which is close to all three, is a quaint village with many restored structures. A thriving business area is clustered along the main street and the family will enjoy walking along this business district. Don't miss the Admiral Nimitz Museum and Historical Center, which was built to resemble a ship. Many local homes offer overnight accommodations. The Chamber of Commerce offers a list of lodging services. Contact the chamber at 210-997-6523. Also nearby is the town of Blanco, another small town worth investigating, and Blanco State Park, a 110-acre park in the Blanco River Valley.

A Search for the Past

Belknap can be reached by taking State Highway 251 three miles south of Newcastle. Marked on your map as Fort Belknap, the site is preserved by the state. The state also publishes ghost town information in the *Texas State Travel Guide*. You will find six original structures and one replica, plus a museum and archives. In the 1850s, Fort Belknap protected settlers living close to the Brazos Indian Reservation. The fort also provided protection for those delivering mail on the Butterfield Overland Mail Route. When the fort was abandoned, after the Civil War, the town lost many of its inhabitants. The fort was restored during the Texas centennial in 1936. Stop in Fort Belknap's museum for a look at the preserved past and enjoy a picnic in the park.

Next stop is Thurber, which became one of the first towns to have complete electric service in 1895. Established in the late 1880s, Thurber, owned and operated by a company, grew as employees were recruited from around the world to work in a coal mine and brick manufacturing plant. Thurber supplied brick for paved roadways throughout the state, including Austin's Congress Avenue and Camp Bowie Boulevard in Fort Worth. At the top of New York Hill, you can see a large brass plaque that shows the location of significant structures. The restored 100-year-old St. Barbara's Church, Thurber Cemetery, a furnished miner's house, and an authentic Italian bocci ball court give a glimpse into the past. Restaurants display photos of Thurber in its heyday. You can also enjoy the restored Main Street. Interstate 20, U.S. Highway 80, and State Highway 108 bisect Thurber, which is a National Historic Site.

Also in the area, you can visit Fort Griffin, which is considered to be a ghost town. More about Fort Griffin is in Chapter 20. Other preserved ghost towns include Helena, which has several restored buildings in the town square. You can see the courthouse that houses a museum, a farm house from the late 1800s, the town's post office, and one of the four original jail cells. The town of Helena was established

Winter

in 1852 on the Chihuahua Trail and near the Indianola–San Antonio Road. A lively little town with many gunfights in its saloon, Helena met its own demise after a young Emmett Butler was shot. Colonel William Butler vowed to kill the town that killed his son. Using his considerable wealth, Butler offered free land to the railroad to locate miles away from Helena. Like many other Texas towns, being bypassed by the railroad caused Helena's demise. You can find Helena on State Highway 80 between Karnes City and Gillett.

Today's Boys Ranch, which has a population of 550, is a home for boys and girls in trouble. Established in 1939, the first boys who came to live there stayed in the abandoned courthouse of Old Tascosa, a Texas ghost town from the 1870s. The courthouse is now the Julian Bivins Museum. Visitors are allowed to see the ranch and museum, which is open daily. You can see Boot Hill Cemetery where some of the unfortunate gunfight losers were laid to rest. The town was on the trade route and was the shipping point for some of the state's largest cattle ranchers. Known as the "Cowboy Capital of the Plains," some of the most notorious of the time came through town. Kit Carson and Billy the Kid were a couple of those who passed through Old Tascosa. As with many Texas towns, Old Tascosa died fairly quickly after the railroad was established too far away. Boys Ranch is on U.S. Highway 385 just north of where the Canadian River crosses the highway.

Other ghost towns found in the *Texas State Travel Guide* include Harmony Hill, Study Butte, Terlingua, and Old Springfield. Harmony Hill is 18 miles northeast of Henderson on State Highway 43. The town was an important trade center known as Nip and Tuck in 1850. Only a cemetery remains as storms destroyed many structures left behind when the railroad bypassed the town.

Study Butte, a good side trip when visiting Big Bend National Park, was a mining town. Around 1900, deposits of mercury were found and Will Study managed the Big Bend

A Search for the Past

Cinnabar Mine until it became unprofitable in the 1940s. Today, a few families live among the remaining adobe structures on State Highway 118 at the western edge of Big Bend National Park. Nearby, you can find the ghost town of Terlingua, off Farm to Market 170. Terlingua also started with the discovery of mercury and died with the decline of mercury sales. Every November, look for about 5,000 chili lovers as the International Championship Chili Cookoff is held in the desert region of Terlingua.

Old Springfield is located near Old Fort Parker State Historic Site and would be a nice side trip while visiting Fort Parker. Old Springfield was the county seat from 1838 to 1873 and the only town in the county for 32 years. You will find a historical marker on State Highway 14 near the entrance of Fort Parker State Park. The marker details the history of Old Springfield. Nearby, you can visit the town's cemetery.

For an extensive guide to ghost towns, read T. Lindsay Baker's *Ghost Towns of Texas*. *Ghost Towns of Texas* by Jim Wheat and *Texas Graveyards, a Cultural Legacy* by Terry G. Jordan are two other sources to check out. Be prepared to find just an open field where towns used to thrive as ghost towns decay and disappear with time. Be sure to enjoy the drive and other attractions along the way.

Winter

10

Great Golfing

SAN ANTONIO

"FORE!"

Keep your head up in San Antonio because "fore" may be more commonly heard than "¿Como esta?" The San Antonio area is home to 45 golf courses. For seasoned golfers, San Antonio is known for the Quarry and Pecan Valley golf courses, rated among the top public courses in the state. San Antonio is also home to La Cantera and the Texas Open.

The list of players entered in the La Cantera Texas Open has included such notables as Eldrick "Tiger" Woods in 1996. At 22, Woods didn't walk away with the $1.2 million purse in San Antonio, but gained his fame as he won eight tournaments. Six of those tournaments were on the PGA Tour, including the 1997 Masters Tournament. He was the youngest Masters champion ever. The San Antonio purse has increased since then. In 1998, Hal Sutton took $1.7 million at the La Cantera Texas Open. Since then, the La Cantera Texas Open has been changed to the Westin Texas Open.

If you would rather play golf than watch it, La Cantera Golf Club is one of the premier resort courses in Texas and the Southwest. Designed jointly by architects Jay Moorish and To Weiskopf, the 7,000-yard, par 72 course spreads over

1,600 acres of San Antonio's northwest side with several panoramic views of the city skyline.

Six natural ponds, running streams, and several signature holes create a remarkable experience. Golfers can look forward to unique holes like the seventh hole, which overlooks Fiesta Texas amusement park. This course, host for the La Cantera Texas Open since 1995, was named best new course the same year by *Golf Digest*.

Five sets of tees on each hole accommodate every golfer's skill level. Six holes expose great views of San Antonio, Fiesta Texas, and the Hill Country. Limestone outcroppings, live oak trees, and 75 white-sand bunkers make this course one of the most beautiful places in San Antonio for golfers to enjoy a game.

The first professional tournament in San Antonio was held in 1922 with a purse of $5,000. San Antonio is also credited with the creation of the Professional Touring Golfers' Association. In 1928, weather delays during a tournament allowed Tommy Armour and other players to incorporate the PGA, which is the governing body in charge of the PGA Tour. From 1960 through 1962, Arnold Palmer set a record by winning a third straight Texas Open title and was also the only player to win three years in a row in San Antonio. For more information about La Cantera Golf Club at 1604 La Cantera Parkway in San Antonio, call 800-446-5387.

While golfers feel La Cantera can't be matched for its beauty, many also enjoy playing at Pecan Valley Golf Club. Pecan Valley plays long with multi-tiered greens. The layout is traditional and the scenery isn't anything special. It's a collection of 18 tough golf holes. The course is affected by drought more than others in town, but if you are looking for a challenge, then try it. You will probably need to use

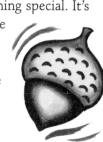

every club in the bag. The course can be difficult for high handicappers because of the length and hazards. Low handicap players will enjoy this well-run course. Pecan Valley Golf Club at 4700 Pecan Valley Drive can be reached at 210-333-9018. Pecan Valley was closed for nine months in 1999 for renovations. Expect some changes in the course.

Near San Antonio and worth mentioning is the 18-hole scenic Tapatio Springs Resort and Country Club with a par 72. Call 210-537-4197 for the pro shop or 800-999-3299 for the reservations desk and information about this course, which has panoramic views of the Hill Country. The reservations desk at the hotel can connect your call to the pro shop. Tapatio is a nice resort to visit with a peaceful country setting where wildlife can be seen. The property also has a nine-hole executive course, a championship course winding through Frederick Creek Valley. Tapatio Springs Resort and Conference Center is a 27-hole course in Boerne, north of San Antonio.

The 18-hole Quarry Golf Club with a 71 par was designed by Keith Foster. Call 210-824-4500 or 800-347-7759 for information. It has an open front nine, and links style with heather roughs. A number of creeks and lakes add to the hazards, and wind is always a factor. The back nine are very rugged as it was a quarry. The jagged rock of an old quarry combined with a lake create another beautiful setting for a game. The Quarry Golf Club is located at 444 E. Basse Road.

Situated near the airport, the 18-hole Olmos Basin Golf Course is at 7022 N. McCullough Avenue in San Antonio. Call 210-826-4041 for more information about this municipal course established in 1963. It has some water in play and a 72 par.

The 18-hole Cedar Creek Golf Course, 8250 Vista Colina, with a 72 par is a busy place. Call 210-695-5050 for infor-

Great Golfing

mation. It is a great municipal course, which has rocky roughs and a number of blind shots.

The Hyatt Regency Hill Country Resort has a 72 par course with 18 holes. Call 210-520-4040 for information. This course is 170 acres with rolling fairways, groves of oak, and meadows. Arthur Hills designed this course with a wide-open layout. It has 45 sand bunkers, grassy hollows, four water hazards, and rock-lined gulches.

Other courses in San Antonio:

Brackenridge Park Golf Course is an 18-hole public course with a par 72 at 2315 Avenue B in San Antonio. Call 210-226-5612.

Canyon Springs Golf Club, an 18-hole public, spikeless course with a 72 par, is at 24400 Canyon Golf Road in San Antonio. Call 210-497-1770.

Carmack Lake Golf Course is an 18-hole public course in Converse near San Antonio. Call 210-658-3806.

Fort Sam Houston Golf Course, the Laloma Course, is an 18-hole course, par 72. It is located on a military base at 2901 Fort Sam Houston in San Antonio. Fort Sam Houston Golf Course, the Salado Course, is an 18-hole course in the same location. To play you need to be a retired or active duty member of the military, or a Department of Defense employee. Call 210-222-9386.

Gateway Hills Golf Course, an 18-hole military course at 1800 Dimsted Place, San Antonio, is located on the Lackland Air Force Base. You can play if you are active in the military or retired, or a Department of Defense employee. Call 210-671-3466.

Max Starcke Park Golf Course, an 18-hole public course, is at 1400 S. Guadalupe Street in Seguin, near San Antonio. For information, call 830-401-2490.

Mission Del Lago Municipal Golf Course, an 18-hole par 72 public course, is located at 1250 Mission Grande in San Antonio. Call 210-627-2522.

Northcliffe Country Club is an 18-hole course at 5301 Country Club Boulevard, Cibolo. Call 830-606-7351.

Oak Hills Country Club, an 18-hole private course, is located at 5403 Fredericksburg Road in San Antonio. This is a private course, par 71, but does reciprocate with other courses. Call 210-384-7700.

Randolph Air Force Base Golf Club, an 18-hole military course, is located in Universal City. You need to be active or retired in the military, or a Department of Defense employee to play. Call 210-652-4570.

Riverhill Country Club is an 18-hole private course at 100 Riverhill Club Lane in Kerrville, west of San Antonio. You can play at the Riverhill Country Club if you rent a cottage there. Call 830-792-1143.

Riverside Municipal Golf Course, an 18-hole public course, is at 203 McDonald, San Antonio. Call 210-533-8371.

San Pedro Golf Course is a nine-hole public course at 6102 San Pedro, San Antonio. Call 210-349-5113.

Scott Schreiner Municipal Golf Course is an 18-hole, par 72 public course, at 1 Country Club Drive in Kerrville. Call 830-257-4982.

Willow Springs Golf Course is an 18-hole public course at 202 Coliseum Road, San Antonio. Call 210-226-6721.

Woodlake Golf and Country Club, an 18-hole semiprivate course, is at 6500 Woodlake Parkway in San Antonio. The public is welcome to play on this course. Call 210-661-6124.

Great Golfing

11

Dive into the Deep

GULF COAST

FOR AN UNUSUAL SIGHTSEEING TOUR, TAKE A SCUBA DIVING trip off the Texas Gulf coast. One hundred miles from Galveston you can find an underwater garden. Called the Flower Gardens by Texans, the gardens appear as a paradise in the midst of the desert. The Flower Gardens are part of the northernmost coral reefs on the continental shelf of North America. The reefs could not exist in conditions found any farther north.

The Flower Gardens have a variety of animal life for divers to encounter, including baby moray eels, manta rays, whale sharks, and huge schools of silvery jacks. In February and March, divers have the opportunity to swim with the hammerhead sharks during their annual schooling. Another popular time to go diving is in August during coral spawning. Some of the most prolific and highly predictable spawning is found the Flower Gardens' reefs. It happens each year eight evenings after the August full moon, usually between 8:00 and 11:00 P.M. *Montastrea annularis* corals release packets of egg and sperm during the annual spawning event at the Flower Gardens. The packets break apart on the surface to allow fertilization, and resulting larvae drift for days or weeks before sinking. If the larvae settle on a reef or other suitable place they can begin growing into mature corals.

In 1990, divers at the Flower Gardens first saw mass spawning, the synchronized release of gametes by a variety of coral species. Spawning by any corals was rarely seen before, and mass spawning in the Atlantic had never been observed. The divers reported their experience to scientists. Since that 1990 discovery, continued annual reports have stimulated "spawning expeditions" and scientific observation there and on reefs in the Caribbean Sea. Mass spawning at the Flower Gardens by three different types of coral allowed researchers to find out if the corals can reproduce with one another. What scientists discovered is the three have slightly different spawning times within the limited window of several hours each year.

Local dive tour companies plan trips during this time at a much lower cost than taking dive trips outside the country. Some tours include transportation to the dive site, air-conditioned quarters, air compressors, and food. Packages can also include training for the novice. Ask what specific areas you will dive in the package offered, and find out how many dives are included. Be sure to see the East and West banks, Stetson bank, and if possible, an oil rig. Oil rigs are unique marine ecosystems. You should see the Ruby Brittle Star and the Great Star Coral spawn at the Flower Gardens reef.

Stetson Bank National Marine Sanctuary is approximately 70 miles off the coast where you will find an offshore reef dive. Depth is limited by divers and dive operators. Typically dives range from 60 to 90 feet with a maximum depth of 100 feet. Visibility is 30 to 110 feet. Water temperature is 65 to 85 degrees, and the sanctuary is accessible by boat. Stetson Banks is closer to shore and a shallower dive than the Flower Gardens and is usually used by dive operators as the second dive site on a trip. A good spot for macro photography, you will see a diverse and large collection of sea life. There are many nooks and crannies in the rocks with lots of eels, worms, shrimp, and smaller fish. Stetson is home to the largest French angelfish you will ever see. It's teeming with critters. In addition you will likely see larger game fish including barracuda, amberjacks, and groupers. There are sometimes even sharks and giant stingrays visiting the area. The terrain is really different, with pinnacles of rock that rise 20 to 30 feet above the main floor, and raised ridges of sandstone that run several yards long in parallel lines.

The Flower Gardens, which is almost 42 square nautical miles, was designated a National Marine Sanctuary by the National Oceanic and Atmospheric Administration in 1992. There are 12 marine sanctuaries in U.S. waters: Stellwagen Bank, the Monitor, Gray's Reef, the Florida Keys, the Flower Gardens Banks, the Olympic Coast, Cordell Bank, the Gulf of the Farallones, Monterey Bay, the Channel Islands, Fagatele Bay, and the Hawaiian Island Humpback Whale National Marine Sanctuaries.

Few places in the world can boast the pristine condition of the Flower Gardens. Fortunately for science, this has allowed the study of natural processes that should characterize healthy ecosystems. With an increasing awareness of the Flower Gardens, the reef will continue to attract scientific attention. Humans have not yet had a significant impact on these reefs. The Flower Gardens are still a natural place where the unpredictable is common. Because of the natural wildness present at the reef, people need to have a healthy respect for the ocean. Currents and waves are not going to cooperate with divers. The annual hammerhead shark schools will not wait for calm weather. Coral diseases and whale sharks have no boundaries. Be prepared for anything.

Scientists continue to study the reef as well as fish in the area. Almost 150 reef fish species inhabit the Flower Gardens' reefs, a low number compared to reefs farther south. Yet this reef has a biological control mechanism not available on many reefs, due to overfishing of grazers and other reef

Dive into the Deep

fish. The Flower Gardens have a significant amount of coral covering their surfaces in comparison with other reefs.

The Flower Gardens' corals have been studied by Texas A&M. Scientists have used coral cores up to five feet long to study historical atmospheric and oceanographic conditions. Corals secrete seven to eight millimeters of limestone each year, analogous to trees adding annual rings. In each annual layer the corals leave chemical records of water quality. Water chemistry varies with changing temperature, salinity, and elemental composition, all of which reflect changes in climate. The cores contain several hundred years of data that can reveal climate conditions in times before people kept records. These findings may help scientists and others predict future weather conditions.

Texas A&M volunteers and Mobil Oil Company officials have begun a joint effort in the area to study the sea life around a gas production platform. A common sight off the coast, production platforms are a part of Texas coastal life. This prototype platform, anchored next to the Flower Gardens reefs, was designed to reduce marine pollution caused by gas production. Scientists and volunteers use donated space on the platform as an on-site laboratory and living accommodations. Scientists teach volunteers how to filter a sediment-trap sample using a vacuum apparatus, to look for changes in the amount of organic carbon on the seafloor during coral spawning. At the Flower Gardens, 10 to 20 volunteers collect samples each year in the study of spawning, larval development, and the use of laboratory-raised corals for reef restoration. The volunteers also provide samples for toxicology research for the National Biological Survey. The studies will determine the level of contamination reefs can

Winter

tolerate before environmental deterioration begins to harm them.

In their work on the reef, volunteers installed mooring buoys to limit damage caused by anchoring, and are involved in a census of fish, manta, and turtle populations coordinated by Texas A&M graduate students. Scientists captured, tagged, and tracked a loggerhead turtle on the West Bank to increase understanding of this threatened species. Scientists from many organizations have worked together on oil spill risk assessment and spill clean-up policies. The Coast Guard and the National Marine Fisheries Service cooperate with the sanctuary on enforcement, while the Environmental Protection Agency regulates industrial discharges and supports scientific efforts. Area industries have donated funds for research and education projects to the Flower Gardens Fund, a sanctuary support group established by the Gulf of Mexico Foundation. In addition, Mobil provides free transportation, food, lodging, and logistical support for scientists conducting research from their gas production platform in the sanctuary.

For more information about current research contact the Flower Gardens Banks National Marine Sanctuary, 216 W. 26th Street, Bryan, Texas, 77802, 409-779-2705. For information about Galveston area dive cruises, call the Galveston Island Convention and Visitors Bureau, 2106 Seawall Boulevard, 409-763-4311. Local divers say they prefer the Flower Gardens to dive locations farther south.

For freshwater experiences, look no further than Balmorhea State Recreation Area in Toyahvale. Balmorhea has what may be the world's biggest spring-fed swimming pool. Having almost two acres and holding more than 3,000,000 gallons of clear San Solomon springwater, this swimming hole is heaven during a hot West Texas day. It differs from public pools in size and depth. Ropes divide the pool into

Dive into the Deep

three sections designated for different uses. Descending 25 feet in one section, divers with tanks swim freely about the pool's deepest waters, while other swimmers splash around the 3- to 5-foot-deep section of the pool. A large area with a 3-foot-deep shelf and a sharp drop to 20 feet is filled with snorkelers catching glimpses of fish. Balmorhea has a variety of aquatic life you can see in its clear waters, which keep a constant temperature of 70 degrees. Located in the foothills of the Davis Mountains, San Solomon Springs has provided water for travelers for thousands of years. Artifacts indicate Indians used the spring. In 1849, the springs were called Mescalero Springs for the Mescalero Apache Indians who watered their horses along its banks. Today's name was given by Mexican farmers who used the water for their crops and hand-dug the first irrigation canals. The park is located four miles southwest of Balmorhea on State Highway 17 in Toyahvale.

Jump In

There are many other great places to dive on the Gulf. Here are a few suggestions.

- Lake Amistad is a popular spot near Del Rio. Contact the headquarters at 830-775-7491. Depth is 80 feet and visibility is 10 to 35 feet. You can see sunken cemeteries, buildings, and wrecks with rocky hills and beaches surrounding you. A line of buoys down the middle of the lake marks the international boundary between the United States and Mexico.

- Aransas Jetties in Port Aransas are rock mounds a half mile apart extending out one mile. It is 10 to 30 feet deep with 3 to 20 feet visibility. There is a lot of marine life to observe, including octopus, barracuda, sharks, sea urchins, and sponges. But beware, this site has several hazards including many people fishing, unpredictable currents that can be strong at times, boat traffic, sharks, and the rocks that form the jetties. Only divers with intermediate skill levels or above are advised to dive this site.

- Frio River at Garner State Park in Uvalde, 830-232-6132, is a spring-fed river with a maximum depth of 20 feet. Most of the river is three to four feet deep. Visibility is 10 to 20 feet, and water temperature is about 70 degrees.

- At Dive Valhalla Missile Silo, reservations are required to dive. The abandoned Atlas Missile Silo has a depth and visibility of 130 feet. You could dive day or night as there is constant low light. The looks of the silo earned its Norse name, Valhalla, which is what Norwegians called Heaven for Vikings. Divers are required to bring lights to use while diving at the site run by Family Scuba Center of Midland. Call 915-686-7333 for information and directions.

Other possibilities include National Seashores, Laguna Madre near Corpus Christi, Athens Scuba Pit in Athens, Blue Lagoon in Huntsville, Lake Travis in Austin, Lake Caddo, Spring Lake in San Marcos at Aquarena Springs, Lake Whitney State Park in Whitney, and Toledo Bend Reservoir on the Texas-Louisiana border.

Dive into the Deep

12

Spring into Action on the Bluebonnet Trail

HILL COUNTRY

EVERY YEAR HILL COUNTRY CITIES BOAST OF WILDFLOWERS blanketing hills surrounding their location. Photography contests begin, and the search for the best picture of bluebonnets, Indian paintbrush, or cactus flowers heats up more than the mild spring weather. Several towns plan festivals around the spring event. These towns are on what locals call the Bluebonnet Trail, including the towns of Burnet, Llano, and Marble Falls. In the spring you will find sunny, breezy, cloudless skies with highs in the 80s and lows in the 50s. The weather is perfect for seeing the natural attractions of the area.

Photographers will enjoy shooting pictures of a variety of wildflowers at this time of year. You may see American lotus, black-eyed Susan, cacti, coreopsis, fleabane, gayfeathers, grass pink, Indian blanket, Indian paintbrushes, Mexican hat, mountain pink, pink evening primroses, prickly pear cactus, rain lilies, sand verbena, tahoka daisy, Texas bluebonnets, Texas dandelion, wild foxglove, winecup, and white prickly poppy. Beginning in late March, the hills and fields should be brimming with bluebonnets, Indian paintbrush, winecups, and primroses in and about Marble Falls,

Llano, and Burnet. Almost any highway in Central Texas will be bordered by an array of wildflowers. The credit for this natural display goes to the Texas Department of Transportation, which spreads wildflower seeds along highways.

Some of the best views to be had are on your drive between attractions. Park Road 4, which services Inks Lake State Park and Longhorn Caverns State Park, linking State Highway 29 with U.S. Highway 281, is a good road for viewing wildflowers. The field near the Smith Visitor Center at Inks Lake becomes flooded with bluebonnets, as do the roadsides within the park.

Some say the drive from Port Aransas to Marble Falls offers the best wildflower viewing of all. Other good viewing roads include State Highway 71 west from Austin as far as Llano; U.S. Highway 281 between Burnet and Johnson City; Farm to Market 1431 from Marble Falls to Kingsland; Farm to Market 2147 from Marble Falls to Horseshoe Bay along Lake LBJ. Request your free guide to the wildflowers of Texas by writing to Texas Department of Transportation, P.O. Box 5064, Austin, TX 78763.

Easter weekend is usually the time set for the annual Bluebonnet Festival in Burnet. Call the Burnet Chamber of Commerce at 512-756-4297 for more information. Burnet is a small city of about 3,500 people located on State Highway 29 and U.S. Highway 281, just over 10 miles north of Marble Falls and 12 miles east of Buchanan Dam. There are several good restaurants and many antique and gift stores surrounding the Courthouse on the Square. The Riverwalk is a landscaped area along the river where you can go for a stroll, have a picnic, or just sit and enjoy the scenery and people. The Riverwalk is within walking distance of the downtown square.

Marble Falls, a town of 5,000, is another city in the bluebonnet area to visit. The city's name is rooted in the rock of the Texas Hill Country. A 20-foot fall in the Colorado River over marble ledges gave rise to the name, but it was the huge stone monolith called Granite Mountain looming on the town's western edge that secured Marble Falls' place in Texas history. Here is where the famed pink granite of the State Capitol Building was quarried. It was a donation from progressive area citizens in exchange for a rail connection with Austin. Today, the natural assets of prized rock and rolling river are still combining with progressive citizens to make the Marble Falls/Lake LBJ area one of the most attractive and popular in all Texas.

Llano, a small town with a population of 2,900, is known for deer hunting and antique stores, as well as good barbecue at Inman's and Cooper's. It is also located in the heart of the Hill Country, making it a great wildflower viewing spot. It is about 70 miles northwest of Austin, and about 40 miles north of Fredericksburg. You can visit the Lightening A Ranch or Enchanted Rock State Park.

In the 1890s, Llano was known as a town without a church, which was a code-phrase for a "party town." Llano had several hotels, including the luxurious Don Carlos with its grand ballroom and tennis courts. Clyde Barrow stayed at the Dabbs in the 1930s. Brothels were an important part of the local scene. The wealthy and elite would hitch their private railcars to trains from New York or San Francisco when traveling to Llano.

If you are anxious to see wildflowers and learn more about them, you can stop by the Lady Bird Johnson Wildflower Research Center in Austin. Make it a Saturday excursion to take advantage of the longer hours, between 9 A.M. and 5 P.M. You can stroll the gardens with numerous courtyards, terraces, arbors, and meadows. Or you can see the Visitors Gallery, the Wild Ideas store, and a great view from an observation tower. You can find something to eat at the Wildflower Cafe. No pets and no smoking allowed. Educational workshops for teachers, youth, and others are available. Contact Lady Bird Johnson Wildflower Research Center at 4801 La Crosse Avenue, Austin, Texas 78739, 512-292-4200 for more information.

Hot Spots

The Hill Country   In an area about the size of the state of New Hampshire, you will find hilly, rocky terrain, wildflowers in the spring, and wildlife year-round. While Burnet, Llano, and Marble Falls may be the best towns for viewing bluebonnets and other wildflowers, other attractions in the area may be worth including in your trip.

Pedernales Falls State Park   Enjoy a beautiful park along the Pedernales River near Johnson City. The falls are a mere ripple, depending on the water level, but the pools they form are spectacular. There are abundant deer, birds, swimming holes, hiking trails, and fishing spots.

Enchanted Rock State Natural Area   The natural beauty appeals primarily to hikers and rock climbers who scramble up, around, and over the granite faces. If you hike to the top of the dome, you can squeeze into Enchanted Rock Cave. The dome mountain held great significance for the area's Native Americans, who believed it was occupied by spirits. Take a seat on the summit as the sun goes down and you can watch the buzzards lifted by strong currents.

Fredericksburg   Known for both its German heritage and its peaches, this town is full of antique shops, restaurants, and bed-and-breakfasts. You can tour the Admiral Nimitz and Pacific War Museum with the Japanese garden and the Pioneer Museum.

Kerrville   Here you find a great place to begin a scenic drive. Take Highway 16 to Bandera, then Highways 470 and 462 to Hondo; return to Kerrville by taking U.S. Highway 90 west a mile or two and then head north on 1796. Routes 187 and 39 will also take you to Kerrville. Watch for armadillos, deer, roadrunners, vultures, and blackbucks (antelope from India introduced into the region).

Lake Buchanan   Huge and deep, this lake was created by a dam in the Colorado River. It is the site of the Vanishing Texas River Cruise. Bring binoculars on this cruise to spot bald eagles and other birds during the winter.

Lost Maples State Natural Area   Found in Vanderpool, south of Kerrville, discover a colorful place to hike in the fall when the leaves turn an array of colors. Arrive early in the day as a limited number of people are allowed in the park.

Wimberley   The beautiful town is filled with antique and craft shops. Take the scenic Ranch to Market 32, also called the "Devil's Backbone" to get there and you won't regret the trip. Two other Hill Country scenic routes close by are Ranch to Market 337, from Medina to Leakey, and Ranch to Market 1431 in either direction out of Marble Falls. In Wimberley you can stroll through an art colony with many galleries. Artists at work will take time out to visit with you as you find souvenirs crafted from silver, wood, or a variety of materials. A bonus for this trip may be to see the Wild Basin Wilderness area, the "Lost Pines" of Bastrop State Park, or McKinney Falls State Park.

13

Canyon Country

RIO GRANDE AND BEYOND

TEXAS IS FULL OF DEEP CANYONS WITH WALLS EXPOSING strata of the past 200 million years of geological activity and a land rich with history. Indian tribes and others lived in canyons during the past 12,000 years. Ash piles, pieces of woven mats, and broken pottery inside shallow caves are traces ancient inhabitants left behind. Indians have worn rough rock surfaces until smooth while grinding corn into meal. Deep canyons afforded some break against high winds of the plains for the inhabitants and some protection and cover from their enemies. The canyons also were used effectively to hunt game without guns. Buffalo were run off canyon cliffs, plunging to their death.

To take in Texas canyons, start big. Start with the nation's second largest canyon, Palo Duro. The 800-foot-deep Palo Duro Canyon is second only to the Grand Canyon. Located down in the canyon is Palo Duro Canyon State Park, one of the largest state parks. South of Amarillo, the canyon is easily accessible by car. Steep inclines winding down into the bottom are manageable for most cars. Jeep tours can take you to the places hard to see by car. Riding stables located at the entrance and in the canyon can take you even closer to some of the red canyon walls.

The Prairie Dog Town Fork of the Red River flows down the caprock to the east. Together with the wind, this small fork of the Red River has spent a few million years carving the rugged canyon walls you can see today. Spanish explorer Coronado could have found the canyon in 1541, but Captain R. B. Marcy is credited with discovering it in 1852.

Palo Duro was the location of the decisive battle between Comanche and Kiowa Indians and U.S. Army troops under General Ronald Mackenzie in 1874. In the 1930s, land was donated for the park and the Civilian Conservation Corps constructed stone buildings to house a store, restrooms, and other facilities. The Pioneer Amphitheater, which seats about 1,700, is the scene of the annual summer production of the drama *Texas* and a big attraction for visitors. Summer is by far the busiest season.

Horseback riding is one of the more popular activities in the park. On the canyon floor you will find Goodnight Riding Stables, named after the famous cattle rancher Charles Goodnight, who also had a part in Palo Duro history during the 1870s. You can ride to the Lighthouse Rock formation, a distinct feature of Palo Duro Canyon. It's a four- to five-hour trip to the Lighthouse and includes a chance to explore Sunday Canyon and picnic near Castlerock. To take the tour a minimum of six people must be signed up. While exploring the canyon, you will see part of the Texas longhorn herd kept by the state parks. There are 23 miles of trails for horses, bikes, or hikes, and 10 trails designated for bikes only.

There are many spots to pitch a tent or park a trailer in Palo Duro, with closeup views of the rough, red canyon walls. Few cabins are available. For primitive camping you can hike a half mile to two miles to reach different remote spots. There are primitive campsites with designated areas for horses available. In the park you can also learn more about the area's geology and history in the visitors center. You can see the restoration of a line shack used by the first commercial cattle ranch in the Texas panhandle in 1876. Camping supplies, snacks, souvenirs, and mountain bike rentals are all available at the Goodnight Trading Post at the bottom of the canyon.

Palo Duro is best seen on bike, horseback, or foot. If you want a good place for climbing, you might look elsewhere. The park is located about 12 miles east of the Canyon on State Highway 217. From Amarillo, take Interstate 27 south to State Highway 217, and go east eight miles. Highs in July reach 92 degrees. With the drier climate, Palo Duro is not as hot as other Texas spots during the summer and shows at the Pioneer Amphitheater are only during summer months. If you want to avoid summer crowds and take advantage of milder weather, then visit the canyon in fall. With the added color of fall foliage, the already breathtaking scenery will be even more beautiful.

To learn more about the history of the area around Palo Duro Canyon, you can go to the Panhandle-Plains Historical Museum. Established in 1933, it is the oldest and largest museum of its kind in the state. Some features of the museum include the limestone used in the structure of its Pioneer Hall. There are more than 100 famous West Texas cattle brands in glazed sandstone surrounding the entrance. Awarded a State Antiquities Landmark designation in 1983 for its unique Art Deco structural style, the museum houses western artwork. The museum is located at 2401 Fourth Avenue in Canyon. For information, call 806-651-2244.

Another famous canyon and spot worth a visit is Seminole Canyon State Historical Park, near Del Rio on U.S. Highway 90. Seminole Canyon preserves Native American pictographs in caves, some dating back eight millennia. The paintings are tucked inside shallow caves where Indians lived, worked, and worshipped, away from the burning sun. Historians believe the weather was milder than it is today in the canyon. The people who lived in the canyon cooked over fire and conducted ceremonies by firelight. The ash pile left by these inhabitants stacked up over the years to reach a height of 30 to 40 feet. On the tour, you take a stairway to the top of the pile and actually walk on it. Evidence of the Indian lifestyle is seen in worn grinding stones and remnants of mats they used to rest on.

Seminole Canyon's cave paintings can be seen only on a guided tour. Tours leave in the morning and afternoon. Pick a very bright, sunny day to visit the caves as paintings have been worn by wind and water over time, and some are barely visible. While the meaning of the drawings is not known, there is much speculation. Pictures of shamans, animals, and hunters are visible.

Seminole Canyon State Historical Park has a few hiking trails where you can appreciate the beauty of the canyon and the river running through the park. The springtime is the busiest season as students from nearby colleges visit the region during spring break. The best part about visiting in the spring is seeing the brilliant colors of the blooming flowers. The canyon has more color then than any other time of the year. During other times you will see more wildlife, enjoy the serenity of standing above deep canyons, and hear the call of circling vultures. Deer walk through campgrounds during the less crowded times of the year. Deer will approach tents, jarring light sleepers out from under their covers.

There are two hikes worth taking in Seminole: one is a short one-and-a-half-mile jaunt to a spectacular view of three intersecting canyons, and the other is a six-mile hike to the Rio Grande. The first hike is not very challenging unless you go during the summer. Bring plenty of water as you will get thirsty and there are no watering holes along the way. The view of the three canyons is worth walking the short distance. You will see jackrabbits and possibly deer along the way.

The hike to the Rio Grande is fairly easy, but allow yourself plenty of time to hike out and back; the return trip takes much longer. The halfway point is where you can see the Rio Grande. It's fairly easy to climb down to the water. On the other side of the river is Mexico. Be sure to pick up a trail map at the headquarters and ask park rangers about trail conditions. But don't believe any stories rangers tell you about desert alligators.

The best of the cave drawings are seen from the Pecos River. To see these you need to go on a guided tour. The hike in and out isn't easy. You need to be in good shape for it, say tour guides from the Rock Art Foundation. The trek is worth it. Members of the foundation also guide tours for Seminole Canyon. The Rock Art in Panther Cave, located on the Rio Grande near Seminole Canyon, is accessible only by boat.

Reservations can be made for any of the state parks by calling the Texas Parks and Wildlife Department at 512-389-8900. For more information, call 800-792-1112.

If you plan to do some climbing in Texas canyons, remember to follow a few basic rules. Canyons are a scarce resource and subject to flooding, so don't destroy vegetation when hiking or riding through. When climbing in canyons do not mark canyon walls. Stop by the park headquarters to learn rules for climbers.

Canyon Country

Spring

14

Rattlesnake Roundup

RIO GRANDE VALLEY

CARNE ADOVADA, CALABACITAS, POSOLE, SOPAIPILLAS . . . ARE
you hungry yet? Maybe you don't know how good these
South Texas food items are yet. How about enchiladas, bur-
ritos and tacos? Most Americans have heard of these Mexican menu items, which are offered in just about every state.
But for a real south of the border taste without ever leaving
the states, head for the Rio Grande Valley of South Texas.

The Rio Grande Valley is between the southern coastal
area of South Padre Island and McAllen, the largest, oldest
and westernmost town of the Valley. Citrus groves, scrub
brush, rattlesnakes, and Tex-Mex food are Valley staples.
When in the Valley, don't be in a big hurry. The pace is slow
but friendly. Spanish is spoken by a large number of Valley
residents. Many people in the Valley are only part-timers
who return to their northern home during the long, hot, and
dry summers.

Tex-Mex cooking was born nearly five centuries ago
when the Spanish brought European spices and animals to
combine with local food. The result can be a hot and spicy
meal. Remember to order extra tortillas, so when the chile
gets too hot you can chew on one. Liquids increase the fire
in your mouth, the starch in tortillas cools it down, and a
few cervesas quench your thirst afterward.

Tex-Mex can be a combination of hearty foods like carne asada (a grilled meat), frioles or refried beans, guacamole, flour tortillas, and pico de gallo (tomato and chile salsa). Fajitas—grilled steak strips wrapped in tortillas and topped with onion, green peppers, cheese, sour cream, salsa, and guacamole—were discovered in the Valley.

If the food doesn't provide enough excitement for you, try a rattlesnake hunt in the Valley, which has plenty to spare. The best time for catching the dangerous fellows is during the cool part of the day. During summer months, start after the sun is down, when rattlers are out looking for small animals like rats and mice. Wear a pair of snake guards to avoid any trips to the emergency room. You can drive slowly through the brushy pastures with a spotlight to illuminate the dark terrain.

To catch a live rattler, take a snake pole, that is, a long pipe with a tip on the end. Out of the end of the pole comes a small noose to be looped around the rattler's head. You can pull the noose tight because the thin rope goes through the pole to the top end. Once the rattler's head is looped, pull the thin rope tight to secure the snake. The pole enables you to keep your distance and catch the snake live.

However, you may *not* want to keep the critters alive. In that case, you can shoot the ones you see. Be careful handling dead snakes since venom still in them can be dangerous. Rattlers are in season all year in Texas. There is no game limit, but you do need a hunting license. On a fair night you could catch more than a dozen. The snakeskins are commonly made into belts and boots. You can find many people who will make these for you in the Valley. Valley people are always ready for a good rattlesnake roundup, such as the one held yearly in Freer, a small town on State Highway 44, north of the Valley.

About 20,000 visitors descend upon the 3,200 year-round residents of Freer every April for the roundup. Rattlesnakes are the main feature of this gathering, but not the only one. The event sponsor, the Freer Chamber of Commerce, puts on a big party. Besides snakes, you can see Miss Texas, a talent contest, a beach party show, rope tricks, bullwhip play, gun spinning, comedy shows, and juggling. You can listen to gospel, classic rock, and country music.

Of interest to you snake lovers, the heaviest rattlesnake brought in for the 1998 roundup weighed 9.5 pounds and measured more than six feet long. One person brought in 367 pounds of snakes! In 1998, more than 1,500 pounds of rattlesnakes were brought in and sold at $3 per pound. More than 700 pounds of fried rattlesnake meat were consumed.

You have to go to the Freer Rattlesnake Roundup at least once. Besides all the entertainment and excitement you will experience, the event helps the youth of Freer. Local non-profit groups such as schools and churches make money on refreshments to give scholarships, purchase uniforms, and provide many other services for youth.

The sounds of the Valley include more than the buzz of a rattler. In the 1800s, traveling musicians with either a flute, guitar, or drum would sing songs originally sung in Spain and Mexico. As these traveling musicians mixed with Germans, Poles, and Czechs, they incorporated the styles of polkas and waltzes. Dancing in a circle is popular with Texas Tejano and country music.

In the 1960s and '70s, Tejano took in the orchestra sound, as well as remnants of pop and rhythm and blues. When the disco scene hit in the early 1980s, a Brownsville native and his group known as Joe Lopez y El Groupo Mazz introduced the keyboard sound to Tejano. More recently, the accordion has been used.

If you are more interested in a less exciting adventure, there are things to see in the Valley not shown on the map. Stop at McAllen, a city on the Rio Grande with a population of 90,000. McAllen began as a railroad stop in 1904. Just across the Rio Grande is the Mexican city of Reynosa with a population of 375,000.

Many tourists cross into Reynosa daily. If you plan to cross, it is a good idea to park your car on the U.S. side of the International Bridge and walk across. You will enjoy shopping for bargains at mercado central or around the zocalo, the town square. Reynosa also has two bullrings. You can call the McAllen Convention and Visitors Bureau for information on bullfight schedules. For dining in Reynosa, Sam's at Allende and Ocampo are known for inexpensive steak dinners, Mexican platters, and quail.

In McAllen, you will want to see the 1886 courthouse and jail, botanical gardens and nature center, the McAllen International Museum, and the Hudson Museum, which features vintage cars. Near McAllen is the Santa Ana Refuge, a good place to bird-watch. Take U.S. Highway 281 south to find the refuge, which is close to the border.

McAllen has a large number of motels to choose from, or you can stay in a small town between McAllen and South Padre. McAllen also has a large number of restaurants where you can make your own taco or have fajitas, frijoles a la charra, grilled onions, and peppers. In nearby Pharr, Armando's Taco Hut at 106 N. Cage has inexpensive Tex-Mex food, as well as a Tejano jukebox and live music.

From McAllen, you can take U.S. Highway 83 across the Valley to Harlingen. In Harlingen you will find museums dedicated to the military and the history of the Valley. The Rio Grande Valley Museum showcases the heritage of Texas and the Rio Grande Valley. Within the same complex is the New Museum, the Historical Museum, the 1905 historic Lon C. Hill home, the Paso Real Stagecoach Inn, and Harlingen's Hospital Museum. The complex is located at Boxwood and Raintree streets.

The Texas Air Museum displays aircraft and memorabilia from World War I through Desert Storm. The museum, located on Farm to Market 106 one mile east of Rio Hondo, has a research center and a library. The Iwo Jima Memorial Monument and Museum is dedicated to the Battle of Iwo Jima. It is located next to the Valley International Airport at 320 Iwo Jima Boulevard in Harlingen.

Rattlesnake Roundup

15

A Place for Salvation

ABILENE

ABILENE IS A CENTER FOR RELIGION. ABOUT 150 CHURCHES representing more than 30 denominations serve the city's population of 106,000. As a center for religious activities, education, and growth, local Christian music groups entertain on a regular basis in the area. Seminars, educational programs, and Christian universities, as well as a Christian camp reach out to many souls in Abilene and beyond.

Abilene wasn't always a bastion of religious activity. The city was established by cattlemen as a stock shipping point on the Texas and Pacific Railroad in 1881. Named for the city of Abilene in Kansas, the original end of Old Chisholm Trail, Abilene became a major cattle producing and farming area. Much later, the discovery of oil boosted the city's economy. To celebrate its centennial in 1981, the city set up a demonstration oil-drilling rig on the county fairgrounds to illustrate the techniques of "making hole." By pure accident, it struck oil and generated a small profit.

The culture of the city has developed from raising cattle for market to educating youth and saving souls. Abilene Christian University, Hardin-Simmons University, and McMurry University, all religious based universities in Abilene, add a large number of young adults to the population.

Founded in 1923 and supported by the United Methodist Church, McMurry University is a four-year, coeducational, liberal arts college with nearly 1,400 students. Combine these with other university students, and you will see why entertainment, businesses, and recreational activities are aimed at college students. Christian punk rock bands like Big 13, a local favorite and local contest winner, are popular in Abilene. The group credits their success to God. Band members find support from the local Crossroads Community Church, an interdenominational and interracial church that supports many events. Another band, Servant's Piercing, promote themselves as God's servants and attract a following in Abilene.

While salvation of the soul is a chief occupation, Abilene's residents also have preservation of the city in mind. The old Drake Hotel, a large, four-story building located downtown, stands as a symbol of this preservation effort. Once considered Abilene's grandest hotel, the building sat dilapidated and was a target for vandals for years. But a dedicated small group had other plans for the 1909 "revival style" mission building. First named Grace Hotel, it is one of the oldest structures in Abilene. In the mid 1930s, a fourth story was added, the name changed to the Drake Hotel, and dances and parties were held on the rooftop. The doors closed in the 1970s after ownership changed hands many times, and the building sat rotting for 15 years. The Abilene Preservation League joined the Abilene Fine Arts Museum to plan a new life for the building and the downtown area. Using colors and architectural details from 1909, the hotel was restored to its original grandeur. The Main Gallery on the first floor exhibits art, and the old hotel guest rooms are offices for museum staff. The Grace Museum, as the hotel is known now, also houses a historical museum and a children's museum.

Another historical adventure is just 14 miles south of Abilene off State Park Highway 89. Turn right on Elm, go two

Spring

blocks, and you will find Buffalo Gap Historic Village, which preserves the early West Texas heritage. Before the Civil War, a favorite buffalo run for Indians was through the big gap in the Callahan divide. Settlers and outlaws attracted by water, good soil, and ranch land came after the Indians left. Pioneers built the village, which today consists of a collection of century-old buildings. A log cabin is the oldest structure in the area, which also includes the first courthouse. The courthouse and jail were built with gun ports to fight off Indians. The Buffalo Gap Chapel is one of the earliest churches. Inside these 19 buildings, you can see Western and Indian artifacts. Also see the train station, the church, a doctor's office, a cabinet mill, a blacksmith shop, a barbershop, a printshop, a wagon barn, a filling station, an art gallery, a school, a bank, a post office, and a Buffalo Gap Store and Trading Post. The home of the first marshall of Abilene has been restored with its original contents. In the 1880s, law and order were badly needed. Buffalo Gap, selected as Taylor County seat July 3, 1878, was the only town in a county of 200 people. Today, the town of Buffalo Gap has good restaurants and unusual stores. Abilene State Park and Lake Abilene are nearby. You can camp in Abilene State Park just four miles from Buffalo Gap Historic Village. For more information about the village, call 915-572-3365.

The city's zoo, dedicated to preservation of plants and animals, is another attraction not to miss. The Abilene Zoo, located in Nelson Park, has animal exhibits surrounded by plants native to South Texas. You can compare animals and habitats from the Southwestern United States and Central America to similar regions in Africa and Madagascar. The zoo cares for more than 800 animals representing over 200 species, including African elephants, giraffes, and aquatic life. The zoo education department provides classes, tours, and special events year-round. For more information, call 915-676-6085. Ask about zookeeper programs for youth and adult classes on bird-watching.

A Place for Salvation

Another side trip could be a stop at the Old Jail Art Center in Shackelford County's first permanent jail. Restored and expanded, the Center is open year-round. One block west is the Shackelford County Courthouse, built in 1883 with the Aztec Theater. Fort Griffin State Park has ruins of a historic frontier fort and is just 15 miles north on U.S. Highway 283.

In Abilene, you can stay at BJ's B&B at 508 Mulberry Street. Numbers to call are 800-673-5855 or 915-675-5855. BJ's has four units, two with private bathrooms and two with a shared bathroom. Only children 16 and above can stay at BJ's. For couples in search of a romantic spot, BJ's has one honeymoon suite, which bears the name Love. All rooms at BJ's have names. The other three are Joy, Patience, and Peace.

A nearby place to stay is the Old Nail House Inn in Albany, 800-245-5163. About 35 miles from Abilene, the inn is located across the street from the Shackelford Courthouse, one of the most photographed courthouses in the state. The inn was the home of Robert Nail, who originated the *Albany Fandago*, a musical produced annually in Albany during the summer. Opened in 1990, the inn has three rooms upstairs, two rooms with sunporches, and full breakfasts served. You can stay in a cottage with a kitchen and living room if you are after more space. You can enjoy relaxing in a hot tub, or sit in a gazebo or on a deck where breakfast is served when the weather permits. Children can stay on a limited basis. Call ahead for more information.

For a Western dining experience, try Fort Griffin General Merchandise's mesquite grilled steaks and chicken, on U.S. Highway 180. Call 915-762-3034 for information. The restaurant serves choice Black Angus beef that is wet aged for 14 days, then rubbed with olive oil, salt, pepper, garlic and onion powders, oregano, nutmeg, and cinnamon, and grilled over mesquite. Tommy Lee Jones and Clint Eastwood

Spring

dined there while shooting movies in
the area. Robert Duvall liked the style
of the restaurant's bar so much he built
one like it in his house. Also, you can
try the Ice House Restaurant, which
serves Tex-Mex, as well as mesquite grilled
steaks and chicken, at 200 South 2nd Street, across from the
courthouse. For home cooking, try High Lonesome at 233
North Main.

Nearby attractions include Possum Kingdom State Park;
historic Albany with numerous historical buildings and small
shops; Kuhn's Wildlife Refuge in Breckenridge; and the aviation museums in both Breckenridge and Abilene.

The Western Heritage Classic is held in early May and
features ranch rodeo, campfire cook-off, sheep dog trials,
horseshoeing competition, Cowboy Poet's Society, Western
art show, and many other activities recalling early Western
heritage. The first weekend in April features Celebrate Abilene, an outdoor festival held in the historic downtown area.
The festival combines the arts, history, railroads, and family entertainment into one. Abilene is on U.S. Highway 84,
a segment of the Ports to Plains Highway connecting the
state's heartland to coastal ports. It can also be reached on
U.S. Highways 83/277 and Interstate 20.

A Place for Salvation

16

The Place Without People

BIG BEND

INDIANS IN WEST TEXAS BELIEVED THE GREAT SPIRIT DUMPED all the leftover rocks in Big Bend after making the Earth. Spanish explorers who ventured into this mountain region thought the land was uninhabited. The Mexicans, who lived nearby, called it "the place without people." On an August afternoon when temperatures may exceed 100 degrees, Big Bend National Park may *appear* uninhabited. But there is life in Big Bend.

You will find species that exist only in Big Bend because wildlife has been cut off from the rest of the world by the Chihuahuan Desert, which is too difficult to cross. In Big Bend, you can find a desert amphibian called couch's spade-foot toad, the sierra del carmen white-tailed deer, a mosquito fish, the kangaroo rat that metabolizes water, and a large bird known as the roadrunner because it runs rather than flies. You can see winged insects that live their entire lives in, on, and off one species of plant. Coyotes, jackrabbits, and the panther, for which parts of the park are named, may be seen.

Some plant species here are found nowhere else in the world. The chisos oak grows only in Blue Creek Canyon. The chisos agave, a hybridized century plant, grows only in these mountains. A number of other plant species, such as the drooping juniper, which always appears to need a good watering, grow only in the Chisos Mountains in the United States. You know you are in the desert when you see lechuguilla, a plant that looks like a clump of dagger blades sticking out of the ground. The coarse, strong fibers of the lechuguilla were once used in matting, ropes, bags, and household items.

You might see the mysterious resurrection plant, which can be dried and stored without water for many years without damage to the plant. Ocotillo, or the "Devil's Walking Stick" is symbolic of Big Bend. It was once used instead of barbed wire by Mexican cattlemen to construct fences. The plant has dark green leaves from top to bottom after a rainfall, and will produce a bright red flower at the end of each limb two or three times a year.

Big Bend is best described as a piece of desert with the Chisos Mountains at its heart. With vast distances separating Big Bend from the rest of the world, you have to plan carefully for arrival in the park. Be sure to make reservations for lodging far in advance as the available places are booked up quickly. Lodges can be booked as much as a year in advance. Trains, airplanes, or buses will not take you all the way to the park, but do go as far as Alpine, 108 miles from the park headquarters. Plan ahead for driving in by packing water, gas, and tools for car repairs in case of a breakdown. In the desert you can expect the temperatures to be extreme.

Volcanic rock forms some surfaces in Big Bend National Park. Dinosaur bones from 60 to 80 millions years ago have been found in the park. The area isn't completely dry since the Rio Grande flows through the land. Water slowly carved out the canyons of Big Bend. The area was inhabited by nomadic Indians who arrived in 6000 B.C.

When the Spanish came in the 1500s they tried to enslave the Indians. Tribes changed over time and the Apache Indians drove out other tribes in the 1700s. The Apaches terrorized residents by making monthly runs across the border to steal cattle and other things from Mexican farmers. Many Mexicans died during these bloody excursions, and some were brought back as prisoners. The U.S. National Guard tried to prevent raids and fought with the Apaches in later years. The Texas Rangers were called in to protect ranches in the Big Bend area. Photographs in the park's museum depict the Old West days.

Before the Apache Indians ended their reign of terror in Big Bend, they began one of the area's biggest mysteries—the location of the Lost Mine. Spanish explorers found a rich mine in Big Bend. To excavate the mine, the Spanish hired Mexicans to work for them. In order to keep the location of the mine a secret, the Spanish would put bags over the Mexicans' heads before taking them to work. For days they went to and from the mine without seeing where they were going. Nobody knew the exact location of the mine. The Apaches decided they didn't like the intruders, so they killed every man. To prevent others from trying to work the mine, the Apaches covered the entrance. You can hike the Lost Mine trail, but you probably won't find the mine. You will have a scenic hike with shady spots surrounded by mountains. Today there are two other reminders of the Apache era in Big Bend. The Chisos Mountains were given their name by the Apaches because of the trees growing on them. In spite of the bloody past, you can walk peacefully on the Apache Trail through the park.

Comanche Indians pushed the Apache out and started raiding parties for supplies. The Comanches attacked both Mexican and American settlers, as well as wagons passing through the area. When gold was discovered in California, a route was built through Texas. Military posts were established along the

A Place Without People

way to protect those heading west, and the soldiers were able to stop the Comanche attacks.

The park is almost 800,000 acres with about a 200-mile border to Mexico formed by the Rio Grande. Most people start their tour of the park in the Chisos Mountains, which tower over the desert. Emory Peak, at 7,835 feet, is the highest point of the Chisos. Boquillas Canyon to the east and Santa Elena to the west are highlights in the Chisos Mountain area. For a glimpse of geologic time, you can visit the Fossil Bone Exhibit or take a look at rock strata in the canyons.

Another canyon view can be had by taking Ross Maxwell Scenic Drive, which winds down to Santa Elena Canyon. Between hikes, or as a full day of fun, you may want to bathe in the historic hot springs.

You can find the remains of two historic ranches at Panther Junction in St. Elenor Canyon. A trail leads a mile into St. Elenor Canyon, which is deep and narrow. You will enjoy hearing your voice echo as you enter the canyon. There's a primitive campsite at Panther Junction, but you will probably prefer renting a cabin as temperatures after dark can drop.

From Panther Junction, the road continues to the Basin. The Basin is the trailhead for all other hikes in the Chisos. The length of trails in Big Bend start at about a quarter mile and stretch as long as 30 miles. From a cliff at the end of a 15-mile loop passing the highest peak in the Chisos, you can have a spectacular view of the mountains and Mexico. Horses are allowed on designated trails. Other places to see include Castolon, Dagger Flat, Dagger Mountain, Hannold Grave Homesite, Old Sam Nail Ranch, and Sotol Vista. Near the park, and worth seeing, is the Big Bend Ranch State Natural Area, a massive park west of Big Bend.

The desert is surprisingly green due to summer rainfall. In spite of the rain, you need to drink a gallon of water a day

Spring

to keep from becoming dehydrated. After you have seen the desert and the mountains of Big Bend, take a river ride on a float. The park is named for the U-turn or bend you will see on the Rio Grande. Teethmarks on cottonwood or willow trees made by beavers who live in bank burrows as well as garfish and turtles can be seen on the nearly 200 miles of river designated for recreation.

Extended float trips on the Rio Grande can be arranged in Lajitas, Terlingua, and Study Butte. There are no equipment rentals in the park. Guided raft, canoe, and kayak adventures may be a great way to spend a weekend without any planning headaches. Some companies only rent gear, but others pamper guests with gourmet meals and unique experiences. You can try Texas River Expeditions, 800-839-7238; Big Bend River Tours, 800-545-4240; or Far Flung Adventures, 800-359-4138.

Thunderstorms from July through October can raise river levels and increase the rate of water flow. For white-water enthusiasts this can make a trip very exciting. For those looking for a leisurely pace, this could be a hair-raising experience. When you go to the park headquarters to obtain a free river float permit, ask for current river information. You can expect to find Class 1 to Class 4 water in Big Bend.

The river is good for bird-watchers, with summer tanagers, painted buntings, vermilion flycatchers, and cardinals serving as accent colors to the background greens of river banks. On the river's sandbars and cliff banks are the sandpiper, killdeer, and cliff swallows. If you wanted to see all the birds that are in the United States, eventually you would have to come to Big Bend to see the colima warbler.

State Highways 118, from Alpine, and 385, from Fort Stockton and Marathon, lead south into Big Bend National Park from Interstate 10. For overnight lodging in the park at the Chisos Mountains Lodge in the Basin or various campgrounds, call 915-477-2291. There are backcountry roadside

A Place Without People

campsites along some park dirt roads with a free permit required. Some sites require a four-wheel-drive vehicle to enter. Lodging can be found in Lajitas, which was reconstructed to resemble an Old West town. Also Terlingua, Alpine, Marathon, and Presidio are interesting towns nearby with lodging possibilities.

Supplies are available in the park on a limited basis. The Chisos Mountains Lodge has a gift shop. There are no medical services in the park. The nearest hospital is in Alpine, 108 miles from park headquarters. A paramedic service is available at Terlingua, 26 miles from park headquarters. If you have any questions, the best source for answers is the Big Bend National Park Office at 915-477-2251.

Spring

17

A Capital City in Outlaw Country

AUSTIN

IF ELVIS PRESLEY WERE ALIVE TODAY TO SING THE BLUES HE wouldn't be singing about heartbreak hotel. He'd head for Sixth Street in Austin, Texas. Whether you have the blues or just like listening to the blues, Austin is where you need to go.

Austin, located in the center of the state, is the capital of Texas and home to the 50,000 students attending the main campus of the University of Texas. Austin isn't the largest city in Texas, but it has a population of 1,057,000 in the metropolitan area and 567,566 within the city limits. Austin is located within 200 miles of San Antonio, Houston, and Dallas. Best known for its laid-back atmosphere and live music, Austin is where "outlaw country" music and "redneck rock" originated.

But a statue of the late Stevie Ray Vaughn stands in testimony to Austin's dedication to the blues. It is home to Austin City Limits, which began with Willie Nelson in 1974 as a fund-raiser for public television, and has grown from there. When Vaughn played the Austin City Limits for the first time in 1984, he was so loud that hunks of fiberglass sound insulation vibrated loose and floated down from the studio ceiling. If it's a musical production or event you seek, then you might want to visit Austin during the South by Southwest (sxsw) music festival in March. Similarly, each summer droves of blues fans gather on the Arboretum lawn to be a part of Blues on the Green, a free live performance series dedicated to the art form.

While obtaining tickets to Austin City Limits is almost impossible for out-of-town visitors, Austin has rock, reggae, alternative, salsa, jazz, folk, cabaret, and heavy metal groups that can also be heard most evenings. Clubs are concentrated around downtown's Sixth Street. Austin also was the starting ground for the late Janis Joplin, Jerry Jeff Walker, Shawn Colvin, and the Fabulous Thunderbirds. Called the "Live Music Capital of the World," you can find out why Austin got the name in places like Antone's, Blues, or the Broken Spoke, a typical Texas roadhouse with country music.

Or you can go to the symphony in Symphony Square, a collection of four 19th-century limestone buildings along the banks of Waller Creek near the Capitol Building. Home to the Austin Symphony Orchestra and Cafe Serrano, it is the site for the Symphony's Summer Music Festival. Steamboat, Maggie Mae's, and La Zona Rosa are typical Austin places to hear good music. But where do people go to be seen? Some say it is the Copper Tank at 5th and Trinity, a block off of Sixth Street.

At dusk during the summer, pause and watch possibly the world's largest urban bat population—about 1.5 million Mexican freetail bats—fly out from under the Congress Avenue bridge to begin their nightly search for dinner. On the bridge the bats may only be 10 feet over your head. More comfortable locations to view this mass exodus are the lounge of the Four Seasons Hotel, or the patio of the Shoreline Grill.

Another must-do when in Austin is to see the Capitol, which is seven feet taller than the nation's capitol in Washington, D.C. Reopened in 1995 after a three-year, $180 million renovation, the state Capitol mirrors the original structure when it was completed in 1888. The pink granite structure is decorated with historical paintings and several Elizabet Ney statues. You can start at the Capitol Complex Visitors Center, 112 E. 11th Street, on the southeast corner of the Capitol grounds. Call 512-305-8400 for information. It features historical Capitol exhibits and guided tours. The Center is located in the newly restored 1857 General Land Office Building. The Capitol Complex, which covers 26 acres, is best seen with a tour by a Capitol guide.

William Barton settled in Austin in 1837, but recorded history of the city begins with the visit of Mirabeau B. Lamar to Jacob Harrell in the fall of 1838. Lamar, then vice president of the Republic of Texas, was in the area to hunt buffalo, but while camping along the Colorado River, he fell in love with the landscape. When he became president in 1839, succeeding Sam Houston, Lamar sent his agent, Edwin Waller, to build a new capitol city to be named for Stephen F. Austin, the father of the Republic of Texas.

In 1842, Mexican troops invaded San Antonio. Fearing Austin might be next, President Sam Houston, back for a second term, moved the capital first to Houston and then to what is known as the "Washington-on-the-Brazos." People in Austin feared President Houston was trying to permanently move the capital. Loyal Austinites hid the government archives from President Houston's men. Two men President Houston sent to retrieve the archives returned empty-handed with their horses' manes and tails shaved off. So, President Houston sent an armed force of about 30 men to Austin. As these men were loading their wagons, hotel keeper Angelina Eberly fired a cannon near a wagon. The blast alerted townspeople, who went after President Houston's men, overtaking them near Brushy Creek, not far from

A Capital City in Outlaw Country

Austin. The archives were retrieved and stored in a safer place.

When Texas joined the United States on July 4, 1845, Austin was reaffirmed as the temporary capital. It passed two statewide voter referendums, one in 1850 and another in 1872, before the issue was finally settled. The staggering proportions of the building were so dramatized by the elevated site that visiting Texans had the feeling their Capitol was not only capable of dominating Austin, but the whole so-called Texas Empire.

The Governor's Mansion, near the Capitol, was first used in 1856 as home of the state's chief executive. This antebellum-style house underwent massive restoration and was completed in 1982. Some rooms are furnished with items dating back to the early years. Not all rooms are open to tours as the mansion still serves as the governor's residence. It is located at 1010 Colorado. Call 512-463-5516 for a 24-hour recording with updated information before visiting.

On the banks of the Colorado River in the heart of Austin, you will find Town Lake, Zilker Park, Barton Springs, and Zilker Botanical Gardens with flowers, shrubs, trees, and ponds integrated into a design that provides inspiration and tranquility. Zilker Park was deeded to the people of Austin in the early 1900s by A. J. Zilker, a merchant who purchased the land. The park complex has a spring-fed swimming area, a Japanese garden, a miniature train, and hiking or biking trails. Take a canoe for a water tour and some exercise. Or for a romantic water cruise, try paddle-wheel riverboat rides from March through November. Don't miss the view on top of Mt. Bonnell, at 3800 Mt. Bonnell Road. Climb the 99 steps of Mt. Bonnell to savor a violet-tinged sunset over Lake Austin and see Westlake Hills from the most scenic and highest point in the city limits. Open

Spring

daily to visitors from dawn to dusk, the view is 800 feet above sea level.

Barton Springs, a 68-degree spring-fed pool, actually has dinosaur tracks in the shallow end. The springs probably opened around 9,000 years ago and changed very little from then until the European colonists arrived. The Balcones fault can be seen under the lifeguard stand to the west of the diving board. Buffalo herds were a common sight at the springs before the city was established. Spanish friars located three missions on the southeast side of the pool in the 1730s. More than a century later, in 1837, William Barton built a small cabin near the springs and named each of the three main springs after one of his daughters, Parthenia, Eliza, and Zenobia.

The springs are home to catfish, carp, bass, turtles, eel, crawfish, tetras, silverback darters, and salamanders. The springs also attract a variety of birds, including belted kingfishers, great blue herons, mallards, red-bellied woodpeckers, red-tailed hawks, rock doves, ring-billed gulls, cormorants, golden-fronted woodpeckers, great-tailed grackles, starlings, northern cardinals, bluejays, cedar waxwings, and wood ducks. For more on nature go to the Austin Nature and Science Center at 301 Nature Center Drive, 512-327-8180.

Places of historical interest are East Sixth Street and Congress Avenue to Interstate 35, which by day give you a look at the past when "Old Pecan Street" was the center of business. There are many landmarks along this National Historical Register District, which houses a wide variety of restaurants and shops. Treaty Oak at 503 Baylor Street is a 600-year-old tree once called North America's most perfect tree specimen. It was poisoned in 1989, which brought an outpouring of gifts, prayers, and experts to save it. One massive branch of greenery remains. This is the last of the Council Oaks where treaties with Indians were signed.

A Capital City in Outlaw Country

Everyone who is new to Austin needs to stop at the Old Bakery and Emporium, 1006 Congress Avenue, 512-477-5961. Built in 1876 and listed in the National Register of Historic Places, the Lundberg Bakery occupied the building until 1936. After restoration, it opened as a bakery, gift shop, and visitors information center.

Other places to see include:

O. Henry Museum, 409 East 5th Street

Old German Free School Building, 507 E. 10th Street

Republic of Texas Museum, 510 East Anderson Lane

Texas Military Forces Museum and All-Faiths Chapel, 2200 W. 35th Street

Austin Children's Museum, 201 Colorado Street

Austin Museum of Art–Downtown, 823 Congress Avenue

Austin Museum of Art–Laguna Gloria, 3809 West 35th Street

Dougherty Arts Center Gallery, 1110 Barton Springs Road

Elisabet Ney Museum, 304 East 44th Street

George Washington Carver Museum, 1165 Angelina Street

French Legation Museum, 802 San Marcos Street

Mexic-Arte Museum, 419 Congress Avenue

Umlauf Sculpture Garden and Museum, 605 Robert E. Lee Road

Lyndon B. Johnson Presidential Library and Museum, 2313 Red River

Symphony Square, 1101 Red River, 888-462-3787

Texas State Cemetery, 909 Navasota Street

Texas State Library and Archives, 1201 Brazos

Austin History Center at 810 Guadalupe

Women and Their Work, 1710 Lavaca

The University of Texas is home to the Center for American History, the Harry Ransom Humanities Research Center, the Archer M. Huntington Art Gallery, and the Texas Memorial Museum. For more information about Austin's attractions, call the Austin Convention and Visitor Bureau Hotline at 800-888-8287.

A Capital City in Outlaw Country

18

Hot Times in Texas

CHIHUAHUAN DESERT

IF YOU ARE LOOKING FOR HOT TIMES IN TEXAS, HEAD FOR THE desert—the Chihuahuan Desert. Traveling west of San Antonio on U.S. Highway 90 can fulfill your desire for desert terrain or turn just a little north of 90 to check out Monahans Sandhills. In the summer, the desert can be hot, dry, and cruel with its ceaseless wind beating on your face, arms, and legs. The desert seems deserted because people don't tend to travel to desert regions at that time. This can make the summer an ideal time to see desert regions undisturbed by tourists, giving you a real chance to see wildlife. As night falls, deer, jackrabbits, and other animals come out to search for food.

On a hot desert night, white-tailed deer will come up to your camp to see what is there. Don't be surprised if you come face-to-face with a deer, who may be more surprised than you. Deer have been known to circle tents at night to investigate what there may be to eat. In Seminole Canyon State Historical Park near Del Rio in August, jackrabbits and deer let visitors walk fairly close before taking off at high speed. Desert regions in Texas aren't just acres and acres of sand; you will see plenty of cactus and scrub brush. In the spring, you will see an array of color painted on desert plants as flowers bloom.

The desert is filled with a variety of plants like the prickly pears and Mormon tea that are prevalent in the Chihuahuan Desert. Tarbush can be seen along with honey mesquite bordering washes. White-thorn acacia, allthorn, and ocotillo are other large plants living in the desert. Upon first glance, you may think the desert only has plant life, but on closer examination you can find a variety of animal life. Mammals populating the area include bats, bobcats, coyotes, gray foxes, kangaroo rats, Mexican gray wolves, mountain lions, mule deer, prairie dogs, and wild burros.

Look up and see one of these many birds in the desert: barn owl, black-necked stilt, desert woodpecker, hummingbird, quail, red-tailed hawk, roadrunner, and turkey vulture. Or how about a fish in the desert? Look for a desert pupfish. While looking for the desert fish, you may also see one of these: black-collared lizard, chuckwallas, common king snake, and the desert iguana.

One recognizable figure is the tortoise, but you can also see gila monsters and horned lizards, also known as "horny toads." These lizards are on the endangered species list and can't be handled without a license. Keep an eye out for rattlesnakes, sidewinders, western banded geckos, and western coral snakes. There really are black widow spiders, scorpions, and tarantulas, too. Probably the most misunderstood of the bunch, the tarantula, is actually harmless—if you leave it alone. Make a tarantula nervous and watch out. One sign of just how hot it is in the desert is the whine of the cicada, an insect resembling a rather large fly. The buzz or constant hum of the cicada almost seems to swell with the heat.

The Chihuahuan Desert covers more than 200,000 square miles. Although most of it is south of the border, a good piece is found in South Texas, New Mexico, and Arizona. But when you are driving west on U.S. Highway 90 through the desert on a summer day with the heat waves and pavement always seeming the same, it may feel like the entire Chihauhaun Desert is in Texas. The lowest point in the desert region is 1,000 feet above sea level, but most of it lies between 3,500 to 5,000 feet above sea level. Winter can be fairly cool, with temperatures reaching down to about 29. The summer temperatures rise above 100 degrees. Less than a foot of rainfall each year replenishes the dry, dusty land made up of mostly limestone. It is a shrub desert with yuccas and agaves, growing with grasses and often creosote bushes.

What can you do in such an oppressive environment that would be any fun? Many people actually flock to the desert for their fun. About 800 people show up with bicycles in February to take part in a "Classic Mountain Bike Race." The four-day event attracted a record number of bicyclists to the 10th Annual Chihuahuan Desert Challenge and Mountain Bike Festival held in Lajitas. About 60 showed up for the first race in 1987. The Challenge leads off the nine-event Texas State Championship Series. Call Desert Sports in Terlingua for more information at 915-371-2727. If you go to the desert, you should see Terlingua, which is marked as a ghost town on the map. The town makes an interesting stop along Ranch Road 170 west of Big Bend National Park. Lajitas, also a good stop, is a little farther south and west of Terlingua on 170. Lajitas borders the Rio Grande River and Mexico.

Also in this desert region east of Big Bend, halfway between Del Rio and San Antonio where U.S. Highway 90 intersects U.S. Highway 83, you will find Uvalde, home of former vice president John Nance "Cactus Jack" Garner. You can visit the Ettie R. Garner Memorial Museum in Garner's former home at 333 N. Park. Garner, a colorful character, was once quoted as saying the office of vice president "isn't worth a bucket of warm spit." He served as Franklin Delano Roosevelt's vice president from 1933 to 1941. His death

Hot Times in Texas

came in 1967, just shy of his 99th birthday. Next, you can tour the 1891 Grand Opera House, which Garner purchased. He used the second floor for his office, while keeping the downstairs open for theater productions. The theater, which seats 390, is open for tours and is still in operation. Another famous former resident of Uvalde was Dale Evans, a Hollywood cowgirl paired with Roy Rogers.

Traveling further back in time, you will be able to see where the San Antonio–El Paso Trail crossed U.S. Highway 90 in Uvalde, founded in 1855. The town is still centered around a broad square that originally served as a wagonyard for teamsters and travelers. Uvalde was the home of Billy the Kid's killer, Pat Garrett, during the 1890s. The corrupt lawman's house site is marked off U.S. Highway 90 a half-mile east of U.S. Highway 83.

With a population of 15,000, mostly Hispanic, Uvalde offers some spicy menus in its restaurants. Try a classic South Texas menu of fajitas, migas—eggs scrambled with chiles, onions, and tortilla strips—or fried catfish. With the Rio, Sabinal, and Nueces rivers flowing through it, there are plenty of river-oriented activities to indulge in when the heat and chiles prove to be too much. You will pass through Uvalde at the halfway point if you are driving to Del Rio.

If you want to see the classic sand dunes of desert terrain, then go straight north of Big Bend and the junction of Interstate 20 and State Highway 18 to Monahans Sandhills State Park. There you will find nearly 4,000 acres of sand dunes, some up to 70 feet high. You can surf West Texas style by stopping at the park headquarters to rent a toboggan or disk. Take a dune tour in a 4 × 4 utility vehicle or stroll along on a nature trail and take the museum tour. Bring your horse to enjoy 600 acres of equestrian trails. Bring the whole clan to feast in a 1903 railroad section house transformed into a dining hall. Monahans was a watering stop along the Texas and Pacific Railroad line between Pecos River and Big Spring in the 1880s.

Spring

Indians roamed freely in the wind-sculpted dunes before the railroad cut its path and led the way for explorers and settlers. Various Indian tribes used the area for temporary campgrounds and a meeting place. They found game and, beneath the sands, fresh water. Indians ground acorns and mesquite beans into paste with stone tools. The sand dunes, which stretch another 200 miles south, west, and north beyond Monahans, were first documented by Spanish explorers about 400 years ago. Humans lived in this area as far back as 12,000 years ago.

Today these vast hills remain relatively quiet even though they are home to many different animals and birds. To hear nature's sounds, you have to wait patiently by shallow pools of water for the inhabitants to appear. You can listen to the wind slowly change this landscape. In much of the park you will see shinoak, a plant and stabilizing force in this desert. Shinoak stands up to four feet tall and produces acorns. You will find one working oil well in the park. Oil production started here in the 1920s. The park, which is a half hour west of Odessa, is leased from a private company until the year 2056. For more information, call 800-792-1112 or 512-389-8900 for reservations. Monahans is near Balmorhea State Park and the Million Barrel Museum is in Monahans.

While in the Odessa area, you have to stop by the Odessa Meteor Crater. A shower of meteors plunged to earth some 20,000 years ago, shattering the limestone bedrock. The impact left an explosion pit that is 500 feet in diameter with many smaller pits. Over the centuries, desert winds filled the large crater with silt until it was almost level with the surrounding plains. The site was not identified as a meteor crater until the 1920s. It was first discovered in 1892 by a rancher and thought to be a "blow hole" created by a natural gas explosion underground. Research conducted at the site included digging a 10-by-12-foot shaft that went 165 feet down. Scientists were hoping to find the meteor or some remnants. There were no remnants of the largest meteor but they collected pieces of meteors from the smaller craters. The large crater attracts attention because of its size and ease of access. A marked nature trail winds through the crater and a free brochure interprets the unusual sight. Just west of Odessa, take Interstate 20, exit Farm to Market 1936 south, and then drive west on the frontage road about three and a half miles. You should see signs indicating the location of the crater.

The city of Odessa also has many attractions to see. A mid-size city with a population just more than 90,000, Odessa, like many Texas cities, was established in the 1880s as a railroad stop. The city's name originated from the area's resemblance to the region around the Ukraine in Russia. The area is part of the Permian Basin, which once was the heart of an ancient sea.

Attractions on the University of Texas of the Permian Basin campus include the Art Institute for the Permian Basin, two galleries featuring works of regional artists, and traveling exhibits; the Globe of the Great Southwest, a replica of the original Shakespearean Globe Theater; and the world's largest jackrabbit statue and favorite photo spot located in the university administration's parking lot.

Also in Odessa

- Don't miss the Brass Lamp Auto Museum, a collection of antique cars made before 1916 with such models as Flanders, Brush, Saxon, Oakland, and Overland, as well as Cadillac and Ford. Included in the exhibit is a 1903 Ford Model A with two cylinders and a chain drive, which was built the first year Ford Motor Company made and sold autos. The museum is located at 701 N. Grant Street.

- Another attraction worth stopping for is a cable tool drilling rig re-created to resemble ones used in 1920. In the driller's shack by the rig is a collection of photographs and relics of West Texas oil boom days. You can find the rig just north of Ector County Coliseum at Andrews Highway and 42nd Street.

- In Prairie Pete Park you can view rare prairie dogs in their own town. The park is located in Sherwood Park at 44th and Dixie.

- The Presidential Museum, 622 N. Lee Street, is devoted to the presidency and presidential political campaigns, from George Washington to the present. Campaign slogans, buttons, and posters are included in the collection. You can see a collection of dolls with every first lady's hair-style and inaugural gown, which took 20 years of research and work to create.

- Another historical site to visit is the White-Pool House at 112 E. Murphy Street. The two-story brick home constructed in 1887 is the oldest existing house in Ector County. On the Register of National Historic Places, the home includes period furnishings from the original and second owners. The interior reflects the lifestyles of the 1880s ranching period and 1920s oil era. Outside the house is a windmill.

Hot Times in Texas

19

Through the River of the North

El Paso

El Paso, once a gateway for Spanish explorers to the wild and unsettled country that became the United States, has grown up between the mountains with the influence of three cultures. El Paso is a shortened version of the name given to this river valley by a conquistador. El Paso del Rio del Norte, The Pass Through the River of the North, was the name Don Juan de Onate gave the area more than four centuries ago.

Get acquainted with the tricultural heritage of the city at the El Paso Museum of History. The people and events that shaped the city's 400-year history are depicted in dioramas featuring settlers, conquistadors, Indians, Mexican vaqueros, and the U.S. cavalry. To beat the heat and take advantage of the warm winter, visiting El Paso in February will be most comfortable. Some events occurring in the summer may be intriguing enough to sweat a little.

Tigua St. Anthony Day in June at Ysleta del Sur Pueblo is a ceremony in which the Tigua Indians pay tribute to their patron saint. The Annual El Paso/Juarez International Mariachi Festival takes place in June at the Civic Center. The event features traditional dancing and is sponsored by the

Hispanic Chamber of Commerce Tourism Division. The Annual Coors Light Mariachi Festival in June is at Wet 'N' Wild. The International Festival de la Zarzuela in late summer at Chamizal features Spanish operettas from Latin America.

El Paso grew from settlements dating back to the Juan de Onate expedition in 1598 and a settlement by Juan Maria Ponce de Leon in 1827. Area missions predate that civil settlement by almost 150 years. El Paso's neighbor, Juarez, is Mexico's fourth largest city. The combined population of these sister cities is almost two million. Like many large metropolitan areas, El Paso has a symphony orchestra, theater, museums, libraries, and diversified sporting activities including horse and greyhound racing, and polo. The city is home of the University of Texas at El Paso, noted for Bhutanese-style architecture and the Sun Bowl Stadium.

The city lays claim to the first Thanksgiving and celebrates the holiday in the spring. The first celebration was 23 years before the Pilgrims' celebration, according to city historians. Gasper Perez de Villagra documented the difficult journey of Juan de Onate. The explorer crossed the Rio Grande near El Paso on April 20, 1598, and feasted in thanksgiving. The El Paso Mission Trail Association celebrates the occasion in April in Chamizal National Memorial Park.

Another part of El Paso's history can be visited at Tigua Indian Reservation: Ysleta del Sur Pueblo. The oldest community in Texas, now part of El Paso, was established in 1681 by refugees from a bloody Indian uprising that expelled Spanish missionaries and Christian Indians from present-day New Mexico. The missionaries and Tigua Indians settled in El Paso and built Isleta Mission. The church is still part of the Tigua Indian community.

The Ysleta del Sur Pueblo Cultural Center is owned and operated by the Tigua

Indians. It features a museum, gift shop, Indian social dancing, the Cacique Cafe, and fresh baked Indian bread. It is located at 305 Yaya Lane. Also operated by Tigua Indians is the Speaking Rock Bingo Entertainment Center, but patrons must be at least 21 years old to enter. There are three levels of play and jackpots vary. The bingo hall is located on the Tigua Indian Reservation. For information, call the Tigua Indian Reservation at 915-860-7777.

Pueblan tribes inhabited the area before Spanish explorers arrived in 1851 to establish a series of missions along the Rio Grande. Ysleta Mission is located next to Ysleta del Sur Pueblo. It was built in 1681 by Franciscan padres and the Tigua Indians. It is the oldest mission in Texas. Socorro Mission is the oldest continuously active parish in the United States. The original mission was constructed in 1681. The handcarved roof beams were sculpted by the Piro Indians.

The San Elizario Presidio Chapel is about 22 miles southeast of El Paso. It is a white stucco chapel that wasn't technically a mission, but has pretended to be one for a long time. Visiting the chapel and town is a journey back in time. Rich in history, San Elizario also claims to have been the site of the first Thanksgiving when Onate traveled through the area. Billy the Kid is also thought to have broken one of his friends out of the town's jail.

Across the border is the Guadalupe Mission in downtown Juarez. It was constructed of adobe between 1658 and 1668 by a Spanish missionary and local Indians. According to legend, shadows from the mission point to the Lost Padre Mine in the Franklin Mountains where Spanish gold is said to be hidden.

Walk across one of the international bridges to Mexico or take the El Paso–Juarez Trolley. Indulge in an authentic Mexican meal, wander around the marketplace, and take advantage of bargains. Juarez is linked to El Paso by three bridges over the Rio Grande. Visitors find a variety of shopping such as the Pueblito Mexicano Shopping Mall, which is an indoor mall re-created as a Mexican village or pueblito. There is the Juarez Race Track and the Museo de Arte y Historia that displays excellent collections of pre-Columbian art, historic and contemporary.

The El Paso–Juarez Trolley will take passengers past many of the attractions mentioned, as well as the Rio Grande Mall; Silver Castle, where you can purchase silver handcrafted jewelry; J. J. Market for wholesale and retail arts and crafts; Chihuahua Charlie's famous bar and grill; Casa Onate leather shop; City Market; and Export Free, a duty-free shop. The trolley enters and exits on two different bridges and passes by Chamizal National Park, both the United States and Mexico parts. The trolley company offers special tours. For more information call 800-259-6284.

Visiting El Paso and Juarez can shed light on issues at an international border between the United States and Mexico. The Chamizal National Memorial, in El Paso, commemorates the settlement of a border dispute. The U.S. Border Patrol Museum documents the history of law officers who have the job of preventing illegal immigration and smuggling.

When in El Paso, be sure to stop by the El Paso Saddle Blanket trading post at 601 N. Oregon. For 25 years, this unique store has been an El Paso fixture featuring blankets, rugs, Indian artifacts, and Mexican imports.

Interested in a two-pound steak? Inquire about the Indian Cliffs Ranch and Cattleman's Steakhouse 30 minutes east of the city on Interstate 10. Take Fabens, Exit 49, and turn north. Nearby attractions are the Franklin Mountains State Park, Magoffin Home State Historical Park, and Fort Bliss.

For full details and literature on city attractions, contact El Paso Convention and Visitors Bureau, 1 Civic Center Plaza, 915-534-0600.

20

Frontier Forts

ALAMO–BOGGY–CONCHO

A BIG PART OF TEXAS HISTORY IS CONNECTED TO MILITARY action and establishments. Having flown six flags since its inception, Texas had many forts out of necessity. While people turn to the Alamo as a famous Texas fort, it wasn't actually a fort at all. It was a Catholic mission established to save the souls of Indians. Here you will find some forts that are still with us today, partially in some cases, as a replication in other cases. But their history and story live on in museums and state parks dedicated to preserving the past.

A U.S. Army post was established in Fort Davis in 1854 at the crossroads of the Chihuahua Trail and the Butterfield Overland Mail Route. Today, the restored army post has costumed staff and a ghostly dress parade that is heard over the fort's public address system three times a day. The ruins and restored structures of the Fort Davis National Historic Site portray the struggles of the settlers who lived there. After wandering through the ruins of the old fort, you can hike through Davis Mountains State Park. Take State Highway 166 for a scenic loop around the 8,382-foot Mount Livermore. You might see antelope along the route. You can stay at the Indian Lodge within the park. Try the Prairie Theater in nearby Albany for Western-style entertainment. Call 915-762-3642 to reach the Albany Chamber of Commerce for information and reservations. Also in Albany is The Old Jail Art Center, an art museum housed in Shackelford County's first permanent jail, now restored and expanded. One block east of the 1884 Shackelford County Courthouse; the Center is open year-round. For information, call 915-762-2269.

The ruins of a frontier fort as well as recreation facilities are in Fort Griffin State Park. From Albany, go 15 miles north on U.S. Highway 283. The town of Fort Griffin grew around the military post and served as trade center in the 1870s and 1880s. It was a rough, wild settlement frequented by cavalry troopers, trail-herd cowboys, buffalo hunters, and outlaws. More than 200,000 buffalo hides were shipped from the town. Gunfights were a common cause of death during the late 1800s. There were 34 recorded deaths in a decade attributed to gun duels. Only a few scattered farms exist today. Partially restored ruins of Old Fort Griffin include a hand-dug well, a mess hall, a ghost building, a barracks, a library, a rock chimney, a store, an administration building, a cistern, a hospital, a powder magazine, the foundation of the officers' quarters, and a bakery. You can see replicas of enlisted men's huts. The fort structures are on a bluff overlooking the townsite of Fort Griffin and Clear Fork of the Brazos River Valley. Ruins of other structures still can be seen.

Famous commander Pecos Bill, also known as William Shafter, served at Fort Concho, which was founded in 1867 at the junction of the North and Middle Concho Rivers to protect frontier settlements and transportation routes. All four regiments of the Buffalo Soldiers were stationed at Concho. A frontier army post for 22 years, Fort Concho can be seen in 23 restored structures at Fort Concho National Historic Landmark. You can see the headquarters building, soldiers' barracks, officers' quarters, chapel, schoolhouse, and the post hospital. The Fort Concho National Historic Landmark is located at 630 South Oakes in San Angelo. San

Spring

Angelo is a few hours' drive from Albany, south on U.S. Highway 283, and then southwest on U.S. Highway 67. Call 915-481-2646 for more information. General William T. Sherman called Fort Concho "the prettiest post in Texas." Each spring, spectacular blooms of bluebonnets and other wildflowers cover the area.

Fort McKavett State Historical Park was originally called Camp San Saba because it overlooks the headwaters of the San Saba River Valley. The fort was established by five companies of the Eighth Infantry in March of 1852 to protect frontier settlers and travelers on Upper El Paso Road. Later, it was named for Capt. Henry McKavett, who died in the battle of Monterey on September 21, 1846. Abandoned during the Civil War, it was reoccupied for several years from 1868 to 1883. No camping is allowed in the park, which is located 23 miles west of Menard. Take U.S. Highway 190 west of Menard for 17 miles, then go south on Farm to Market 864 for 6 miles to the park. Fort McKavett is about an hour and a half from Fort Concho if you take U.S. Highway 277 south and U.S. Highway 190 east.

In 1840, settlers moved into the area of Fort Boggy, north of the Old San Antonio Road and between the Navasota and Trinity Rivers in Fairfield. When one resident was killed in an Indian raid, the settlers built a fort. The fort was constructed of upright logs set in the ground. The Keechi and Kickapoos, who lived there, regularly raided settlements for the livestock. Starting life out with a different name, the fort became Fort Boggy because it is close to Boggy Creek. By the end of 1840, 75 people lived in two blockhouses and 11 dwellings within the 75 square yards enclosed by the fort walls. Republic of Texas President Mirabeau B. Lamar authorized the formation of a military company for the fort. When Indian attacks decreased the fort was left in disrepair. You can see the fort in Fort Boggy State Park by traveling about two hours south of Dallas on Interstate 45.

Frontier Forts

Established in 1855 to guard against hostile Indians, Fort Lancaster protected the movement of supplies on the El Paso–San Antonio Road. West of Ozona in Crockett County, the fort was abandoned in 1861 after Texas seceded from the Union. Fort Lancaster State Historical Park offers exhibits on history, natural history, and archaeology; nature study on a nature trail; historic ruins; and places to have a picnic. The park is located eight miles east of Sheffield, off Interstate 10 on U.S. Highway 290. Take Exit 343 and follow U.S. Highway 290 to the park. It is near Fort McKavett and Fort Leaton.

Fort Leaton State Historical Park has a pioneer trading post built in 1848 by Ben Leaton. It was a fortified adobe trading post, which helped Leaton dominate border trade with the Apache and Comanche Indians before he died in 1851. The site was recognized in 1936 by the Texas Centennial Commission. Besides historic ruins and an interpretive center, Fort Leaton serves as the Western Visitor Center for Big Bend Ranch State Park. The park is located four miles southeast of Presidio on the River Road to Big Bend. Farm to Market 170 is a scenic highway route in the area.

Fort Parker State Historical Park is the site of a well-known Indian attack in 1836. Cynthia Ann Parker, who was captured by the Comanches, gave birth to the last Comanche chief, Quanah Parker. Ms. Parker had taken on the Indians' customs and married Chief Peta Nocona. A century later, in 1936, the old fort, which guarded the area's settlers, was reconstructed by the Civilian Conservation Corps. The original fort was erected for protection in 1833 by Elder John Parker and other settlers from Illinois. The park encompasses the historic town of Springfield, established in 1838. Springfield began to die in the early 1870s, after the railroad bypassed the town and the courthouse burned. It soon became a ghost town. The cemetery remains with the graves of many East Texas pioneers, an American Revolutionary War veteran, and two veterans of the Battle of San Jacinto fought during the Texas Revolution. The oldest tombstone is dated 1849. To reach the park, take State Highway 14 out of Groesbeck four miles north to Park Road 35 to park headquarters.

In Fort Parker Park, a second park bearing the Fort Parker name, you can canoe the Navasota River, camp, swim, hike, or bike. The canoe trip from Confederate Reunion Grounds to Fort Parker is a three-mile trip. The park is located seven miles south of Mexia or six miles north of Groesbeck on State Highway 14. The entrance is on Park Road 28. The city of Groesbeck oversees this park.

Fort Richardson State Historical Park is located northwest of Fort Worth in Jack County. Fort Richardson was established in November 1867 to stop the Indian raids. Named for General Israel B. Richardson, who died in the Battle of Antietam during the Civil War, the fort was the northern-most post of Civil War federal forts. Orders in 1866 called for a fort at Buffalo Springs, but due to unhealthy conditions and the possibility of Indian attacks there, the soldiers returned to Jacksboro. New orders came to establish a fort on Lost Creek. The fort served the area for 12 years. Fort site structures include a restored post hospital, officers' quarters, powder magazine, morgue, commissary, guardhouse, and a bakery, which baked 600 loaves per day. There are replicas of officers' and enlisted men's barracks. The park is a half mile south of Jacksboro on U.S. Highway 281, a little more than an hour's drive northeast on U.S. Highway 281 from Fort Worth.

Historic Fort Stockton is located two blocks east of Main Street in Fort Stockton. You can see the officer's row, guard house, enlisted men's barracks, and the parade grounds. A museum and visitors center is maintained in the barracks. The guard house, one of the first buildings constructed, was completed in 1868. Military presence began here with the establishment of Camp Stockton in 1858 by U.S. Army troops of the 1st and 8th Infantry. It was named for Commodore Robert Field Stockton, a naval officer who distinguished himself during the Mexican War. The post protected travelers and settlers as they crossed the Comanche War trail. The U.S. Army withdrew from Texas during the Civil War and abandoned Camp Stockton in 1861. Confederate troops briefly occupied the fort, but by the end of the Civil War, nothing remained. The "Buffalo Soldiers," black men fighting in the U.S. Army in the 9th Calvary, came to the fort in July 1867 under Colonel Edward Hatch. The fort's lands were leased from civilians.

For more information about Texas State Parks, call 800-792-1112. For camping reservations, call 512-389-8900.

Spring

21

Stargazing

OBSERVATORIES

I wish I may, I wish I might, make a wish on the first star I see tonight. . . .

Texas would be a good place to make your wish as Texas skies overflow with stars. The best viewing may be the vast open ranch land and mountain ranges of West Texas. From almost any area in West Texas, you can put a blanket down, lie back, and watch the show. Countless shooting stars pass overhead while the Milky Way provides a background. The constellations stand out brightly and even amateur stargazers can distinguish the more well-known ones. Pick out the Big Dipper and go from there.

For the best viewing, take advantage of observatories open to the public. Many are located in scenic areas with many other activities to fill up daylight hours. While at Fort Davis State Park, in the midst of the Fort Davis Mountains, you can use the University of Texas' McDonald Observatory. Great views day or night spread before you from the top of Locke Mountain.

At McDonald Observatory there is a self-guided tour. Several telescopes are available for gazing at the stars. Amateur star parties are held on Friday or Saturday night. The parties are for the whole family and open to all without reservations. The party begins at sunset at the Public

Observatory. Take your tour of the constellations and view the moon, planets, stars, and galaxies through a telescope. Dress warmly as it gets cool after sunset up on top of Locke Mountain. Also, bring your binoculars. Reservations are required to use the big telescope, but the general view from the McDonald Observatory has improved.

Construction has been completed on the most powerful instrument yet at the West Texas observatory, the third largest telescope in the world. Astronomers are ready to explore the universe with it, and scientists want to get their hands on it. What's so special about the new telescope? The Hobby-Eberly Telescope atop Mount Fowlkes in the Fort Davis Mountains is 10 times more powerful than the next largest telescope at the observatory. It may be smaller than two telescopes in Hawaii, but astronomers can probe deeper into space to seek new celestial objects. Astronomers have faith they will see new planets with this $13.5 million telescope, which was named after its two principal benefactors, former Texas Lt. Gov. William P. Hobby and Pennsylvania philanthropist Robert E. Eberly.

The new telescope operates differently than other telescopes when tracking objects. Instead of turning on its tracks, the telescope has a hexagonal mirror composed of 91 smaller hexagons. This mirror remains stationary in the bottom of the telescope dome and a tracking device mounted above the mirror array follows the light of the target object. Astronomers can observe about 70 percent of the sky and track an image for an average of about an hour. The University of Texas owns more than half of the telescope, which five universities worked together to develop.

Locke Mountain and the observatory are near the Chihuahuan Desert Research Institute, a good place to learn more about West Texas desert terrain. Since the University of Texas McDonald Observatory is one of the world's major astronomical research centers, its primary purpose is to provide a place for astronomers to live, work, and learn about the universe. McDonald Observatory sponsors educational programs to help people learn about astronomy. If you have children with stars in their eyes, be sure to boost their enthusiasm with a visit here.

McDonald Observatory is located 6,800 feet atop Mt. Locke in the heart of the Fort Davis Mountains of West Texas. From El Paso, go east on Interstate 10; from San Antonio, go west on Interstate 10. You can take State Highway 17 south at Balmorhea to Fort Davis, then State Highway 118 north 16 miles to Mt. Locke. If you are coming from Big Bend National Park, take State Highway 118 north from Alpine to the observatory. For more information, call the W. L. Moody, Jr. Visitors Information Center in Fort Davis at 915-426-3640.

While at the observatory and in the Fort Davis Mountains for the weekend, you should have lunch at Indian Lodge in Fort Davis State Park. The Fort Davis Mountains are a hidden jewel in West Texas. Nearby you can see Big Bend with 800,000 acres, set up camp, and view a sky unpolluted by city lights.

Another popular stop for stargazers is Fort Griffin State Park. The park is used frequently by stargazers because it has electricity for those who bring telescopes and accessories, but no observatory. A 200-foot, 110-volt extension cord is needed to reach the observing area. The park is located about 15 miles north of Albany on U.S. Highway 283. Park headquarters will be on the left and the campgrounds will be located a little farther down on the right.

Brazos Bend State Park in Needville is home to the George Observatory. Located near Creekfield Lake amidst one of the most scenic parks in Texas, the George Observatory houses several telescopes, including a 36-inch reflector that is usually available for public viewing on Saturday evenings from 3:00 to 10:00 P.M.

The George Observatory in Needville, with its white domes rising out of the cypress trees, looks like an abandoned outpost from another world. At the observatory, a dollar buys you time on the larger telescope under the dome. Smaller telescopes can be used at no charge. The observatory has a casual atmosphere with a few small displays.

George Observatory is for people who like to look at stars. The observatory is open on Saturday from approximately 5:00 P.M. until 10:00 P.M. While it is closed during the week and on Sunday, a stargazing group meets from about 7:30 to 10:00 P.M. on Friday. George Observatory is located at 21901 Farm to Market 762 in Needville. You can call 409-553-3400 for more information about scheduled activities.

Other features of Brazos Bend State Park include more than 20 miles of hiking and mountain biking trails. Several trails are paved to increase the ease of use for handicapped visitors. The Creekfield Lake Nature Trail, a half mile walk, includes special signage for the visually impaired. You can fish from lighted piers along Elm Lake, Hale Lake, and Forty-Acre Lake.

Numerous lakes and the Brazos River create a unique environment for wildlife. With more than 270 species of birds, as well as deer, raccoons, bobcats, and alligators, the park is a great place to take in nature during daylight hours. Located 30 minutes from Houston, the park has several hundred campsites to choose from, ranging from RV and tent sites to screened shelters.

22

Great Parks

CAMPING TO CAMELS

TEXAS HAS A WIDE VARIETY OF TERRAIN FROM DESERT TO mountains, forests to marshland. You can see it all in Texas and mostly with great weather. Here are some parks that need to be highlighted in addition to those already mentioned in other sections. A brief description of each is included.

Pedernales Falls State Park, just over 5,000 acres, in Blanco County east of Johnson City, is located along the banks of scenic Pedernales River. While considered to be one of the most beautiful spots in the state, it is subject to flash flooding. This could be a problem if you are planning to camp in the park. Calling ahead to ask rangers about conditions will help avoid disaster. The water in the river can rise from a placid stream to a raging torrent in a few minutes. If you are in the river area and notice the water beginning to rise, you should leave immediately.

Pedernales Falls can be seen from an overlook at the north end of the park. The elevation of the river drops about 50 feet over a distance of 3,000 feet to form the falls. Water flows over the tilted and layered limestone much like rolling down a stairway. The limestone was tilted by what is known as the Llano Uplift and the river's limestone belongs to the 300-million-year-old Marble Falls formation. Millions of years of erosion have played a part in moving the sand, gravel, limestone, and fossils found there.

The park used to be the Circle Bar Ranch and is a great place for camping, picnicking, hiking, river swimming, tubing, mountain biking, bird-watching, and horseback riding. The park includes typical Hill Country wildlife: white-tailed deer, coyotes, rabbits, armadillos, skunks, opossums, and raccoons. More than 150 species of birds have been seen with 30 percent of them making the park their permanent home. Hawks, buzzards, herons, quail, dove, owls, roadrunners, and wild turkeys are a few you can see. The endangered golden-cheeked warbler nests in the park.

The park is nine miles east of Johnson City on Farm to Market 2766. Fall, spring, or summer would be ideal times to go; rain is more likely in May, August, and September. Nearby is Inks Lake, Longhorn Cavern, Blanco, and Guadalupe River State Parks.

Garner State Park, Concan, in the scenic Rio Frio Valley, is ideal for fishing, swimming, paddleboating, hiking, biking, camping, and miniature golfing. Cabins are available in the park, which was named for John "Cactus Jack" Nance Garner of Uvalde. Garner served as vice president of the United States from 1933 to 1941.

During the summer season the Friends of Garner State Park have introduced a new program called *Cowboy Sunset Serenade*. The history of the American cowboy through songs and poetry is presented three nights a week from Memorial Day weekend through Labor Day weekend. There are cabins with fireplaces available.

White-tailed deer, Rio Grande turkey, mourning dove, eastern bluebirds, golden-cheeked warblers, black rock squirrels, fox squirrels, raccoons, and many other animals can be

Spring

spotted. A variety of trees gives the park a unique quality. You'll see Texas redbud, bald cypress, western ash juniper, Spanish oak, lacey oak, Texas madrone, cedar elm, pecan, mountain laurel, and agarita shrubs. Adding to the scenery are canyons with cliff walls, high mesas, and streams.

The park is located in Uvalde County, 31 miles north of the town of Uvalde, 9 miles south of Leakey, or 8 miles north of Concan on the Frio River. From U.S. Highway 83, turn east on Farm to Market 1050 for a half mile to Park Road 29.

Sea Rim State Park, Sabine Pass, is divided into two parts, a five-mile beach and a 4,000-acre marshland. A boardwalk nature trail cuts through the marsh for a close-up view of it. Camping, airboat rides, and bird- or alligator-watching are some activities you can enjoy. The beach part of the park has campsites with water and electricity, but the marsh area does not have any facilities for campers.

The marshland waters are home for migratory waterfowl, a prime wintering area for many varieties, and part of the park is closed during migratory season. Shrimp, crabs, and various fish make the lake area home, as well as muskrat, the rare river otter, raccoon, alligator, mink, nutria, rabbit, skunk, and opossum. No swimming is allowed because of alligators. There are observation blinds for bird-watching. Fishing is permitted during daylight hours.

The park is located 20 miles south of Port Arthur on State Highway 87. You're at sea level with an elevation of six feet. Nearby is Sabine Pass Battleground State Historical Park, Village Creek State Park, McFadden National Wildlife Refuge, Pleasure Island, Big Thicket, and the J. D. Murphree Wildlife Management Area.

Huntsville State Park was slow in the making but worth the effort to visit. The heavily-wooded park adjoins the Sam Houston National Forest and encloses the 210-acre Lake Raven. The lake, an artificial one, took more than a decade

Great Parks

and the sale of $250,000 in lumber to complete. The park offers camping, hiking, biking, boating, miniature golf, horseback riding, fishing, swimming, boat rentals, and nature study. Waterskiing is prohibited and there are restrictions on boat size. Lake Raven, fed by three major creeks, offers fishing for crappie, perch, catfish, and bass.

Hiking trails have been constructed so that wildlife and birds can be observed in a natural setting. White-tailed deer, raccoon, opossum, armadillo, migratory waterfowl, and fox squirrel are just a few of the creatures that may be discovered in their natural environment. Occasionally, alligators may be observed in the lake. The park is six miles southwest of Huntsville off Interstate 45 on Park Road 40. The park is very popular and can be crowded at times.

Kerrville-Schreiner State Park is along the Guadalupe River, three miles southeast of Kerrville. The most notable attraction is Camp Verde, on Verde Creek. It was a base for the U.S. Army's experiment using camels for transportation in the desert Southwest. It was active from 1855 to 1869 and had about 75 camels stationed there. Also, Bandera Pass, 12 miles South of Kerrville, is a noted gap in the chain of mountains through which passed camel caravans, wagon trains, Spanish conquistadors, immigrant trains, and U.S. troops.

Boating, fishing, camping, swimming in the river, birdwatching, hiking, walking, and cycling are all things you can do in the park. You can rent tubes and canoes year-round. A sampling of Hill Country landscape includes juniper, live oak, Spanish oak, and several varieties of flowers. The Texas bluebonnet is one of the most plentiful and colorful of the native plants you can see. The park can be reached by traveling three miles southeast of Kerrville on State Highway 16 to State Highway 173 for three miles. The park headquarters building is on the left.

Mission Tejas State Historical Park was built in 1934 as a commemorative representation of Mission San Francisco de los Tejas, the first Spanish mission in the province of Texas, which was established in 1690. Also in the park is the restored Rice Family Log Home, built in 1828 and restored in 1974. The home, which Joseph Redmund Rice, Sr., constructed between 1828 and 1838, is one of the oldest structures in the area. The home served as a stopover for immigrants, adventurers, and local residents traveling the Old San Antonio Road across pioneer Texas.

Near the edge of Davy Crockett National Forest, the park is filled with tall pine trees. The dogwood are beautiful the last week or so of March, usually around the 25th. You can fish for perch and bream while in the park. It is a hilly terrain with elevation ranging from 167 to 552 feet.

The park is located 21 miles northeast of Crockett and 12 miles west of Alto on State Highway 21. The entrance to the park is in Weches, where Park Road 44 intersects State Highway 21. Nearby attractions include Caddoan Mounds, Jim Hogg, and Texas State Railroad Historical Parks; Rusk and Palestine State Parks; Ratcliff Lake; Texas Forestry Museum in Lufkin; and Ratcliff Lake Recreation Area. Ratcliff, a U.S. Forest Service park 12 miles away, has a nice swimming beach.

Palmetto State Park is named for the tropical Dwarf Palmetto plant found there. The San Marcos River runs through the park. If you bring a canoe you can put in at Luling City Park and travel 14 miles to Palmetto, portaging around one dam along the way; or put in at Palmetto and take out at Slayden bridge, 7.5 miles downriver. It is a two-day trip from Luling City Park to Slayden bridge, overnighting in Palmetto along the way. There are no rapids, but almost always a steady current. Check river conditions at the park. Bring your own canoe and arrange your shuttles.

Palmetto resembles the tropics, but eastern and western plants and animals merge here. Artesian wells produce sulphur-laden water. Wildlife in the park includes white-tailed deer, raccoons, armadillos, squirrels, and numerous birds. To

Great Parks

reach the park, go six miles southeast of Luling on U.S. Highway 183, then southwest on Park Road 11 for two miles. Nearby attractions include Pioneer Village Living History Center with 1800s reenactments; Lockhart State Park; and Sebastopol State Historical Park.

For reservations at any state park, call 512-389-8900. For more details about any state park, call 800-792-1112.

Spring

23

A Weekend Whirl

HOUSTON

To outsiders, Houston looks like a densely packed skyline of mirrored glass-and-steel skyscrapers. Most of the impressive buildings you see downtown have been constructed during the past 20 years. To take in the entire landscape of this megacity, try the top of the Texas Commerce Tower. If you are interested in architecture, then you will appreciate I. M. Pei's design of the tower and Philip Johnson's Pennzoil Place. In the sky lobby on the 60th floor of Texas Commerce Tower you can see the entire shimmering collection of towers in downtown Houston, the city named for Sam Houston. Houston was general of the Texas army that won independence from Mexico and president of the Republic of Texas. Another good view of the city of Houston can be had from the top of the Transco Tower on Post Oak Boulevard.

After you take it all in, you can come down to take a closer look at the real Houston. The city is a collection of everything you can imagine from all around the world. Cityscapes range from the old buildings of Market Square and the Victorian homes in the Heights neighborhood, to the artsy Montrose area with small but charming older homes, specialty shops and boutiques, trendy restaurants and clubs. South of downtown you can find a collection of authentic Vietnamese restaurants.

Go east of downtown to take a boat tour of the Houston Ship Channel and the Port of Houston. Have a seafood dinner while watching the sunset on the water from the Bay Brewery, Landry's, or one of many restaurants on the waterfront of Seabrook, Kemah, and El Lago. Most Houstonians will tell you to drive through the River Oaks neighborhood to see a nice collection of mansions. Some homes in River Oaks were built by noted architect John Staub.

If you are looking for an unforgettable weekend for two or a family weekend filled with fantastic entertainment, great cuisine, and fine shopping, you can easily create it in Houston. The fourth largest city in America, Houston has just about any kind of entertainment, cuisine, and shopping you want. For the fantastic, try a night at the opera. Many of the country's finest operas are produced right in Houston, Texas. This cowboy capital also has its fine arts, including the Museum of Art of the American West with Western art, located downtown in the lobby of One Houston Center.

You can see all the well-known productions, such as *Phantom of the Opera* and *Cats* in the Bayou City. But there are new productions, both homegrown and imported, in Houston theaters. You will find a Theater District with a variety of entertainment choices. Clustered around the district are Jesse H. Jones Hall, Brown Theatre, Ariel Theatre, Houston's Opera Studio, Nina Vance Alley Theatre, the Music Hall, and the Wortham Center with two theaters. Jones Hall, at Louisiana and Capitol Streets, houses the Houston Symphony Orchestra. The Jones Hall lobby features Richard Lippold's *Gemini II* sculpture floating in a gleaming curve toward a 66-foot ceiling. The Alley is an ultra modern the-

Spring

ater and the Wortham Center, which houses both the Houston Ballet and Houston Grand Opera, has a 12,000-square-foot foyer built above Prairie Street. In the Wortham Center, you can see productions of the Society for Performing Arts, the Gilbert and Sullivan Society, Texas Chamber Society, and others. In the Civic Center you will find plenty of parking to use while attending events. Near the Wortham Center is Sesquicentennial Park, a three-story pavilion surrounded by a waterfall cascading into a pool. Hiking and biking trails throughout the park are enhanced by gardens. A boat landing in the park provides access to Buffalo Bayou. The Theatre District is easily accessible if you take Memorial Drive off Interstate 45. There are many fine hotels inside and nearby the district.

If you plan to stay in the downtown area, you should get a map of Houston's underground tunnel system. Houston has six miles of underground tunnels and skywalks connecting 55 buildings, including three hotels. A variety of shops and more than 100 restaurants are accessible during daytime hours.

Although it appears to be a typical modern city, Houston has some unique spots you have to see to believe. First, not too many cities can boast of having a beer can house. But at 222 Malone you can see one. The beer can house is a private residence owned and created by John Milkovisch, a retired upholsterer. Milkovisch started with the yard. He filled the yard with concrete blocks, each inlaid with a pattern of marbles, rocks, or metal pieces, so he wouldn't have to mow the grass. Milkovisch used his beer can collection as aluminum siding for his home. The tops, bottoms, and pull tabs were fashioned into curtains. When the wind blows hard enough you can hear the tinkling of the 50,000 beer cans.

While the beer can house is a private residence and admirers need to respect the residents' privacy, you can see another unusual home in Houston up-close. The Orange Show at 2401 Munger is one man's tribute to the orange and

A Weekend Whirl

the benefits of eating oranges or drinking orange juice. Bright red gates mark the entry to this unusual concrete structure. Go through the turnstile made of bicycle handles. You will find a colorful maze with narrow stairways, passages, observation decks, and amphitheaters. You will see colorfully painted wrought-iron railings, birds, and wagon wheels. Brightly painted tractor seats are arranged in rows. A steamboat on wheels plies an empty reservoir. Retired postman Jeff McKissack began work on the site in 1954 and opened it 25 years later.

After building his tribute to the orange, McKissack was sure the people would come. But just eight weeks after opening day, he died. The crowds never came. The Orange Show is preserved and operated as a cultural and educational resource by The Orange Show Foundation. Thousands of people visit The Orange Show each year. It is open weekends from mid-March through mid-December. For information about The Orange Show, call 713-926-6368.

Once a year, usually in late summer or early fall, The Orange Show Foundation organizes a bus tour of Houston's folk art environments. On the tour you can see Hog Heaven, a purple house that is a shrine to swine; a tower of corrugated steel, which is a house designed by Italian-born architect Frank Zeni, called the "temple of the spirit"; and the Flower Man's House, one man's tribute to his mother and a promise to God.

Another unusual stop not on the tour directed by The Orange Show, but worth a stop, is the American Funeral Service Museum, 415 Barren Springs Drive, 281-876-3063. The nation's largest collection of funeral service items includes horse-drawn hearses, a funeral sleigh, a 1941 hearse, and a 1915 Packard "mourning bus," which carried everything necessary for the funeral including the pallbearers and at least 20 mourners. To lighten your spirits after this tour, stop by Anheuser-Busch Brewery for a tour. One of the largest breweries in the state, it will show you the brewery process from start to finish. The brewery is located at 775 Gellhorn. Call 713-670-1695 for more information.

If you are looking forward to seeing the museums, park your car in the Museum District. Within walking distance of each other are the Houston Zoo, the Houston Museum of Fine Arts, the Contemporary Art Museum, the Museum of Natural Sciences, and Cotrell's Butterfly Museum. Herman Park is in the midst of the Museum District.

The Museum of Natural Science has extensive displays relating to paleontology, petroleum sciences, space sciences, biological sciences, and gems and minerals; it is home to the Burke Baker Planetarium and the Wortham IMAX Theater. In Hermann Park, you'll also find the new Japanese Garden, a Zenlike setting with native plants and Japanese garden structures that came about through the combined efforts of Japanese and American business communities in Houston.

The Museum of Fine Arts has rotating exhibits, a permanent collection of notable masters, pre-Columbian and tribal arts, and a restful sculpture garden. The Contemporary Arts museum, housed in a stainless-steel building, has more recent works by artists and groups of artists exploring different techniques.

The Children's Museum, the Burke Baker Planetarium, and the open-air Miller Theatre are also in the Museum District. The Miller Theatre has regularly scheduled concerts and plays open to the public. You can get a ticket for the seating around the stage, or take a blanket, sit on the grassy slope facing the stage, and enjoy a picnic during the performance. The Houston Arboretum and Nature Center has five miles of trails for walking.

For a look at the best architectural examples in homes besides the River Oaks neighborhood, stop by the Bayou Bend, the family home of Ima Hogg, a Texas philanthropist. For a taste of Texas history, take a look inside the stately

A Weekend Whirl

1927 mansion designed by John Staub. The completely restored 28-room mansion displays American antiques from the 17th through 19th centuries, including works by Duncan Phyfe, Gilbert Stuart, and Paul Revere.

Two other museums with strong connections to the city's history are the Menil Collection and the Rothko Chapel. The Menil Collection was the private collection of John and Dominique De Menil. It has works from prehistoric to pop art, with an emphasis on 20th-century art. The Rothko Chapel, also built by the De Menil family, is said by many to evoke a great spiritual experience. Inside, the chapel contains a handful of Rothko's monochromatic paintings. You can see one of Barnett Newman's *Broken Obelisks* in the reflecting pool outside the chapel.

Another place in historic Houston is Market Square, where you will find restaurants and shops. While Market Square has been designated a National Historic District, the site of the original Market Square is a public park. You will find historic photographs and materials salvaged from nearby buildings displayed in the park. The Visitor Information Center for the city is across the street. West of downtown is Sam Houston Park, the city's oldest park. You will find a set of restored historic structures there.

A final stop before leaving Houston, and great place to take a picture, is the wall of water, a fountain next to the Transco Tower. This massive waterfall is traditionally used as a background for portraits, wedding photographs, and family pictures. For more information about Houston and events in the city, call the Greater Houston Convention and Visitors Bureau at 713-227-3100.

24

Catchin' Cajun Shrimp and Fish

ARANSAS PASS

ARANSAS PASS IS SITUATED IN THE COASTAL BEND OF THE Texas Gulf coast and was named for the pass between Mustang Island and St. Joseph's Island. The area around Aransas Pass is some of the best fishing in the coastal waters of Texas. But fishing is not what helped build the city in the 1880s when it was first known as Aransas Harbor. The town was first promoted as a farming area, but that didn't take hold. The railroad moved into town in 1892 to connect today's Aransas Pass with Harbor Island. With the railroad came development. The construction of jetties and deepening of the pass spurred growth. The real boom for this coastal city came when oil was discovered.

The town's name changed, its business changed, and the pass for which the town is named changed as well. Many years ago the pass was nearly a mile farther north than it is today. Evidence of this shift can be seen in the grandest of monuments to the past. The lighthouse on Harbor Island was constructed opposite the inner end of the original pass. But shifting sands slowly moved the pass south until a stone barrier was built across the head of Mustang Island in 1888.

This stopped the roaming pass and explains why the lighthouse is some distance from the pass it is supposed to serve.

The lighthouse typifies problems threading through Aransas Pass history. Twice promoted as a farming community, the town took a third try before consumers would buy in. The benefits of fresh sea air were promoted the third time in 1909. Land was purchased for $100 a lot, sight unseen. But promoters oversold property by $3 million and were forced to return money. After everything was settled, only 78 people were on the mail route for Aransas Pass. Nearly 30 years later, the discovery of oil pumped new blood quickly into the sleepy village.

On most days, Aransas Pass still appears to be a sleepy little coastal town with a single main street lined with small businesses and cafes. Conn Brown Harbor is relatively quiet on most days as you pass along piers where shrimpers dock when day is done. At first glance, the harbor seems to have only a small population of boats moored. But Conn Brown Harbor is home to 250 shrimp trawlers. The seafood industry is the lifeline of Aransas Pass with a large number of local businesses to support shrimpers and the industry, including fueling and ship repair. Aransas Pass shrimpers landed 22 million pounds of shrimp in 1993 with a dockside value of $41 million.

A boat launching ramp is open to the public in Conn Brown Harbor Park and it is a good place to find boats to rent. With average July temperatures just over 80 degrees, Aransas Pass is a great place for fun and fishing from the bays. Beaches and piers bordering the intercoastal canal and tributary channels are home to large redfish, speckled trout, drum, sheepshead, and flounder. Shallow bays also are good places to hunt ducks and geese.

For fishing fanatics, the best event of the year is Annual Shrimporee, a celebration of the city's ties to the fishing industry. You will find arts and crafts, entertainment, and plenty of fresh seafood. Some seafood dishes to try out include the always tasty, traditional fried shrimp. For a little Cajun flavor, sample some Shrimp Creole, Cajun Style Shrimp, or Gumbo. For the no-frills way of eating shrimp there's boiled shrimp and plenty of sauce. If you aren't a seafood lover, then you can have turkey legs. Follow the whole meal with something sweet like funnel cakes, cotton candy, or candy apples. Wash it all down with lemonade.

Aransas Pass is a tropical paradise in the winter and summer. Gentle breezes and towering palms are a welcome relief from the workweek. It is a small community with beaches and parks for exploration. San Patricio Navigation District Park has fishing piers, a small beach area, boat ramps, and a children's play area. Nearby attractions include Aransas Wildlife Refuge, Caldwell Fishing Pier, Corpus Christi, Nueces State Park, and Padre Island National Seashore.

For more information about fishing guides, boat rentals, and accommodations, contact the Aransas Pass Chamber of Commerce, 130 West Goodnight, 800-633-3028.

Catchin' Cajun Shrimp and Fish

25

Thrills, Chills, and Spills

AMUSEMENT PARKS

SIX FLAGS ASTROWORLD PASSED ITS 30TH BIRTHDAY WITHOUT the same worrisome thoughts most of us experience at this milestone. The park is growing every year with new rides and attractions. A new four-loop, steel roller coaster named Taz's Texas Tornado greeted the park's 30th season opening. Taz's Texas Tornado is 112 feet tall, making it one of the steepest roller coasters on earth.

Astroworld, located off the 610 Loop at the Fannin Exit across from the Astrodome, is too big to miss when you come to Houston. The park is large enough to be divided into sections with different themes. This may make it easier for some to find their way around, but take the map they give you at the gate just in case. There are a few restrictions on riders under 54″ tall, and more restrictions for those measuring under 42″. There are a limited number of rides for children under 42″ to enjoy.

- Nottingham Village is home to Excalibur; the Dungeon Drop, a free fall from a 230-foot tower; and games in a carnival atmosphere where you can win prizes.

- The Oriental Village is home to the Mayan Mindbender, Texas' first indoor roller coaster, that is, an in-the-dark roller coaster. Thunder River with its white water also awaits Oriental Village visitors as does the Bamboo Shoot, similar to log rides where you travel in a log on water. Expect to get wet on both of these. The Oriental Village Train Station gives you a chance to ride around the park in a much less frightening fashion as does the Oriental Astroway, unless you have acrophobia. The Astroway gives you a bird's-eye view of the park. The Serpent is a fun roller coaster designed for smaller children. The Viper is a steel roller coaster for coaster lovers. Runaway Rickshaws also is in this village.

- Mexicana is home to the wettest ride in Astroworld, the Tidal Wave. Want to stay dry? Try Warp 2000, a galactic journey through space. XLR-8 is a suspended roller coaster where you are hanging underneath the track instead of sitting in a cart on top. It also provides an interesting view as you hang below the track. This section is home to Taz's Texas Tornado and Mexicana games.

- At Western Junction, Greezed Lightnin' is ready to shake you up with instant acceleration as you are catapulted through a 360-degree loop forward and then backward. Empty your pockets, take off your glasses, and hand everything you are carrying to someone else before getting on Greased Lightnin'. Gunslinger is a Texas-styled swing; Wagon Wheel is best described as a spinning wheel; these rides and a train depot are also in Western Junction.

- The European Village is home to Batman the Escape, a stand-up roller coaster. The sights along the route to this ride are also fun for Batman fans to see. Ultra Twister is another challenge for hard-core riders. Dentzel Carousel, an original 1895 hand-carved wooden carousel, is a good place to catch your breath. The Astroneedle won't take your breath away, but will give you a panoramic view of Houston's skyline.

- Looney Tunes Town is a cartoon-town with nine different rides for anyone under 54″. If you are taller, then you must be accompanied by someone under 54″. In the USA section, the Texas Cyclone, a taller and faster version of the original Coney Island roller coaster, awaits coaster lovers. Take a 360-degree loop in space on the Looping Starship or drive a car without going to the driver's license bureau first on Antique Taxis. Some of the latest games can be found here and in other sections. In Americana Square check out the latest in virtual reality.

An additional fee is charged to try the Barnstormer. It's a flying experience that blends skydiving and hang gliding from 173 feet above the park. Also for an additional fee, take the rock climbing challenge of the Rock Wall. Scale the wall up to 30 feet above the ground and battle the law of gravity.

Astroworld and Waterworld are separate parks next to each other. The best way to experience Waterworld is to enjoy it during the heat of the afternoon while at Astroworld, or take a full day there. Go ahead and rent tubes, one for everyone. It's a little extra, but well worth it. Three water slides require tubes and these same three slides are three of the best reasons to come to Waterworld. You can wait in a line to use some of the tubes provided, but the wait may get long.

Start by getting wet at Breaker Beach, a 30,000-square-foot wave pool that produces a steady surge of 4-foot waves. The Lagoon Activity Center is a pool with slides, diving platforms, swings, and more. Wipeout is two 283-foot speed slides that tower 60 feet high. You fly so fast down the slide it's easy to lose your bikini top. On Run-a-way River, tubers descend through five pools, chutes, and rapids before shooting into a splash pool. Water slides named Hurricane, Typhoon, Tsunami, and Pipeline spiral and twist down 400-foot chutes.

Squirts Splash is an activity center for children under 48″ tall. It includes a giant water maze and water cannons. The Mainstream is a 900-foot river you float down without any effort. It travels in a circle, so you don't have to stop. The Edge is an 82-foot slide with a sheer drop that makes you feel weightless as you fall. Waterworld is open May to September only during the daylight hours.

If you are looking for fun in the Dallas/Ft. Worth area, Six Flags over Texas in Arlington has added Mr. Freeze, a high-tech roller coaster named after Batman's archrival. Mr. Freeze launches you to speeds of 70 mph within 3.78 seconds and to a height of 236 feet. Mr. Freeze uses linear induction motors to propel riders at high speeds. The linear induction launch was part of the Star Wars military defense program. The park has 10 roller coasters. It is also divided into sections.

- In El Sombrero everyone can ride the twirling, tilting Mexican hat. La Vibora, Spanish for "the viper," is designed like the bobsled to take you on a fast-moving, twisting ride. The Conquistador is a swinging Spanish ship that starts calmly, but quickly picks up the pace. El Aserradero was the world's first log flume ride. Plan on getting wet.

- In the Texas Section you will find the Texas Giant, a monstrous wooden roller coaster that towers 14 stories and reaches a top speed of 62 mph. Yosemite Sam's is an animated boating Gold River Adventure where this Wild West cartoon comes to life. Sheriff Bugs Bunny is after the bandit who stole the gold. Chaparral Antique Cars, old cars on an old road, gives the young a chance to drive. Board the Six Flags Railroad at the Texas Depot and take a ride while admiring the century-old Jefferson Patton steam engine.

- Tower Section is home to Shock Wave, the world's first roller coaster with back-to-back vertical loops, and the Oil Derrick, which towers above the park. You can ride to the top for an exciting view that includes the skylines of Dallas and Fort Worth. Take a ride up on the Air Racer where open-air biplanes circle the air at a height of nine stories before landing. Dive Bomber Alley sends you soaring into a 150-foot drop at high speeds for an additional fee. Rock Wall is for rock climbers. Scale the side of this simulated rock wall for an additional fee.

- In Old South and France you will find Runaway Mountain, a roller coaster enclosed in a 65-foot-high mountain. If you are afraid of the dark, it's not for you. LaSalle's River Rapids will take the whole family on a wild, whitewater adventure. It can be a cool thing on a hot day. In USA and Looney Tune Land everyone can ride the Silver Star Carousel, each turn-of-the-century wooden horse was restored by hand. Still sweating? Then try the Splash Water Re-Entry Test Simulation. After you take your place in the test module you rise high in the sky before splashdown. Too tame? Then try G-Force, a cliffhanging experience that shoots passengers 10 stories straight in the air, then races down in a free fall. The Right Stuff gives you a chance to break the sound barrier and travel over land at high speeds in the cockpit of a jet.

- Looney Tunes Land is for anyone under 54" tall. Rides are designed for children. In Goodtimes Square and

Boomtown, step on the Texas Chute Out, float up 200 feet in a parachute before plummeting toward the ground. Don't worry, it's a soft landing. Flashback is a loop steel roller coaster that turns you upside down six times, three going out and three going back in reverse. Judge Roy Scream is a classic wooden roller coaster spread over eight acres with speeds reaching 50 mph. Mr. Freeze, the tallest roller coaster in Texas, can be found here. Bumper cars provide old-fashioned fun. The Chameleon, a virtual reality arcade game, lets you race through time and space for an additional fee. The Mine Train was the world's first tubular steel roller coaster. The Mini Mine Train, a smaller version of the Mine Train, is full of fun for children. Texas Tornado swings send you twirling in a circle while going up.

All that make you too hot to go on? Then, get a ticket to Hurricane Harbor, a Six Flags Water Park open May to September. Some of the wild and wet fun you'll find there includes the Black Hole where two tentaclelike 500-foot tubes twist from a black flying saucer. Ride two at a time through the dark tentacles to splash down.

Next, the Sea Wolf, with four-passenger flexible toboggans powered by water blasted at a rate of 4,000 gallons per minute. Toboggans race down 830 feet of open, high-banked turns and drops. The ride was inspired by the speedy raiders of the Caribbean and is still the tallest, fastest water slide of its kind. Blue Raider is another two-passenger tube ride that takes you down more than 500 feet and ends in a big splash. Powered by 3,000 gallons of water per minute, half of the ride is through a dark tunnel.

Bubba Tub, a 300-foot-long slide, with bumps, can be ridden in multiple passenger tubes. Shotgun Falls, four separate slides, sends you through the barrel. Climb a seven-story tower to reach Der Stuka, take the northern or southern route, then lie down and get ready for a free fall. It's designed for only the bravest or craziest. Atlantic Panic and Caribbean Chaos, both with a speed of 25 mph, are open flumes with a push of 1,500 gallons per minute.

Slides aren't for you? Then take the Lazy River, a one-mile, gentle flowing, continuous river for floaters. Surf Lagoon, filled with more than a million gallons of water in a football-field-sized pool, is sent into motion by six wave makers. Surf up to four feet high is created for an oceanlike experience without sand. The Children's Water Playground has six kid-sized flumes, dozens of water cannons, and a fort filled with water and surrounded by an 18″ deep wading pool that covers more than an acre. Shaded tables are nearby for parents who want to stay dry and watch. Lagoona Beach Volleyball has four professional quality sand courts for tournaments, groups, and open play.

To contact Six Flags Astroworld, call 713-799-8404; to contact Six Flags Over Texas, call 817-640-8900.

Thrills, Chills, and Spills

26

Three Palaces

PALACIOS

PALACIOS MAY BE ONE OF TEXAS' NEWER TOWNS, FOUNDED IN 1903, but its history goes back centuries to when it was the coast's best port of entry. Indians who greeted many explorers were the last sight for some adventurers. Many newcomers were slaughtered by Indians before they could travel past the coast. Palacios' name comes from shipwrecked Spaniards who supposedly saw a vision of *tres palacios* or "three palaces." When the sailors saw this mirage of palaces, they swam toward the shore. The palaces disappeared, but the name did not.

French explorer Rene Robert Cavelier, Sieur de la Salle, landed on these shores more than 300 years ago. A statue of la Salle marks the same barren sand beach he found then. The memorial is made of Kingsland pink granite and stands 22 feet tall. Starting with la Salle, history has proved the area difficult to settle.

The county of Matagorda, for which the bay is named, was organized in the 1800s when the Republic of Texas was alive. Like much of Texas, it quickly became ranch land and cotton fields. When the 1900s were ushered in, so was the railroad. Real estate agents cashing in on the coastal location had a hand in developing the bay area you see today. Look for Bull Pasture, which was part of the famous

Shanghai Pierce Ranch. There, a town was established at Hamilton Point in 1902 and named Tres Palacios. The Tres was later dropped.

For those who have an interest in Texas history and ghost towns, Indianola should be a stop. You can find where Indianola was located at the end of State Highway 316, south of Port Lavaca. The area is clean and quiet after the sea has washed many settlements away. At one time, concrete and wooden structures lined what was the best harbor on the Gulf of Mexico. Piers reached a half mile into the bay, serving as docks for cargo laden ships. In the 1800s, the German settlers landed with Prince Carl of Solms-Braunfels, who settled New Braunfels. By the mid-1800s, an army depot supplied Texas from this central location. The camels deposited here were used in the Jefferson Davis effort to replace horses with the hump-backed creatures. Ice shipped from the Great Lakes was stored in Indianola warehouses and used by sweltering Texans.

The town flourished with the help of the shipping industry. It survived the Civil War despite the South experiencing massive destruction. Yellow fever epidemics could not kill this prosperous coastal city. The Gulf of Mexico gave Indianola its life and also took it away. The benefits of the seaside location could not outweigh the destructive forces of a hurricane. On September 17, 1875, the sea rose against the town and the wind beat it down. When all was said and done, 900 died and almost the entire city was destroyed.

Indianola, the prize of the coast, was rebuilt with even larger warehouses. But the wrath of Mother Nature returned for a second and final devastation 11 years later. Indianola disappeared in the storm. The few who survived did not return. Indianola has proved difficult to tame and residents over the years have lost houses and cars to the gulf waters there. You can see the tide working on the few stones left of the courthouse foundation. Just inches above the smooth

sand, you can find outlines of broken concrete cisterns. Indianola County Historic Park in Port Lavaca is located on
the same grounds as the old town of
Indianola. The park is also a great place
for picnicking, fishing, boating, and
camping. It is located at State Highways 238
and 316.

Palacios is located halfway between Corpus Christi and
Houston by Matagorda Bay, one of many on the Gulf Coast.
The bay is host to many sailing regattas and sport fishing
events. With the second largest fleet in the state, fishing is
the prime source of income. Seafood-processing plants have
sprung up to accommodate this industry. The bayfront park
that stretches along Tres Palacios Bay can be seen up close
with a mile and a half of railed walkway at the water's edge.
A pier with a covered pavilion, fishing jetty, and boat ramps
make this park a frequent stop for tourists. Palacios, which
is on "The Great Texas Coastal Birding Trail," is home to
several species of birds.

An attraction to include in your weekend in Palacios is
the Calhoun County Museum in nearby Port Lavaca's courthouse annex at 201 W. Austin Street. The museum has relics
from the early days to connect the present-day scenery with
the past.

Halfmoon Reef Lighthouse in Port Lavaca was established
in 1858 on Matagorda Bay. Kept dark during the Civil War
for the benefit of blockade runners, it was turned back on in
1868. The lighthouse was severely damaged in a 1942 hurricane. Although its light kept shining throughout the storm,
it was condemned afterward. Halfmoon Reef Lighthouse
was moved after the hurricane from its location on an old
World War II bombing range to Point Comfort. In 1979,
Halfmoon Reef was relocated next door to the chamber of
commerce on State Highway 35 bypass near the causeway.

Three Palacios

Port Lavaca Causeway State Recreation Park is a popular place for fishing, swimming, and boating. The pier in the park extends 3,202 feet into Lavaca Bay and has lights to allow visitors to enjoy night fishing. You can find the pier alongside State Highway 35. Another fishing pier is the Port Lavaca State Fishing Pier, operated by the City of Port Lavaca, at 202 North Virginia. Call 512-552-5311 for information.

For a historic night of sleep, try the Luther Hotel, built in 1903. The hotel is a recorded Texas historic landmark. Luther Hotel was the headquarters for early land developers. In the past, a formally attired orchestra played at mealtimes along the rambling front porch. Unfortunately, the porch, which was said to be the longest one in Texas, is gone. The hotel is located between 4th and 5th Streets.

You can also visit the Marine Fisheries Research Station where studies include adaptability of saltwater species to freshwater. Newcomers to the Texas coast can find out what is under the surface. But tours are aimed at visitors with a marine biology background and interest. It is a good idea to make an appointment. To reach the facility, go about eight miles west on State Highway 35, then south about six miles on Well Point Road.

As with most coastal towns, you may enjoy looking at sailboats, shrimp boats, and the luxurious yachts moored in the bay area. Palacios is off the beaten path and a quiet retreat. It is a nice town to take the family for a vacation on the beach or to go fishing. For more information, call the Palacios Chamber of Commerce at 512-972-2615.

Summer

27

Forgotten Vacations

LAKE AMISTAD–AQUARENA SPRINGS

FIGHTING CROWDS MONDAY THROUGH FRIDAY IN RUSH HOUR traffic, on the subway, or on a bus, gets old fast. Long days in the office and the rush to clean, cook, and get the young ones to bed can take the fun out of life. Sometimes it's easy to dream of how nice life would be if you were stranded on a deserted island. If you're looking for paradise without the crowd, then try these two forgotten vacation spots. Lake Amistad near Del Rio and Aquarena Springs in San Marcos through time and tragedy have become forgotten vacation spots that can make ideal getaways from daily stress.

Considered an international attraction, Lake Amistad is near Del Rio on the border of Mexico in Southwest Texas. Advertisements build Lake Amistad up as paradise for boaters and scuba divers. While driving from San Antonio to Lake Amistad, watch the landscape along U.S. Highway 90 West disappear into desert. Seeing any kind of water is a welcome relief. Using the map as a guide to find regions of the lake in the summer of '98, it was easy to see how years of drought have taken their toll on the area. Several coves disappeared, and usable docks dwindled to two on American shores. The swimming area in the national park became a dusty bowl.

The water level dropped during four years to 47 feet below normal. One boat dock in Rough Canyon was 200 feet out of water and hasn't been used for four years. The drop in water level created an interesting effect on the terrain. Inside the Rough Canyon Marina store you can see a photograph of the area before it became a premiere resort. The original dam was quite large and the canyon was clearly visible as the river twisted and turned through it. Postcards for sale at the store show a Rough Canyon Cove on Devil's River after the area became a resort. The water is just below the tops of canyon walls, hiding the real beauty of the limestone.

After four years of drought conditions, steep limestone walls jut out of blue water. Explore old foundations, the old dam, and concrete stairways that seem to lead up to the sky. Much of the area's past remnants were only visible to divers in deep blue water. Why visit this once booming tourist spot so deteriorated from drought? Quite simply, this forgotten vacation spot is one of the best places in Texas to really get away. The beauty of the desert cut up with canyons is beyond compare to any city skyline. The peace at night as you lie back to watch shooting stars dart across the sky cannot be found in other vacation spots.

Rough Canyon Marina, run by Hollis and Martha Rogers, provides affordable accommodations compared to other areas where tourists flock. Boat rentals are available with a wide variety to choose from at very reasonable rates. The cost of a weekend there would be half the cost of a weekend of boating in most other areas. Water skis and tubes are also available. Martha says to reserve rooms and boats about two months in advance. Once bitten by the beauty of the area, most people want to return regularly.

Swimmers ought to know that the water temperatures range from 54 degrees in winter months to 83 degrees late in summer. Amistad's exceptionally clear water makes it an excellent place for scuba diving. A dive cove is located at Diablo East. Depending on lake levels, divers can see several submerged ranches. If you are going to the lake strictly to dive, call ahead to find out about diving conditions and register at the park's headquarters. The area suffered severe flooding in the fall of 1998. When diving be sure to register with a park ranger or at park headquarters.

The clear blue water of Lake Amistad also has black bass, stripers, and channel and yellow catfish for those who like to fish. The lake usually extends 74 miles up the Rio Grande, 25 miles up the Devil's River, and 14 miles up the Pecos River. This varies with water levels. Texas fishing license requirements apply when fishing on the U.S. side of Lake Amistad. When in Mexican waters, you must adhere to Mexican fishing regulations, which differ considerably from Texas in terms of size and catch limits. Be sure to find out ahead of time what is required when in Mexican waters.

The store has groceries, fishing tackle, live bait, gas, boat rentals, and a launch ramp. To get to Rough Canyon from Del Rio, take U.S. Highway 277 about 15 miles north and turn left at Recreation Road 2. When traveling to Amistad be sure to carry water and tools for small car repairs on those hot, lonely stretches of road. The people of the Del Rio area are very friendly and love to talk to visitors. Nearby you can see Seminole Canyon State Historical Park, Del Rio, and Mexico. However, once you find Rough Canyon and Lake Amistad, you probably won't want to leave. Call Martha or Hollis at 830-775-8779 to find out about rooms and campgrounds next to the national recreation area.

Another great escape vacation spot came about through a different sort of misfortune. Texans who have been to

Forgotten Vacations

Aquarena Springs Resort in the past remember all the glitz of the amusement park mixed with the great outdoors. But the resort in San Marcos, operated by Southwest Texas State University, proved to be a financial drain because of the number of employees it took to run the amusement park, restaurants, golf course, and stores. When the Southwest Texas University Board of Regents voted to close down the amusement park and stop providing entertainment at Aquarena Springs, the board lamented the loss. Many fondly remember underwater shows at Aquarena that included mermaids. Their loss can be your gain.

Aquarena Springs is located on the scenic San Marcos River, a favorite Texas tubing spot. The Aquarena Springs Inn and the golf course remain open for business. Some of the glass-bottomed tour boats continue to operate, and the endangered species and archaeological exhibits remain open. You won't be charged the $15 admission to visit the amusement park. Golfers will still be charged a fee to play on the course, which will be operated by SWT recreational sports. The university plans to go in a different direction with future development of the resort property. Those looking for some peace in the great outdoors may enjoy the new direction much more. If you have been to Aquarena Springs before, you can expect it to be quite a bit different. The regents plan to sell the amusement park rides and other equipment. Ralph, the Swimming Pig, one of the park's attractions, may stay at SWT.

At the time of purchase, university officials were considering turning the park into a wildlife preserve for educational purposes. The purchase included 90 acres and cost $9 million. Even though 125,000 people visited yearly, the university lost $1.7 million on the park since the 1994 purchase. As the board closed the amusement park, they saw this original idea as the new focus. The new focus is to protect the springs flowing from Edwards Aquifer and to preserve wildlife.

Summer

If you are a bird-watcher, you will enjoy seeing the flock of red-crowned parrots among the cypress trees; green-backed herons, tricolored herons, and western kingbirds are found near Old Main. Also, watch for warblers during migration on Sessom Drive by the stream near the woods. Plants in Aquarena attract hummingbirds. Look for water-fowl and other wild birds at Spring Lake, which contains the headwaters for the San Marcos River. Tubers and swimmers enjoy a popular access point to the river where the lake falls over the dam by Peppers restaurant. To find out more about Aquarena Springs, call 800-999-9767.

Besides Aquarena Springs, the city of San Marcos has a lot to offer you. It is quietly tucked between two well-known cities—Austin and San Antonio. Depending on your direction of travel, San Marcos is 15 minutes away from Wimberley or New Braunfels, Lockhart, or Buda. It is a beautiful one-hour drive to or from Luckenbach, the state's most famous ghost town. Other attractions include the San Marcos River Walk through the city park. The river path is close to the parking lot behind the Chamber of Commerce on C. M. Allen Parkway. The Children's Playscape is also on C. M. Allen.

San Marcos is the gateway to the Hill Country and home to one of the state's best chili cook-offs, the Chilympiad Chili Cook-Off. The cook-off is held the third weekend of September at the Hayes County Civic Center on Interstate 35, a mile south of San Marcos. San Marcos is also known for its outlet malls along Interstate 35.

Tubing down the Guadalupe River or the San Marcos River is a must, especially on a hot summer day. The place to cast off on a tube on the San Marcos River is a few blocks away from Aquarena Springs, the source of the river. Traditionally, tubers haven't been able to get in the water because of the glass-bottom boats showing tourists the fish and springs. If the university is still running the boats when you visit, you will need to circle behind the gym and make your

Forgotten Vacations

way over to the National Guard Armory area. Here you will find everything you need: restrooms, picnic tables, tube rentals, and taxi service back when you finish. The river moves slowly, which allows plenty of time to enjoy the overhanging trees and wildlife. However, the trip will end with a fast chute at Rio Vista Park. Watch others navigate the chute before you go. The water stays a constant 71 degrees, so a dip should be refreshing.

After all that fun on the river, you may be hungry. If you miss the Chilympiad culinary competition, you can find food elsewhere. The locals recommend hamburgers from Grin's, which is one block north of the SWT campus; tacos at Herbert's Taco Hut, near Interstate 35; or Peppers restaurant for a great view of the San Marcos River falls.

Summer

28

The Biggest and Best Lakes

EAST TEXAS

IN TEXAS EVERYTHING IS BIG AND LAKES ARE NO EXCEPTION TO the rule. Lakes mentioned here are some of the biggest and the best in the state for boating, water skiing, scuba diving, swimming, or fishing.

Toledo Bend   With 185,500 acres of surface area on the Texas-Louisiana border, Toledo Bend is so big that many people think it is three lakes. Private and public campgrounds surround Toledo Bend, which is considered one of the best fishing spots. You can catch largemouth bass, striped bass, and crappie. Toledo Bend, which is the largest manmade lake in the South and fifth largest in the nation, is a great recreational lake for all activities. With 1,200 miles of shoreline, you can take many different roads to the lake. The most direct route is State Highway 21 from Nacogdoches or U.S. Highway 59. State Highway 21 intersects the lake in the center of its 65-mile length.

Sam Rayburn Lake   Covering 114,500 acres, Sam Rayburn has a national reputation as a top fishing lake. It is near Lufkin off State Highway 103. You will find 560 miles of shoreline with plenty of marinas and a Corps of Engineers campground. Big enough for boating, the lake is also a good place to catch bass and crappie. Sam Rayburn is the largest lake in Texas.

Lake Texoma   This lake starts at 89,000 acres, but can cover as much as 143,000 acres. Water levels can fluctuate as much as 15 feet per year. Shallow water and shifting sand bars around Red River and Washita River pose hazards to navigation. These two rivers are the lake's source of water. There are many small inlets. The lake was built for fun and to provide hydroelectric power and flood control. Clarity ranges from two to four feet. There are 580 miles of shoreline with varying features, such as cliffs, boulders, sand beach, clay, mud, and marsh. When water levels drop, willows grow on the Oklahoma side across from Treasure and North Islands. It is close to Denison, and Eisenhower State Park borders the lake. From Dallas, take U.S. Highway 75 north from U.S. Highway 82.

Summer

Lake Livingston   This 82,600-acre lake is not far from Houston off North U.S. Highway 59. You will find good marinas, resorts, and camping areas along 52 miles of shoreline, as well as a state park. The lake is fed by the Trinity River and has enough open water for sailing and motor boats. Lake Livingston is known for having largemouth bass and white bass.

Falcon Lake   Spanning across 78,300 acres, Falcon Lake is near Zapata at the intersection of U.S. Highway 83 and State Highway 16. With its distance from any populated areas, Falcon Lake has proved to be great for bass fishing. Part of Falcon Lake is in Mexico, which may affect license requirements for fishing. A state park is located on Falcon Lake. While summertime can be too hot for comfort, campers can enjoy pleasant winter weather and the various birds that winter in the area. While the lake attracts serious fishermen, it also is great for boating. Falcon is the major irrigation source for Rio Grande Valley farmers and water levels vary according to rainfall.

Lake Meredith   The deep blue of Lake Meredith, found in Lake Meredith National Recreation Area, contrasts starkly with its surrounding limestone canyons. The lake lies on the dry, windswept plains of the Texas Panhandle in the Llano Estacado region. This oasis was created by a dam on the Canadian River. Located 30 miles north of Amarillo on State Highway 136, Lake Meredith is more than a pretty lake. You can have a good time boating, skiing, swimming, and fishing.

Inks Lake State Park   Located in the Hill Country, Inks Lake State Park is by Inks Lake on the Colorado River in Burnet County. Inks Lake, surrounded by granite, is a constant level lake. Droughts do not affect water activities such as lake swimming, boating, water skiing, scuba diving, and fishing. You can take nature walks and geology hikes and learn about lakeshore ecology. Junior Ranger programs are conducted on Saturdays in the summer. The Devil's Waterhole Canoe Tour and the Bat Watch program are other park activities. The park has a panorama of cedar and oak woodlands, wildflowers, and pink granite outcroppings in the Central Texas Hill Country. Deer, turkey, quail, songbirds, and other wildlife are in the park. The most commonly caught fish are bass, crappie, and catfish. The park is nine miles west of Burnet on State Highway 29, take Park Road 4.

Cedar Creek Lake   A 34,300-acre lake located about 60 miles southeast of Dallas, Cedar Creek Lake is a favorite weekend retreat for citizens of Big D. Lakeside developments are popular with plenty of marinas and boat rentals. Best known for boating, Cedar Creek is also an excellent

The Biggest and Best Lakes

fishing lake for white bass and crappie. Take U.S. Highway 175 south to Mabank, then State Highway 198 south to Gun Barrel City and State Highway 334 across the lake.

Lewisville Lake   Another lake close to Dallas and Fort Worth, this beauty stretches across 29,592 acres. The Corps of Engineers created this reservoir, which boaters love. Restaurants, clubs, and campgrounds are among the lakeside businesses. Sailing, skiing, or fishing can be fun. The lake level was raised to help fish thrive in Lewisville Lake. To find the lake, take Interstate 35 north from Dallas.

Summer

Choke Canyon Lake   At 26,000 acres, this is one of the biggest lakes in South Texas. You can fish for largemouth bass, channel catfish, and sand bass. If you are a photographer, then you will find the Calliham Unit of Choke Canyon State Park a good place to photograph wildlife. You can feed the white-tailed deer, javelinas, and wild turkeys. Since so many people do feed the animals, they are approachable, but be cautious. Choke Canyon is off Interstate 37 between San Antonio and Corpus Christi, near Three Rivers.

Lake Palestine   Another East Texas Lake to see is Lake Palestine with more than 25,000 surface acres. It is tucked in the Pineywoods on the Neches River. You can enjoy boating and skiing but there are only private boat ramps. From Tyler, take State Highway 155 south.

Lake Buchanan   Another Hill Country beauty is Lake Buchanan at 23,200 acres. Fed by the Colorado River, it is the biggest of the Highland Lakes. If you visit during the winter, you might see bald eagles. During the summer, the lake

is filled with boaters. To get to Lake Buchanan from Georgetown, take State Highway 29 west to Farm to Market 690.

Lake Possum Kingdom   Possum Kingdom State Park is
located in the rugged canyon country of the Palo Pinto
Mountains and Brazos River Valley. Lake Possum Kingdom
has 20,000 acres of the clearest, bluest water in the southwest. Numerous white-tailed deer make their home in the
park. Also, a large portion of the official Texas longhorn herd
is located here. To reach the park, travel U.S. Highway 180
to Caddo, then go 17 miles north on Park Road 33. To make
boat, jet ski, and other rental reservations, call 940-549-5612.

Lake Travis   Just over 18,000 acres, this natural wonder is
on the Colorado River close to Austin. Its serpentine shape
and crowded waters make it a dangerous lake. In spite of
the danger, it is one of the most popular recreation and res-
idential lakes. Its well-developed shores include resorts,
restaurants, golf courses, and marinas. Take Interstate 35
south to Round Rock and Farm to Market 620 to Lake
Travis.

Lake Arrowhead   In the North Central Plains you can find
Lake Arrowhead, a reservoir on the Little Wichita River
with 16,200 surface acres and 106 miles of shoreline. Lake
Arrowhead is a good place for swimming, water skiing, disc
golf, picnicking, camping, studying nature, hiking, and boating. An 18-hole frisbee golf course, horse trail, and camping
areas are some of the features of the park. The park is six
miles south of Wichita Falls on U.S. Highway 281, then eight
miles east on Farm to Market 1954.

For reservations at all state parks mentioned here, call 512-
389-8900. For more details about state parks, call Park Information at 800-792-1112.

The Biggest and Best Lakes

29

Splashdowns and Struedel

NEW BRAUNFELS–GRUENE

FOR A WET AND WILD WEEKEND DURING THE DOG DAYS OF summer, head for Schlitterbahn, a water park in the heart of New Braunfels, a fair-sized Texas city between San Antonio and Austin. You know you are in Schlitterbahn when you hear the screams of excitement and feel a splash of water. A more refreshing day couldn't be had in July. For this kind of fun you need a bathing suit.

Schlitterbahn Waterpark's German castle with four slides was the first attraction built at the New Braunfels park in 1979. Head to the water park today and get ready for Schlitterbahn's 30 attractions, one ride lasting as long as 45 minutes. You will find 65 acres of slides, pools, inner tube floats, kiddie parks, high-tech water rides, and year-round resort rooms all along the scenic banks of the Comal River. It is one amusement park where you won't feel trapped in a cement and steel world, but instead you will be immersed in a forest on a riverbank.

Are you ready to check out the thrills waiting for you? Start by surfing the Boogie Bahn where you will blast through hills and valleys on the uphill water coasters before plunging into the spring-fed Lagoon Pool. Afterward, take a break and swim up to the refreshment bar. Ready for more? Hop a tube on the mile-long Raging River, sweep down body flumes at Schlitterbahn's landmark castle, brave two slides with sheer drops, and feel the thrill of the White-water Tube Chute. Relax and be lulled by the water in the wave pool, or ride an alligator on the Congo River.

Bored? If that's possible, then, race through the Banzai Pipeline or one of three tube chutes. If you're ready for a break, try kicking back in a giant hot tub. You can stay where you play right in Schlitterbahn Park. Step out your door and jump on the tube rides. Schlitterbahn Resorts are right next to Schlitterbahn Waterpark with many different types of accommodations to choose from. The two riverside resorts put you in the heart of the water action.

If you aren't interested in water parks and prefer the natural waterways, take a raft down some rapids. The Guadalupe River's crystal clear, cascading water offers a challenge you dare not pass up. You can paddle rafts, kayaks, canoes, or tubes available on site or bring your own. Guides can be hired, but really aren't necessary. It is a good idea to phone ahead for river conditions before making a trip to ride the rapids. Unlike the water park, the Guadalupe River is subject to changes due to weather conditions. The river ride will take you through a series of falls and rapids, including Huaco Falls, the largest rapids on the Guadalupe River, with stretches of the river gliding downstream through some beautiful country. Mix in an occasional swim or water fight to make an unforgettable experience for the family. Trips are exciting, but not considered dangerous. Wear bathing suits and some old tennis shoes, plus sunscreen. The Texas sun is extremely harsh to untanned skin. Call 830-625-2351 for more information.

Suggested river rafting companies for renting and guides: Gruene River Company, 1404 Gruene Road, New Braunfels, 830-625-2800; and Rockin' R River Rides, 830-629-9999 or 800-55-FLOAT. If you would prefer a calmer tour of the river area, try a scenic drive on River Road, the only road along the river. See the rapids and wildlife without any agony. For those who prefer dry activities, there are seven area golf courses and many special events taking place almost every weekend.

If you are looking for something a little quieter, stay at the Hotel Faust. The hotel caters to many needs, including weekend getaways and honeymoons. Experience the history of Texas in a hotel originally opened in 1929 as the Travelers Hotel. Completely renovated in the original decor and furnishings, Hotel Faust has all the modern conveniences. For reservations, call 830-625-7791. Children are welcome.

You could also try the 1847 Kuebler-Waldrip Haus, a bed-and-breakfast that was a German pioneer limestone and hand-hewn timber home. The 1863 Danville School is an original wooden one-room schoolhouse on the property. The Historic Kuebler-Waldrip Haus property was first owned by Francois Guilbeau, a French-born wine merchant who is credited with saving the diseased French vineyards with mustang grape vine cuttings that came from this property.

The original rock house has walls ranging in thickness from 17 to 23 inches. The rocks added during the restoration of 1980 included originals from the Comma County Jail House and St. Peter and Paul Catholic Church, which is still in operation. The big rock in front of the fireplace was the main front steps into the old jail house. The main building has a total of six bedrooms, six private baths, some with porches and kitchens, and a wonderful view. There are four more rooms in the schoolhouse. The house is set on 43 acres in Hill Country, minutes from attractions in New Braunfels and Gruene. Watch the sun rise and set. Call 800-299-8372 for reservations.

Also while in New Braunfels, don't miss the museum with the largest collection of original art by Sister M. I. Hummel. It has a large collection of Hummel figurines and

Splashdowns and Struedel

collectibles. Charcoals, pastels, and oils displayed at the Hummel Museum were created by a nun who lived in Germany during World War II. Sister Maria Innocentia Hummel entered the Siessen convent in Germany in 1931. Before her death from tuberculosis at the age of 37, her artworks were the inspiration for the popular Hummel figurines.

Other sites to see in New Braunfels and Gruene are

Alamo Classic Car Museum   Take a trip down memory lane and see the cars you've dreamed about, or the ones your dad drove.

Children's Museum   The museum is not a quiet place because the rooms are filled with excited young people learning new things. Exhibits invite you to experiment, imagine, and discover. While you are there exploring, remember to touch everything.

Conservation Plaza   A collection of buildings that have been restored to preserve the natural beauty of the community and its heritage.

Historic District of Gruene, 830-629-5077, features many unique shops, a wine-tasting facility, an antique mall, and two working potters in a late 1800s Texas setting with good places to eat. It is also the home of the oldest dance hall in Texas.

Landa Park   This nearly 200-acre park can be seen as you relax on a miniature train. Feature attractions include the Landa Park Arboretum, Landa Lake, and the Comal River. You can see what's living underwater in a glass-bottom boat.

Lindheimer Home   Check out the gardens blooming at the home of Ferdinand Lindheimer, also known as the Father of Texas Botany.

New Braunfels Marketplace   Go to any of the 48 factory shops for the best bargains, including Fila, American Tourister, Goeffrey Beene, Pfaltzgraff, and Oneida. Call 830-620-6806 for more information.

Museum of Texas Handmade Furniture   You will see more than 75 furniture items handmade in Texas during the 1800s, plus tools used by the early immigrants. Call 830-629-6504 for more information.

Sophienburg Museum and Archives   Walk through the pages of history at Sophienburg and learn about early German immigrants. Artifacts, graphic presentations of words and pictures, maps, documents, and even the hand-crafted model of the prince's castle in Braunfels, Germany, are in this unique museum.

Stage Stop Ranch   See a real 1800s stage stop and stay in a bed-and-breakfast or cabin. The ranch provides a rustic atmosphere with cowhide rugs and fireplaces in cabins. Spend a romantic night in a private cabin about 20 miles west of New Braunfels, and three miles from Canyon Lake. Enjoy a scenic trail ride with the family or relax in a spa. Call 800-STAGE STOP for more information.

When you have finished screaming down every slide and seen all the artifacts gathered to portray German immigrant history in Texas, it's time to taste some traditional German food and take in the incredible views found in New Braunfels. For an unforgettable dinner or lunch, try one of the following:

Castle Avalon   Find your throne and royal treatment at an English style castle located on Highway 46, a little more than 10 miles west of New Braunfels. For more information or reservations, call 830-885-2002.

Splashdowns and Struedel

The Gruene Mansion Restaurant You will find seafood, steaks, and pasta with a wide selection of wines, and a table overlooking the Guadalupe River. Call 830-620-0760 for more information.

Wolfgang Keller Restaurant A romantic dining experience is waiting for you at this restaurant located in the historic Prince Solms Inn. Authentic German food with live piano music on Friday and Saturday nights. Call 830-625-9169 for information and reservations.

For more information call the New Braunfels Chamber of Commerce at 830-625-2385.

Summer

30

Play in Port A

PORT ARANSAS AND MUSTANG ISLAND

IF YOU ARE LOOKING FOR PARADISE, THEN LOOK NO FURTHER than Port Aransas, a barrier reef island near Corpus Christi. Port Aransas is accessible via the John F. Kennedy Causeway from the south end of Corpus Christi by taking South Padre Island Drive to Park Road 22. A more exciting entrance can be made by taking a short free ferry ride from the east off Aransas Pass. The town was called "Paradise" by one of its past residents, Elda Mae Roberts, who managed to still think it a paradise after the Great Depression in the 1930s. Roberts and her family settled on the island by washing ashore during a storm on Roberts' Point, which is now Roberts' Point Park.

Named "Wild Horse Island" by the first settlers, the Karankawa Indians, Mustang Island has been rediscovered by vacationers. Port Aransas was also the little fishing village known as "Sand Point" in 1833. At one time it was ranch land for cattle and sheep. A little more than a decade ago the first condominiums were built in the middle of the 14-mile island. The Seagull and Port Royal provide a secluded and serene atmosphere where couples can enjoy watching the moon rise during a beach stroll. On cool nights you can cuddle by a fire on the beach or by a fireplace in a room with a water view. In the spring, the water glows an

iridescent green at night from algae. But the summer provides the hot weather for enjoying the beach. The average
temperature in July is 85 degrees, but a steady wind on the
island and a place to get wet will keep you cool. Boating,
fishing, swimming, and surfing are favorite island activities.

Suggestions for arranging a boat tour include calling Duke
Nature Boat Trips at 512-749-5252. It is located at 136 Cotter inside Woody's in Port Aransas. You can take a two-hour
trip cruises past the Old Lydian Historical Lighthouse behind
St. Joseph's Island and into Corpus Christi's ship channel. A
shrimper's trawling net pulled behind the boat yields up
samples of the varied marine life, which the staff aboard
will identify, describe, and then release. Another suggestion
would be to contact the Fisherman's Wharf in Port Aransas
at 512-749-5760, 512-749-5448, or 800-605-5448 for deep-
sea fishing, catamaran cruises, daily fishing excursions, birding tours, sunset cruises, and private group charters.

For island sightseeing, you can take a trolley tour from
The University of Texas Marine Science Institute, located
on Cotter Street near the university's visitors center. The
tour begins as the trolley makes its loop at the jetties. The
trip lasts about one hour, depending on traffic and use by
other riders. You can get off and on during the tour. If you
stop, you have an hour before the trolley comes back.

Some people may prefer to stay in town at one of the
many condominiums. Port Aransas is a small town with
2,333 residents. Cline's Landing on the end of McAlister
Street stands seven stories high on the edge of the ship channel, providing a spectacular view from every balcony.
Flanked by a popular fishing pier and docks, Cline's Landing
has a pool and a hot tub for guests to relax in. A great place
to enjoy the sunset and a view of the entire city and the ship
channel is on the seventh floor of Cline's Landing in the Sunset Lounge. You have to ask at the desk for the key to this

private room, which is the only room on the seventh floor of Cline's.

Next to Cline's is the U.S. Coast Guard Station, originally built in 1915. The station weathered the big storm of 1916, which caused much destruction of property on the island. One block from Cline's is another popular place to stay, the Tarpon Inn. A vintage wooden structure from 1886, the inn is 80 percent restored. Famous guests have included Franklin D. Roosevelt and Duncan Hines, who spent his honeymoon in the inn. Accommodations include a seafood restaurant and 26 rooms with baths. Call 512-749-5555 for reservations.

If you want to ride horses down the white sand beaches, crack crawfish to the sounds of live Cajun country music, and watch dolphins play or pelicans dive for fish, then you have three reasons to take a weekend trip to Port Aransas. The love of seafood is another good reason to head there. Just past the Tarpon Inn, next to the city docks, are several restaurants, places to dance, and a fresh seafood market. The Trout Street Inn is a popular restaurant in this part of town.

Mustang Island probably began life as a submerged sand bar about 4,500 years ago. The famous pirate Jean La Fitte spent time on Mustang Island in the 1820s. Legend has it that somewhere on the island is a Spanish dagger with a silver spike driven through the hilt to mark the spot where La Fitte buried a chest of gold and jewels. Today, most vacationers in search of jewels look in stores on the island. But some hunt for treasure with metal detectors. You can discover tales of sunken Spanish ships and lost treasure, which may be somewhere on the island.

For additional history and an overview of Port Aransas and Mustang Island, visit the museum in the Port Aransas City Hall located at West Avenue A and Cutoff Road. For additional information about accommodations, dining, events, and area facilities, contact the Port Aransas Convention and Visitors Bureau at 421 West Cotter, 800-452-6278. To find out more about marine life around Mustang Island go to the University of Texas Marine Science Institute Visitors Center located on Cotter Street at the beach. It is estimated that more than 600 species of saltwater fish inhabit the waters off the island today. The center is along the ship channel between Mustang and San Jose Islands. Call 512-749-6729 for more information.

Mustang Island State Park, which has 3,474 acres of sand dunes, sea oats, and beach morning glory, and five miles of Gulf beach frontage is a good place for seaside camping, surfing, fishing, swimming, and shell collecting. Other facilities include picnic areas, restrooms, showers, dump station, nature trail, and fish-cleaning station. The park is located 14 miles south of Port Aransas on State Highway 361. For more information, call 512-749-5246.

Not far from Port Aransas, and visible from the upper floors of Cline's Landing, is a long, low island named St. Joseph's Island, the alleged headquarters for the pirate La Fitte in the early 19th century. After La Fitte's end, the island remained virtually unknown until the 1800s when cattlemen and seafarers built a town there they called Aransas Wharves, which vanished for an unknown reason. Some suspect the Civil War was responsible for its end. The island remained uninhabited until the early 1900s when it was purchased by Col. E. H. R. Green, the only son of Hetty Green. The Colonel's title was self-selected, and his mother was one of the richest women in the world. Hetty Green had a reputation for being tightfisted when it came to spending, but the Colonel made up for lost time and tried to spend it as fast as he could. He built a mansion on the island, and imported wine and liquor for parties. Fast times caught up with the Colonel, he died, and the island again was left uninhabited. Nobody had any interest in it. More recently, Sid Richardson built a great house on St. Joseph's Island and furnished it with original paintings by Frederick Remington and Charles Russell. He also built wharves and an airstrip for his guests and employed an army of guards to keep the uninvited away. Sid died and the property remains in his family, who raise Santa Gertrudis cattle there. The island is still off-limits to visitors.

Play in Port A

31

Cool Caverns

SOUTH CENTRAL

IF YOU ARE TIRED OF HOT WEATHER ON WEEKENDS IN THE summer and would relish a cool dark spot, maybe you should consider caving this weekend. Texas caves stay a cool 65 degrees year-round. With nearly 3,500 caves documented in Texas, and most commercially developed caves centrally located around Austin and San Antonio, you can see a few caves in one weekend.

If you already know you have Flintstone blood in your veins, or if you need a little experience before you declare your true ancestry, a few hours underground should help. To enjoy caves or appreciate how they were formed, you don't have to be an expert. The National Speleological Society (Huntsville, Alabama) is the largest organization in America for the scientific study, exploration, and conservation of caves. The society focuses on how to explore caves that have not been commercially developed with lights, handrails, and gift shops. But here we will help you map out tour plans for caves with all the modern conveniences. If you venture off into uncharted caves be careful not to destroy formations that took millions of years to form.

Most of Texas' caves occur in the limestone and gypsum areas of central and west Texas. Caves were formed during earthquakes, or formed by water. An estimated 30 million years ago, a major earthquake along the 1,800-mile Balcones Fault Line created a prehistoric undersea earth shift. The fault was named by Spanish missionaries who first explored Texas. The view seen from the fault line appeared to them as balconies on an upper story of a building. This shift during this earthquake formed Wonder Cave in San Marcos.

Inside Wonder Cave you can see the strata of geologic ages that make up the world under our feet. By looking at cave walls you can see how the earth was torn apart, since the cave has remained unchanged since the quake. You will find fossils and an up close view of the Balcones Fault. Some experts say that the earthquake formed a true cave, while the water formed a cavern. Caverns are constantly changing as water continues to create new formations. Others argue against this belief, claiming the water-formed caverns are true caves. Whatever side of the fence you stand on, exploring caves in Texas is a trip into the fanciful.

While you are touring Wonder Cave be sure to exit by the elevator to see the fault line's drop-off point from the top of the Tejas Observation Tower. From the tower you can see the separation point between the Hill Country's Edwards Plateau and the vast Gulf Coastal Plains. You will be looking at the bed of an ocean that vanished. Wonder Cave is part of the Wonder World tourist attraction, which includes a gift shop plus Mexico's World Import Marketplace. Other attractions are train rides and an animal park. Wonder Cave is between San Antonio and Austin off Interstate 35 at the San Marcos exit. Follow the signs. Call 800-782-7653 ext. CAVE for more information.

Natural Bridge Caverns, discovered in 1960, was named for the 60-foot-long limestone bridge at the entrance. While there you will see many fascinating formations suspended from the ceiling or shooting up toward the ceiling from the floor of the caverns, which are registered as a U.S. Natural Landmark and a Texas Historical Site. The most notable formations are the spindly Watchtower, a stalactite "chandelier," and stalagmites that look like fried eggs. Next to the caverns you will find Natural Bridge Wildlife Ranch, a drive-through wildlife park with more than 500 animals from around the world. To find the Natural Bridge Caverns take the exit named for the caverns at mile 175 off Interstate 35 north of San Antonio. Continue on County Route 3009 northwest for almost eight miles. From Natural Bridge's private road it is a mile to the cave. Call 210-651-6101 for more information.

With walls of deep, rich color and brilliant crystalline formations, the Caverns of Sonora have been called some of the most beautiful caves in the country and possibly the world. The Caverns of Sonora is the state's fifth longest cave at 20,000 feet. The caverns are similar to Natural Bridges with many wonderful stalagmites tall enough to almost reach the ceiling, with stalactites hanging down. Don't miss the world famous Butterfly of Sonora. You will find lighted trails and stairway, a gift shop, snack bar, and above ground nature trails. To reach the Caverns of Sonora, take Caverns of Sonora Exit off Interstate 10 at the 392 mile marker. Follow signs seven miles to the cave. Call 915-387-3105 for more information.

Inner Space Cavern, a limestone cave in Georgetown, was discovered in the early 1960s when the state was building Interstate 35. With its sound and light presentation, Inner Space operators put on a show for you. To reach Inner Space Cavern, go north from Austin on Interstate 35, and take Exit 259 onto Business 89 toward Georgetown. If you turn left under the overpass and cross the railroad tracks you should be at the cave headquarters. For information, call 512-863-5545.

Cascade Caverns near Boerne have an underground waterfall. To find Cascade Caverns, take Interstate 10 northwest from San Antonio 16 miles and exit on Cascade Caverns Road. Follow the signs to the cave. For information, call 210-755-8080.

Cool Caverns

Close to Cascade Caverns is the Cave Without a Name, 18 miles northwest of San Antonio on Interstate 10. Take the first exit for U.S. Highway 87 and follow the road into Boerne. At the fourth traffic light, turn right onto 474. Follow this road out of town for six miles, turn right onto Kreutzberg Road, and follow the signs just over five miles to the cave. If you need more information, call 210-537-4212. The Cave Without a Name was purchased by former *Houston Chronicle* photographer and writer Blair Pittman. When asked if he will name the cave, Pittman says it draws too much attention without a name to give it one now. No name fits the cave, which is the deepest, darkest secret in Texas. A cave like Pittman's isn't found anywhere. But each cave is unique in its features, says Pittman, who has been in more than 500 caves around the world.

Longhorn Cavern has the most colorful history of the commercialized caves. It was a hideout for Comanches, housed a Civil War era black powder factory, and was a refuge for the bandit Sam Bass. It also was a church, restaurant, dance hall, and nightclub during Prohibition. Formed by an underground stream millions of years ago, mineral formations do not obscure the beautifully sculpted walls. A cave tour takes about an hour and a half. Longhorn Caverns is near Inks Lake State Park where you can see wildflowers bloom in the spring months. Driving north on U.S. Highway 281 from San Antonio will take you to Longhorn Cavern State Park. Take Park Road 4 just eight miles north of Marble Falls at the Colorado River and follow it for six miles to the park.

Kickapoo Cavern State Park has 15 known caves with two large enough to be worth exploration. The cave named Kickapoo Cavern is about a quarter-mile-long cave with

Summer

impressive formations. Green Cave, slightly shorter than Kickapoo, is a migratory stopover for large numbers of Brazilian freetail bats from mid-March to about the end of October. Bat flights can be spectacular to see, but only by reservation. Kickapoo Cavern tours by staff are all on a pre-arranged basis only. The cave is in an undeveloped state, so you need to be in fairly good shape to take the tour. There are no handrails, elevators, or lighted walkways, and you have to bring your own light for use in the cave. When making reservations, be sure to ask what appropriate gear and clothing are needed for the cave tours. Reservations for Green Cave bat flight observations can be made for early April through mid-October.

The area around Kickapoo is similar to the Hill Country but without water. You can see white-tailed deer, raccoon, ringtail, gray fox, rock squirrel, porcupine, and rabbits. Black-capped vireo, gray vireo, varied bunting, and Montezuma quail are some hard-to-find birds that frequent the area. Also, you might see the barking frog, mottled rock rattlesnake, and Texas alligator lizard. Nearby are Garner and South Llano River State Parks, Seminole Canyon State Historical Park, Devil's River State Natural Area, and Amistad National Recreation Area. Kickapoo Caverns State Park can be reached by taking U.S. Highway 90 west out of Uvalde, then taking Ranch Road 674 north of Brackettville for 22 miles. There are no highway signs indicating the park location. The gate is a quarter mile past the Edwards County line on the west side of the highway. This cave is not very close to the others, but if you map out your trip ahead of time, you can save it for last.

32

A Tale of Two Cities

KILEEN AND WACO

If Waco is mentioned in a conversation it is most likely to be about the David Koresh cult and the two-month-long standoff featured nightly on national news. In Waco, you won't see the Koresh compound, which burned to the ground, but you will find many other things to do and see. If the city of Kileen is mentioned, most Texans remember the 24 killed in a Luby's restaurant by a lone gunman. When you go to Kileen, you won't see the Luby's, which was demolished by its owners in an effort to erase the tragedy. You will find the largest army base in the nation and plenty to do.

To reach Waco and Kileen, travel south of Dallas and Fort Worth on Interstate 35. Waco is a little more than an hour away from Kileen, which is off Interstate 35 on U.S. Highway 190. These cities are centrally located in the state near the Hill Country, with Austin about an hour south of Kileen on Interstate 35.

Kileen

The tragic shooting in Kileen affected the entire state. Suzanna Gratia Hupp, who lost her parents that cold October day in 1991, was eating with them. The loss of her parents combined with the anger over not being able to act during the shooting spurred Suzanna's crusade to fight for an individual's right to carry a concealed weapon. In 1996, a law took effect allowing Texans to carry loaded handguns if they obtain a license and complete a safety course. Hupp went on to serve in the Texas legislature.

Kileen began in 1882 as the railroad's central shipping point for the surrounding agricultural area. The town only grew to 2,000 citizens before a temporary training facility called "Camp Hood" was established to train troops. In 1950, Congress designated the camp as Fort Hood, a permanent installation. The base, which is open to the public year-round, has museums, a drive-through display, and plenty of rough terrain for four-wheeling.

Fort Hood, which covers 340 square miles, has grown into the largest active duty armored post in the United States Armed Forces. Troops work on state-of-the-art range facilities where practically every piece of weaponry in the army's inventory can be fired. Fort Hood was named for confederate General John Bell Hood, who gained recognition during the Civil War as the commander of a Texas Brigade.

With 45,000 soldiers and 6,000 civilians employed by Fort Hood, it is the largest single location employer in the state. Inside the gates of Fort Hood is a self-sufficient city offering military personnel and their families many stores and recreational facilities.

As an open post, Fort Hood allows you to drive through more than 1,000 acres of military equipment on display. The four-mile drive down "Motor Pool Road" features an impressive array of every kind of military vehicle imaginable, including M1A1 Abrams Main Battle Tanks and Bradley Fighting Vehicles. At the base airfield, you can see the Apache Attack Helicopter.

On the base, you can see the First Cavalry Division Museum at Headquarter Avenue and 56th Street. A half hour tour takes you through 70 years of the First Cavalry. Beginning in 1921 at Fort Bliss, the division patrolled the Mexican border. In 1991, the Cavalry headed to the Gulf War. Other events covered are World War II, the Korean War with General Douglas MacArthur, and the Vietnam War when the Cavalry fought in the air.

You need an hour to see the Second Armored Division Museum in building 418 at Battalion Avenue and 27th Street. The unit, activated in 1940 to counter Hitler's invasion of Poland, was nicknamed "Hell on Wheels" after fighting victoriously in Africa. After enduring the Battle of the Bulge, the division was the first American one to enter Berlin in 1945.

Though it is an active military installation, the army will let you use certain areas of land for recreation. You need a pass before using the base, and the staff will instruct you on procedures you need to follow. One problem with planning trips is the army could call for maneuvers at any time with no advance notice. In spite of this, Fort Hood has become a popular four-wheeling spot because the terrain is rough. Hummers and tanks have torn up the land, so you will get into plenty of off-camber and end-over-end roll-over situations while four-wheeling.

Other highlights of Kileen include the annual Festival of Flags and the Vive Les Arts Theater.

For water sports, you can visit Belton Lake, which has a beach and places to fish. You will find a boat marina with rental boats, boat launching ramps, picnic area, horse and pony riding, playgrounds, party pavilions, an archery facility, and a snack bar. If hunting is your game, Fort Hood offers over 190,000 acres of bountiful hunting grounds open to anyone with a Texas hunting license and a Fort Hood permit. Deer, turkey, quail, dove, squirrel, and duck hunting are all permitted. Stillhouse Hollow Lake is a man-made lake with 77 miles of shoreline where you can enjoy fishing, boating, water skiing, or sailing.

A Tale of Two Cities

Day trips from Kileen could include the Texas Safari Wild-life Park in Clifton. This drive-through safari will give you a look at over 30 species of animals from all over the world. The Topsey Exotic Animal Ranch in Topsey has 70 species of animals to see from your car. A petting zoo and pony rides are part of the fun. Nearby, the village of Salado may be of interest. More than 20 historical markers dot the town, and shopping abounds at specialty stores that feature antiques and hand-made clothing. Bell County Museum in nearby Belton is dedicated to Bell County regional history.

For more information, call the Greater Kileen Chamber of Commerce at 800-869-TANK.

Summer

Waco

In Waco you may be able to see the charred remains of the Branch Davidians' compound, which was the focus of national news for nearly two months in 1993. The compound burned on April 19, killing 72. The siege began on February 28 when the BATF raided the compound. Four officers were killed and 16 were wounded. Before the final blaze, 14 adults and 21 children left the Branch Davidian Compound. On May 27, 1993, Koresh's body was buried in a secret ceremony at an unmarked grave. The story lived on in many people's memory.

Waco is located where the Brazos and Bosque Rivers flow together. The city was established in 1849 on the ancient settlement of the Huaco Indians, a friendly tribe that lived at this site before recorded history. Huaco Indians built 70 beehive huts where Waco Drive meets 8th Street today. The Huaco Indians and the Tehuacanas formed allied forces against the Comanches, but couldn't stop them. During one skirmish the Comanches rode off with horses and nearly 50 scalps.

In the year 1542, the Spanish explorer Luis de Moscosco de Alvarado first mapped the location of the "Waco Village." About 300 years later, an Indian trading post was established on a high bluff south of Waco Village, on the Brazos River. The Chisholm Trail crossed Waco at the Suspension Bridge.

A group of businessmen from Galveston invested in land to establish the city of Waco. They hired land agent Jacob de Cordova and Austrian surveyor George B. Erath to design the city. Famed Indian fighter and Texas Ranger Shapley P. Ross was among the first to buy land. Captain Ross served as Waco's first postmaster, carrying the letters under his hat to make deliveries. Ross also built the first hotel and constructed a crude ferry across the Brazos to increase traffic through the village. Large, productive plantations were established along the fertile Brazos River bottomlands.

Waco stuck with the South, sending more than 2,000 of their own to fight in the Civil War. Six from Waco became generals, including Sul Ross, one of the South's youngest generals. After the war, in 1870, Waco opened America's first and largest suspension bridge, 13 years before the Brooklyn Bridge. Cowboys on the Chisholm trail drove their cattle across this bridge, which took almost three million bricks and $135,000 to build. The 424-foot bridge is used only for foot traffic now. The railroad came to Waco and the city's population grew to 15,000 by 1880.

The 1911 Alico Building, which stands 22 stories tall or 246 feet, was the first skyscraper in the Southwest. For many years it remained the tallest building west of the Mississippi. The building was powered by an electric generator with oil wells to fuel the heating system, and an artesian well for water. Still the tallest building in Waco, it was cracked by the 1953 tornado, which devastated downtown Waco. Stores on the low levels have been reinforced by a facade.

A Tale of Two Cities

Waco has many historic homes worth visiting. The Earle-Napier-Kinnard House, 814 South Fourth Street, can be seen from Interstate 35. John Bayliss Earle, an early settler of Waco, began construction on the original part of the Greek Revival–style home in 1858. John Smith Napier, a wealthy planter from Alabama, purchased the home and completed it in 1869. The kitchen section is part of the original building. A John Talman and Sons of Philadelphia rosewood pianoforte is one of the original pieces in the home. A Victorian Teeling Playhouse is a place for children of all ages.

East Terrace at 100 Mill Street was constructed in classic Italianate Villa architecture. The home, built around 1872, belonged to industrialist John Wesley Mann. The Victorian era furnishings include a pier mirror and desk. Set on the banks of the Brazos, the house was named for the terraced grounds.

The Fort House at 503 South Fourth Street was built by Alabama planter William Aldridge Fort in the Greek Revival–style during the Reconstruction period after the Civil War. He brought five major families, their children, relatives, and slaves to Waco from his native Alabama. Empire and Victorian furniture and artifacts from some of Waco's fine old homes and families are on display. You may enjoy seeing the collection of antique glass and Pickard china.

The Greek Revival–style McCulloch House, which took from 1866 to 1872 to build, is located at 407 Columbus Avenue. The home became a gathering place for the entire village of Waco and the location of many dances. The only items original to the house are the McCulloch Family Bible and a silver tea and coffee service.

The Hoffman House is where you can contact the Historic Waco Foundation. The foundation of the Hoffman House was built in the late 1890s by W. H. Hoffmann. Originally located on Webster Street, the house was moved to 810 South Fourth Street. For home tour information, call the foundation at 254-753-5166.

Another historic home not under the foundation's care is the Earle-Harrison House and Pape Gardens, 1901 North Fifth Street. This white-pillard Greek Revival home was built in 1858 by Dr. Baylis Wood Earle and his wife, Eliza Ann Harrison Earle, who were from Mississippi. The last of the great antebellum mansions of old Waco, it stands as a reminder of cotton plantations along the Brazos River Valley. You will also enjoy the Pape Gardens, five acres with a gazebo and many native Texas flowers and shrubs.

Another place you can see wildflowers is Miss Nellie's Pretty Place in Cameron Park. The flowers were planted after former Congressman Bob Poage gave $100,000 to the City of Waco to create a wildflower park in memory of his mother, Nellie Conger Poage. With native Texas trees, shrubs, and flowers surrounding picnic areas, benches, and an observation deck, it is a good place to relax.

Two parks worth seeing in Waco include the 35-acre Fort Fisher Park on Interstate 35 between the Brazos River and University Parks Drive. The park is named after a Texas Ranger outpost located near the site in the 1830s. Besides campgrounds, you can see the historic First Street cemetery. Also, you might want to see Indian Springs Park, which is believed to have been the site of a Huaco Indian village. There is a walking trail located near the Suspension Bridge. The band shell by the water hosts summer concerts. Indian Springs Park is located by University Parks Drive and Franklin Avenue.

Three popular attractions worth visiting are The Texas Rangers Museum, the Texas Sport Hall of Fame, and the Dr. Pepper Museum. The Texas Rangers were charged with dispensing justice and protecting the law-abiding citizens. Rangers had a reputation for being tough and fast enough to handle Indian raids or horse thieves. The history of the Rangers, from 1823 to the present, is presented in slide shows, artifacts, and dioramas. You can see the guns of Billy the Kid, early Ranger Jack Hayes, and Frank Hamer, who

A Tale of Two Cities

ended Bonnie and Clyde's crime spree. Jim Bowie's knife, Indian artifacts, antiques, and a collection of other guns are displayed. Located in Fort Fisher Park, you reach it by taking Interstate 35, Exit 335B. Call 254-750-8631 for more information.

Texas Sports Hall of Fame opened in 1993. Inside you can see the Texas Tennis Museum and Hall of Fame; the Texas High School Basketball, Baseball, and Football Halls of Fame; the Paul Tyson Football Memorial; and the Louis Ritcherson Football Memorial. Texas collegiate and professional sports memorabilia are displayed. Located at 1108 S. University Parks Drive, the complex is occasionally visited by famous athletes.

The Dr. Pepper Museum and Free Enterprise Institute opened in 1991 on the anniversary of the 1953 tornado that devastated downtown Waco and left a permanent scar on the building. Dr. Pepper was invented by Dr. Charles Alderton in 1885 in the Old Corner Drug Store on Waco's Austin Avenue. The museum is in the original 1906 home of Dr. Pepper, a 18,500-square-foot Richardsonian Romanesque structure listed in the National Register for Historic Places and located at 300 South Fifth Street .

Another institution central to Waco life is Baylor University, chartered in 1845 under the Republic of Texas. It is the largest Baptist university in the world. There you can see the Armstrong Browning Library, which is the world's largest collection of materials relating to Robert and Elizabeth Barrett Browning. You will find the library, located on Speight Avenue between 7th and 8th Streets, worth seeing when you catch a glimpse of the 56 stained glass windows interpreting the Brownings' poetry. The library has also become known as a research center and presently includes major Elizabeth Barrett Browning, John Ruskin, Charles Dickens, and Ralph Waldo Emerson book and manuscript collections, and significant research materials in most areas of 19th-century culture.

Strecker Museum on the Baylor campus is a natural history museum focusing on geology, botany, anatomy, and cultural history. It is the oldest continuously operating museum in Texas. Collections were begun in 1856 and include a Living Museum of reptiles, amphibians, and a stream habitat. Also in the Strecker Complex is the Governor Bill and Vera Daniel Historic Village. It is on the corner of Fourth Street and Speight Avenue. While on campus, don't forget to stop by the Bear Pit, housing the school's mascot, on South Fifth Street across from the Daniel Student Center.

Taking the Walking Tour of Waco is a good way to see the city's historical sites. The Chisholm Trail Blazers Volkssporting Club designed the walk and provides the guides, which can be picked up at the Waco Hilton, 113 South University Parks Drive. From Interstate 35, take Exit 335B, turn west on University Parks Drive, and go a half mile to the Hilton. The registration box is kept behind the hotel desk.

Highlights of the walk include the Suspension Bridge. The old bridge graces Indian Spring Park on the west bank and Martin Luther King, Jr. Park on the east bank. The cable lighting on the suspension bridge at night is a photographer's dream. You can see St. Francis on the Brazos Catholic Church, built in 1931, which is a reproduction of the Mission San Jose in San Antonio. You should see the Clifton house next to it, which is a Greek Revival–style mansion built in 1868. Also on the walk is the McCulloch House and McLennan County Courthouse. The courthouse was built in the Victorian style with Greek-style statues in 1902. You will see the Alico Building, the Dr. Pepper Museum, the First Baptist Church of Waco, the Fort House, and the Texas Ranger Hall of Fame and Museum.

A Tale of Two Cities

If you like bicycling, try Cameron Park's challenging trails. If biking sounds too strenuous and you want something a little more intimate, take the James S. Wood Mule Drawn carriage. Catch it in front of the Texas Ranger Museum, and ride it down to the Suspension Bridge and back. Along the way, James Wood tells the history of Waco, including Six-Shooter Junction, the Chisholm Trail, and the tornado with a few tall tales thrown in. Wood's tour is 45 minutes long.

The Ollie Mae Moen Discovery Center, 815 Columbus, is a children's museum that is a collaborative effort of Strecker Museum and the Waco Independent School District. Waco Symphony, the Art Center, Waco Civic Theatre, the Hippodrome Theater, and the Heart O'Texas Fair Complex give you a choice of entertainment and events to attend. Waco also is home to the Cameron Park Zoo and the Little League State Headquarters.

Taylor Museum of Waco History, 701 Jefferson, is located in the old Barron Springs Elementary School. A classroom with an adjoining principal's office has been retained from the building's days as an elementary school. A room is dedicated to the history of the Branch Davidians through the decades. Rooms with collections of clothing worn by George and Martha Washington, and an exhibit on the Constitution and Declaration of Independence are also featured.

For information about Waco attractions, restaurants, and events, call the Waco Convention and Visitors Bureau at 800-321-9226.

Summer

33

On Location Texas-Style

BRACKETVILLE–MARFA

WHY GO TO CALIFORNIA TO FIND HOLLYWOOD WHEN HOLLY-wood has been coming to Texas for decades? Texas history and terrain have provided the perfect story line or backdrop for some of Hollywood's greatest works. For a look into the past, just head for Marfa and take a look at the location of the great classic *Giant*, starring James Dean, Liz Taylor, and Rock Hudson. *Giant* was Dean's last film before his tragic death. The people of Marfa warmly remember the Holly-wood invasion.

Also, dig into the past and present with a stop in Brack-etville where you can see the replica of the Alamo in the Alamo Village Movie Location. It was the location of the film classic of the same name, starring the late, great John Wayne. The Movie Studios at Las Colinas in Irving are filled with movie memorabilia from more recent films such as *Robocop, JFK, Problem Child, Talk Radio,* and *Leap of Faith.*

If you traveled back in time to the summer of 1955 when the town of Marfa was invaded by 250 cinema stars, tech-nicians, cameramen, and other workers, you could have seen three of Hollywood's most famous film stars in action. Evi-dence of this event can be found in a pile of rubble, which used to be the false front of the film's mansion on the plains.

For fans of James Dean, Rock Hudson, and Liz Taylor, being in Marfa could be interesting.

In 1955, crews had not only constructed a false front for the mansion, they had erected miniature oil derricks and placed them out on the prairie. The Hotel Paisano and houses in town were home for the cast and crew during their brief stay. Today Hotel Paisano displays memorabilia and autographed photographs from *Giant* in the lobby. For the small ranching community of Marfa, the production of *Giant* was an opportunity to be in the movies as extras, as well as watch Hollywood filmmakers in action. The film that caused the stir in town that summer was an adaptation of Edna Ferber's novel, *Giant*, a story of a young wildcatter who strikes it rich when he finds Texas Tea, black gold, that is, oil. During the excitement of the production of a new film with popular stars, the town viewed past works in the Palace Theater, a local cinema still in downtown.

Director George Stevens had cast the young actor James Dean to portray wildcatter Jett Rink. The local teenage girls were delighted with the choice. But just a month after the film's completion, Dean died in a car wreck. The Evans family, owners of the ranch where the mansion was located, also mourned Dean's death. Clay Evans, 19 at the time of the film's production, spent time with Dean. The young actor learned a lot about West Texas life during his brief stay. The Clay Evans ranch is private land and is not open to visitors.

The movie's $5 million budget was of epic proportions. While the exterior scenes were filmed in Marfa, the interior scenes were completed in a Hollywood studio. Stevens spent a year editing the film before its release.

Another Southwest Texas spot worth seeing, the Alamo Village Movie Location in Bracketville was built on James Shahan's ranch. The set was created for John Wayne, who was planning on filming *The Alamo* in Mexico and Peru. After

Summer

two years of negotiations, terms were agreed upon with Wayne and Shahan getting the rights to build the set. Wayne's film was shot on 400 acres of Shahan's 22,000-acre ranch. While Wayne used $12 million of his own to finance the film, Texas businessmen kicked in some, along with $2.5 million from United Artists. During the negotiations, Shahan won the rights to make the set into full-size buildings instead of false fronts. This was how Alamo Village came into being.

Other films made in Bracketville include: *Bandolero*, 1968; *Centennial*, 1978; *Barbarosa*, 1982; *Alamo: Thirteen Days to Glory*, 1986; *Alamo . . . The Price of Freedom*, 1987; *Lonesome Dove*, 1989; *Gunsmoke: The Last Apache*, 1990; *Bad Girls*, 1994; *Texas*, 1994; and *Lone Star*, 1995.

Shahan turned part of his ranch into an authentic Western town and provides horse-drawn vehicles; livestock, including longhorn steers; and Western accessories for filmmakers. Commercials and televisions shows have also been filmed in the Alamo Village, including the *Roy Rogers Show* and a Brooks and Dunn video. There are more than 30 buildings, including a trading post, cantina, general store, John Wayne and Johnny Rodriguez museums, a blacksmith's shop, and film studio. Memorial Day through Labor Day there are live shows. From San Antonio, take U.S. Highway 90 west for 125 miles. Del Rio is 32 miles west of Bracketville, making it a great stop on the road to attractions near there or on the way to Marfa. Call 830-563-2580 for more information.

A great stop for film buffs in a different direction is The Movie Studios at Las Colinas, at the intersection of O'Connor Road and Royal Lane in Irving, between Dallas and Fort Worth. Tours of the studios are given every hour during the summer, where you have a chance to see how special effects are done during The Addams Family Values Special Effects Show. Times are subject to change, so phone ahead at 972-869-7741.

On Location Texas-Style

You can see the work done behind the scenes of some of today's high-tech films, such as *Independence Day, Superman,* or *The Addams Family Values.* Find out how Superman was able to fly through the air and travel through outer space in real Galactic Hollywood sets. Costumes and sets from *The Wizard of Oz, The Sound of Music, Forrest Gump, Batman, Robocop,* and *Star Wars* are at Las Colinas. While there, you should also see the National Museum of Communications' collection of vintage television, radio, and broadcast equipment.

Summer

34

Legends and Llano

LUBBOCK

THE ROOTS OF ROCK AND ROLL SPRUNG FROM THE DESOLATE, monotonous terrain of West Texas plains in Lubbock. Most budding rock bands today cut their teeth on Lubbock-born Roy Orbison's "Pretty Woman," and many emulate the energetic style of rock legend Buddy Holly. Lubbock stands out on the landscape for its size, not its beauty. An industrial, agricultural center on the Llano Estacado, or staked plain, Lubbock has more to offer than first meets the eye.

Buddy Holly fans may want to explore the places that shaped his life. Start with a trip downtown to see the statue of Buddy at the corner of 8th Street and Avenue Q. Buddy's figure is surrounded by plaques honoring Roy Orbison, Waylon Jennings, Tanya Tucker, and Joe Ely—others from Lubbock who helped shape the music world. While each of these musicians are equally great, rock and roll fanatics of the late '50s and '60s claim "the day the music died" was the day Buddy Holly and Ritchie Valens died together in an airplane crash. Buddy, who was 22 at the time, is buried near the entrance of Lubbock Cemetery at the east end of 31st Street.

Buddy, named Charles Hardin Holley at birth, September 7, 1936, died February 3, 1959, in Mason City, Iowa. Encouraged by his parents, Buddy began playing the piano at age 11, but took up the guitar later. Within a couple of years, Holly and his friend Bob Montgomery were playing a kind of music they called "Western Bop" and country. With a band called the "Crickets," Holly did the vocals and played guitar on the hit "That Will Be the Day." Other hits still played on oldies stations in Texas included "Peggy Sue," "Maybe Baby," and "Oh Boy!"

The Crickets were popular with teenagers and influential in music in America and Europe. The band's Western Bop sound led many to believe the members were black. The Crickets were booked at the Apollo Theater, which had been exclusive to black artists. Although at first the band was booed, the mostly black audiences eventually warmed up to them.

Holly was eventually signed by Decca Records in New York City. On one visit to the New York music publisher, Holly met his future wife, Maria Elena Santiago, a receptionist. Two weeks later, they were married. The couple made their home in Lubbock, but didn't make his hometown a permanent home. Holly broke ties with the Crickets and returned to New York City to form a new band. Not too long afterward, Holly boarded that fateful flight as he and others in the tour were tired from long bus rides between gigs.

Born the same year as Holly on April 23, Roy Orbison enjoyed a long, successful career playing rock. Orbison played in the center arena with the Beatles, was friends with Elvis Presley, and had his songs performed by Linda Rondstandt. Staying in the midst of the happening scene in music, Orbison's classic song "Dreams" was used in David Lynch's film *Blue Velvet*.

Another parallel between Holly and Orbison is in connection with the Clovis Studio in New Mexico. Both had works recorded there in the beginning of their careers. After Orbison recorded "Ooby Dooby" there, he sent it to Sun

Records on the advice of Johnny Cash. Orbison also played with a local band called the Wink Westerners.

In Lubbock's short life there has been some excitement. In 1951, the Lubbock Lights focused the nation's attention on the panhandle. Several college professors saw a formation of blue lights fly quickly overhead twice in one night. The sighting was also seen by a Lubbock woman. A man in Albuquerque, someone in Matador, Texas, and dozens of other people repeated the same description of the blue lights. Photographs of the blue lights were taken by a Texas Tech student. An Air Force investigation into the source of the object never determined its origin.

Another more down-to-earth attraction of Lubbock is Prairie Dog Town in Mackenzie State Park at the northeast edge of downtown. See prairie dogs in action at the park, which is a great place for children. The park is located off Avenue A. For more information, call the Lubbock Convention Center and Visitors Bureau at 800-692-4035.

For thousands of years buffalo and Indians ruled the high plains of the Llano Estacado. The people of the Clovis Culture, also known as Llano, hunted gigantic mammoths, which turned into today's elephants. They hunted large game animals like the reindeer, ground sloth, elk, brown bear, and ox nearly 15,000 years ago. Stop by the Lubbock Lake Landmark State Historical Park at the intersection of U.S. Highway 84 and Loop 289 to see evidence of ancient civilization in Lubbock. Excavations have revealed evidence of humans and animals from as much as 12,000 years ago.

Comanches and conquistadors ruled the plains, hunting bison, buffalo, and other game. Rumors of gold brought Spanish explorers to the Llano Estacado. The fabled seven cities of gold led the early Spanish explorer Francisco Vasquez de Coronado across it in 1541. He was looking for Quivira, the richest of the cities, when he crossed the area that he named Llano Estacado.

Legends and Llano

Estacado means "staked," which may have been used because Coronado's men had to put stakes in the ground to find their way through the featureless plains. Others suggest stakes were pounded into the ground to tie horses up. Some scholars believe that Coronado's journey to Quivira led him through the city limits of Lubbock and the Lubbock Lake site. Most believe that his return trip took him through Yellow House Canyon, through Lubbock. A number of artifacts from the time of Coronado's exploration have been found and are on display in the Texas Tech Museum.

The Spanish used the Comanches to instigate trouble for settlers. Comanches robbed, killed, and kidnapped settlers and their families. Buffalo hunters avoided the area where Comanches roamed and hunted. Lubbock sits on a main Comanche trade route referred to as Ransom Canyon by the Spanish. It has been changed to Yellow House Canyon.

Indian attacks were beginning to ruffle the hair of Americans. Rath City was a target for frequent battles. One famous battle, the first Battle of Adobe Walls, was more of a retreat. The Indians far outweighed the Union soldiers on patrol with Kit Carson in 1864. Carson used the original Adobe Walls trading post to rest his horses after a fight with about 150 warriors. But Carson didn't realize there were nearly 6,000 more Indians nearby. With only 300 soldiers, Carson had to run to escape.

The battles had their effect on buffalo hunters. Many left their trade in the plains of West Texas and headed for safer occupations. The lack of enthusiasm for Indian fighting manifested itself in many ways. One war party fired up on whiskey totaled 500. By morning, when all were sober, 46 men and a barrel of whiskey headed out of Rath City to do battle. They trailed the Indians into "Hidden Canyon," the elbow of the Yellow House Canyon where the Lubbock

Summer

Lake Site is located. When they opened fire on the Indians, it was returned with such vigor their courage dissipated in direct proportion to the exhaustion of the whiskey supply.

Eventually, they retreated to the wagons at Buffalo Springs as the Indians followed at a distance. Even with all this, the hunters sustained no fatalities and only three were wounded. They managed to get the wagons out of Buffalo Springs and headed back eastward as fast as they could. When daylight came, they started great prairie fires behind them as smoke screens. The fighters returned home 23 days after their departure. The Indian trouble came to an end on its own in 1879 when there were no more buffalo.

Mapmakers first venturing into the plains didn't help its reputation when they labeled the area a desert. For 38 years maps had the "Great American Desert" across the Texas plains. In spite of the area's reputation, settlers came in 1909 to work on ranches.

The Causey Brothers built a half dugout at Buffalo Spring and some unknown hunters built a small log cabin near downtown Lubbock. By 1880, there were numerous small ranching operations along the Yellow House Canyon.

When the Indians left, the wolves came. Ranchers around the Yellow House Canyon reported thousands of migrating wolves between 1877 and 1880. These wolf packs, sometimes 20 abreast, solid for several miles, were thought to be escaping the movement of the early settlers.

Before Lubbock was formed, Estacado had a college in 1890 that had up to 100 students. Baylor in Dallas was the next closest college. Although the community of Estacado is all but gone, it was active up through World War II with a glider training base.

A Quaker man named Paris Cox and his wife settled the area. A few others came, but could not survive winters in their tent homes. The Quakers held fast to the plains. In 1880, with his wife pregnant, Cox sent for his friend, Dr.

Legends and Llano

Hunt, who delivered a girl, Bertha Cox. George Singer came to the area and built a store at the northwest end of Yellow House Canyon.

Ranchers bought pieces and began business in the Lubbock area. By 1880 the federal census indicated that there were 25 people in Lubbock County, mostly sheep and cattle ranchers. Of those counted in the census that year, only Zack Williams stayed in the area long enough to be identified with the beginnings of the City of Lubbock. Soon after, the Settlers Act helped attract new residents. For a modern day look at ranching, visit the Ranching Heritage Center, 4th Street and Indiana Avenue.

For fun and a look at another historical aspect of Lubbock, go to the former Fort Worth to Denver Railroad Depot. A collection of restaurants and nightclubs feature pop, alternative, country, and rhythm and blues. A microbrewery and coffeehouse are also a good stop in the downtown area. Lubbock is at the crossroads of Interstate 27 and U.S. Highway 84.

Here are other stops to include:

Lubbock Fine Arts Center at 2600 Avenue P, with exhibits of visual arts from photography to sculpture

Omnimax and Science Spectrum, where hands-on science exhibits and a 58-foot-diameter screen for an all encompassing media experience await visitors; located at 2579 S. Loop 289, children will enjoy the experience

Vietnam Archives in the Texas Tech Library, a collection of materials from the war that is the largest in the country outside of government archives

35

Air Raising Adventure

HOUSTON AND ABOVE

Up in the air about what to do this weekend? Why not try an air raising experience? You can go hot-air ballooning on your own at a Texas event featuring this unique way of seeing the world. Johnson Space Center, known as NASA in the Houston area, hosts the Ballunar Liftoff Festival in August, and the western city of Alpine is the site of Paint the Skies, another balloon festival in September.

If you are looking for a unique, romantic, or family adventure, taking a ride in a hot-air balloon could be just the ticket. With a bird's-eye view of Texas, you could picnic or pop the cork on a bottle of champagne. The average hot-air balloon is as tall as a seven-story building and nearly 60 feet across at the widest point. The average balloon holds up to four adults while large balloons may carry up to 12. A Houston-based company boasts of impressive skyline views from their balloons. A cozy quarters can provide some time for closeness not generally found in other activities. You could also combine other air related adventures and sites with a hot-air balloon ride.

The hot-air balloon reached the skies in 1792 when the Montgolfier brothers sent a duck, a rooster, and a sheep in flight. Two Frenchmen followed with a five-mile flight over Paris using burning straw as fuel for the Montgolfier brothers' balloon. Today, balloons are made of nylon instead of cloth, with propane burners silently propelling them upward. The highest a balloon has ever been piloted is 65,000 feet. While these wonders dotting the sky may appear small as we stand on the ground, most hot-air balloons exceed 100,000 cubic feet in volume.

To appreciate the beauty of hot-air balloons, don't miss the mass hot-air balloon liftoffs during the Ballunar Festival in Clear Lake, a city next to Houston. The liftoffs have been known to stop traffic in the Clear Lake area, so if you are heading for the Ballunar Festival, go early and beat the traffic. Admission and parking are free. To get to Johnson Space Center, go south of Interstate 45, then east on NASA Road 1. Call 281-483-8693 for more information.

During the Ballunar Liftoff Festival the Space Center is open for tours. Inside Johnson Space Center you can see how astronauts are trained, including the underwater training facility. Mission Control, the one used today and the one used during the *Apollo* era, was part of the 1998 tour of about 20 different buildings, including some normally not open to the public. A tram shuffled visitors from one building to another. They were able to see the construction of the crew return vehicle called X-38, a T-38 jet, and the KC-135A plane, which NASA used to simulate weightlessness and camera crews used in the filming of *Apollo 13*.

To see what it felt like to be an astronaut, visitors used simulators to land a shuttle and dock with a space station, or tried out robotic arms and hands. Inside the Neutral Buoyancy Lab astronauts practice in simulated weightlessness. It was also the location of some scenes in the movie *Armageddon*. Some of the real stars of NASA, the astronauts, were at the festival to sign autographs. If you are a big NASA fan and want to keep up to date, you can call the news line at 281-483-5111.

Spectators watched hot-air balloon competitions, evening balloon glows, skydiving exhibitions, or browsed through the commercial exhibits, arts and crafts exhibits, and aviation equipment displays. Local restaurants cooked up something to eat and entertainment was provided by local performing arts groups. The event featured flight—from the simplicity of a hot-air balloon ascent to the high-tech world of space flight. Sponsors aimed to promote education in aviation, space exploration, mathematics, and the sciences. The festival is held annually with activities varying some from year to year. The exhibits featuring state-of-the-art technology used in space change as scientists improve space flight.

Another hot-air balloon festival held in early September is called Paint the Skies, Alpine Texas Balloon Rally. Located in West Texas, the event also features many launches. Each morning of the festival begins with a pilots' briefing, which is followed by the launch of the "Hare" Balloon and the "Hound" Balloons. A citywide sidewalk sale in downtown Alpine sponsored by the city's retail merchants, a pilots' brunch, an awards ceremony, and a "shoot-out" on the courthouse lawn are included in the event. Also, see the Pecos County Cowboys and Desperados, called the "The Hangman's Henchmen." A bonfire in the evening, dubbed the "Basket Burn at Kokernot Park," concludes a day full of activities. With its proximity to Big Bend State Park and Marfa, you can combine stops for a full weekend.

If you don't want to be a spectator but would like to try lifting off, there are companies ready to take you up. Flying in a balloon is like floating in a dream. Since the balloon moves with the wind, there is no sensation of movement, unless you look at the landscape. The air is unusually quiet, between "burns." The barking of dogs below seems to be up

Air Raising Adventure

in the sky around you and people on the ground can hear you speaking in a normal tone.

Airventure Ballooning in Houston is ready to take you on a romantic flight, teach you to fly your own balloon, or take the family on a trip above Houston. Call 713-774-2FLY and book a champagne brunch and balloon flight for a memorable experience. The pilot is a top-ranked FAA professional who can guide you through downtown Houston. Flights last up to one and half hours. Schedule a sunrise flight or afternoon excursion. Morning flights are preferred due to more stable weather conditions. Airventure flight area is mainly on the west side of Houston over the Addicks and Katy area.

While Houston looks good from above, it also has some interesting features on the ground level. After the Ballunar Liftoff Festival, after your own balloon liftoff, or after touring NASA Space Center where the sky is not the limit, don't miss some of the area's attractions.

Attractions near NASA include Old Seabrook, off Nasa Road 1 and Highway 146. There are also antique shops, gift shops, tearooms, and restaurants, and an open air market called "Back Bay Market," which takes place every second Saturday and Sunday monthly. If you are looking for a good place to eat with atmosphere try Kemah's restaurant row on Clear Lake. This waterfront area includes art galleries and shops. Turn on 6th Street off Highway 146. Historic League City is another cluster of shops, restaurants, and historic homes. Go east on Highway 518 from Interstate 45 south. League City is past the railroad tracks.

36

Take Me Out to the Ball Game

COMETS, ROCKETS, COWBOYS, SPURS, ASTROS, AND RANGERS

WHILE NATIONALLY SPORTS FANS HAVE EITHER LOVED OR hated Texas teams, in the state of Texas fans have little to be disappointed about with championship basketball and football teams to watch. Sports fans also will enjoy the future in Texas as Houston won the competition for a new football team in 1999. The addition of a football team to Houston will include a new football stadium. Along with a new football stadium, Astros baseball fans also will have a new stadium in 2000. Look for the possibility of a new basketball and hockey stadium in Houston's future.

Comet Craze

The latest craze in sports in Houston is the Comets, the 1997, 1998, and 1999 Champions of the Women's National Basketball Association. Houston has been dubbed "Clutch City" for the Rockets, who always come through in a clutch. When Houston looked for champions, the Rockets basketball team came through. Now, the Comets are here to join the city's established champions and have been playing before sellout crowds in the Compaq Center. Spectators have not been disappointed with the action. Both on and off the court, the Comets are top-notch.

One of the team's key players is Cynthia Cooper, dubbed the "Michael Jordan of women's basketball." She didn't start playing basketball until she was 16. Cooper was unanimously named the winner of the WNBA Most Valuable Award for the 1997 and 1998 seasons, and chosen for the 1997 and 1998 All-WNBA First Team. She played professionally in Italy where she made the 1996 Italian League All-Star Team. She also played for Spain and was the Most Valuable Player of the 1987 European All-Star Game. Cooper was a member of the 1988 gold medal and 1992 bronze medal U.S. Olympic teams.

Sheryl Swoopes, a guard from Lubbock, worked hard to make it. She's played one-on-one against Michael Jordan, has her own Nike basketball shoe named after her, and scored a NCAA championship game record 47 points to single-handedly lead Texas Tech to an 84–82 victory over Ohio State and to the 1993 NCAA National Championship. Swoopes, a favorite with the fans, was a member of the 1995–96 USA Basketball National Team, on the 1994 gold medal USA Women's Goodwill Games Team, and part of the 1994 bronze medal USA Women's World Championship Team. She is married and a mother. Swoopes took a break after having a baby, but came back for a strong season.

Other key players include Tina Thompson, Racquel Spurlock, Wanda Guyton, and Tammy Jackson. Thompson, who was one of the first women to play in the WNBA, was also the number one draft pick. Thompson, who plays forward, was named to the 1997 All WNBA First Team after ranking in the top 10 in blocked shots. In her youth, Thompson followed her brother to a local recreation center and decided to show the boys up when they said they didn't want her to play.

Comets Coach Van Chancellor was named Coach of the Year for 1997 and 1998. The WNBA Houston Comets play at the Compaq Center, 10 Greenway Plaza East, Houston; tickets are sold at Two Greenway Plaza, Suite 400, and by phone; call Houston TicketMaster at 713-629-3700.

The Rockets Rock Houston

Houston's other great basketball team, which played a short season in 1999, began as the San Diego Rockets in 1967. While the Rockets got off to a slow start after arriving in Houston in 1971, they have become a winning team and a Houston favorite. After five years in Houston, the team signed Moses Malone, who carried the Rockets before the arrival of Hakeem Olajawon and Ralph Sampson. Olajawon and Sampson were known as the Big Men of basketball. Olajawon led the Rockets to championship seasons in 1994 and 1995.

The Rockets have found over the years that some of the best assets were locally grown at the University of Houston: Olajawon, Elvin Hayes, and Clyde Drexler. Olajawon, who never played basketball before attending the University of Houston, became a team leader by the mid-1980s. In 1989, Olajawon made the All-NBA First Team. Coach "Rudy T" Tomjanovich became the all-time winningest coach in Rockets history. Charles Barkley was then added to the team, giving them three players named as some of the greatest players in NBA history.

In all, the Rockets set or tied 32 franchise records and amassed a franchise-best 27 road wins on the way to posting their 13th consecutive non-losing season. But the Utah Jazz denied the Rockets a chance at their third title at the end of the 1997–98 season in the Conference Finals.

The Rockets also play at the Compaq Center at 10 Greenway Plaza. For information on season and group ticket prices and availability, contact Houston Rockets, 2 Greenway Plaza, Suite 400, Houston. For individual game tickets call Houston TicketMaster at 713-629-3700.

The Dallas Cowboys

When it comes to football, America's Team can only be found in Texas. The Dallas Cowboys, a Texas tradition, may have gotten off to a slow start in the early 1960s, but have since made up for it. The Cowboys have been home for such great players as quarterback Roger Staubach, who entered the Hall of Fame in 1985.

The Cowboys had 20 consecutive winning seasons from 1966 through 1985. They were led by Coach Tom Landry for 29 seasons, an NFL record for coaching the same team also held by Coach Curly Lambeau. But Landry's legendary tenure came to an end a year later when Jerry Jones acquired the Cowboys. The Hall of Fame inductee, Coach Landry stepped down and Jimmy Johnson stepped in.

The Cowboys signed quarterback Troy Aikman to a six-year contract in 1989. During the summer of 1989, nearly 100,000 fans visited the Cowboys' first ever in-state training camp at St. Edward's University in Austin. The Cowboys had a good season with Emmitt Smith and Aikman, but missed the playoffs. For the Cowboys, the '90s would prove to be a good decade.

In 1991, the Cowboys returned to the playoffs. Running back Emmitt Smith and wide receiver Michael Irvin became the first two players from the same team to lead the NFL in rushing yardage and receiving yardage in the same season.

Both players were named to the NFC Pro Bowl squad along with tight end Jay Novacek and quarterback Troy Aikman.

In 1992, the Cowboys had their fourteenth division championship; sent six players to the Pro Bowl to establish a Dallas Cowboys' record for most offensive players selected; and won their sixth NFC title. The victory sent Dallas to Super Bowl XXVII in Pasadena, where they won their third world championship.

In 1993, the Cowboys set an NFC record as 11 Dallas players were selected to the Pro Bowl. The team took their fifteenth division championship. Smith earned his third rushing title. The Cowboys captured their seventh NFC title and fourth World Championship. Dallas became one of just three NFL teams to win four Super Bowls by defeating Buffalo 30–13 in Super Bowl XXVIII. The game, played at the Georgia Dome in Atlanta, was the Cowboys' seventh Super Bowl appearance, one-fourth of all the Super Bowl games played.

In 1994, Barry Switzer replaced Jimmy Johnson as the head coach, becoming the Cowboys' third coach. The Cowboys fell short of their third straight Super Bowl. While fans were greatly disappointed, they didn't have to wait long for a comeback. In 1995, taking their seventeenth division championship, their fourth straight NFC Eastern Division title, and eighth NFC title, the Cowboys became the first team in NFL history to win three Super Bowls in a four-year period by defeating the Pittsburgh Steelers 27–17 in Super Bowl XXX. With a fifth Super Bowl title, the Cowboys join the San Francisco 49ers as the only NFL franchises to win five Super Bowls.

The Dallas Cowboys won't disappoint you if you want to see a good game. They play at Texas Stadium in Irving, located off Loop 12 at State Highway 183. Call 972-579-5000 for tickets.

Take Me Out to the Ball Game

The Spurs

San Antonio Spurs, originally called the Dallas Chaparrals, survived the turmoil of the ABA era and the team was rewarded with admittance to the NBA when the league merged with the NBA. In the late 1970s and early 1980s the team featured George "the Iceman" Gervin and won the Midwest Division five out of six years.

In the late 1980s the addition of David Robinson turned the club back into a contender. Despite a great deal of regular season success, the team never prospered in the playoffs until 1999. A postseason participant 22 times in 26 years, the team had survived the first round only 5 times and had never advanced beyond the conference semifinals until winning the NBA championship in 1999. The San Antonio Spurs play at the Alamodome, 100 Montana, San Antonio, 210-554-7700.

Home of the Astros and Rangers

If you are looking for baseball games in Houston, then the Astros are just the ticket. You can purchase tickets in person at the Astrodome Box Office; TicketMaster Ticket Counters found in Foley's, Randalls, and Fiesta stores; or Tele-Ticket Outlets throughout Texas and Louisiana and on the Internet. The Astros Ticket Shuttle Van will also comb the Houston area again this year for the ultimate in ticket-buying convenience, offering fans an opportunity to buy tickets without an additional service charge. The new Ball Park at Union Station should increase the comfort and fun of watching the Astros when it is completed in 2000. The

Astrodome was the world's first covered baseball field when it was built, and is a Houston landmark.

The Texas Rangers

The Ballpark, 817-273-5100, 1000 Ballpark Way in Arlington is the new home of the Texas Rangers. The Ballpark has a wide variety of accommodations for fans, including wait service on the Concourse Level for those who want to eat during games and Friday's Front Row Sports Grill. The Home Run Porch has a great view of the field. Novelties and apparel are sold at the Texas Rangers Souvenir Shop; paintings and autographed memorabilia are available at Sports Legacy—The Gallery of Sports Art. Tours of the Ballpark are conducted year-round. Don't forget to see Legends of the Game Baseball Museum while at the Ballpark. This 17,000-square-foot baseball museum features baseball uniforms, balls, equipment, baseball cards, and photographs depicting the history of the sport. Exhibits include items from the Texas League and Negro League, and items on loan from the Baseball Hall of Fame in Cooperstown, New York.

Take Me Out to the Ball Game

37

Downtown Derby

HOUSTON

FOR THE THRILL OF VICTORY AND THE AGONY OF DEFEAT without leaving your chair, try a day at the racetracks. You can watch greyhounds, horses, or cars run in Texas just about any time of the year. Sometimes the race is right through the streets of downtown, as Houstonians found in October 1998 during their first Grand Prix.

Some of the world's top race-car drivers took to the streets of Houston for a wet show on a rainy day in 1998. The race was exciting for fans, who watched drivers slipping and sliding their way through the turns downtown in their first Houston Grand Prix. Michael Andretti, Al Unser Jr., Bobby Rahal, and other famous drivers braved the slick pavement to give Houstonians and visitors what they came for on a Sunday afternoon. These drivers hit speeds as high as 180 miles per hour through downtown streets while competing in the Championship Auto Racing Teams circuit. Motor sports fans in Houston put their ear plugs in or used fingers as they watched and heard cars worth more than a million dollars whiz by or crash into side walls. That ear-crunching whine you could hear was the car's turbochargers or the sound of engines revving up and down as drivers change gears. Before the Sunday race, fans watched a Trans Am race, a Toyota Formula Atlantic race, and a Houston

Police Officers Bicycle Race. You could see drivers practice speeding through Houston streets in qualifying rounds and go to a "drivers' fair" where the Grand Prix stars signed autographs. Drivers came from five continents. In a Grand Prix weekend you can see who will be first in the race lineup if you watch the qualifying rounds.

The Championship Auto Racing Team directors chose Houston as the spot for a Grand Prix because residents proved to be the biggest race fanatics in television viewer surveys. But the deal seemed even sweeter for the city as officials looked to fill the gap left in local sports with the Oilers' departure. The event was broadcast in Europe, South America, and Japan, placing the city in the international spotlight. But preparing for professional racing on the streets of Houston was no small feat. Weeks of work went into smoothing and perfecting some rough streets. The city and industry teamed up to fund the work, which modified the city's downtown paving plan. Unlike oval track racing, at the Grand Prix there was no prime seat. You couldn't see the entire track from one spot, but you could see hidden action on nearby screens. For comfortable seating and an excellent view, race fans with connections watched from office building windows above the course.

Inside the George R. Brown Convention Center you could see how crews handle cars during pit stops, and watch the mechanics as their pneumatic wrenches whir. Speed counts. So hurry up and don't miss a weekend full of racing events. For more information or to purchase tickets, call 713-739-RACE.

Another alternative for race-car fans is heading toward the Dallas/Fort Worth Metroplex to the Texas Motor Speedway, which contains enough concrete to build a sidewalk from Fort Worth to San Antonio. The $110 million Speedway is the second largest sports facility in the nation. It can accommodate both stock and Indy car racing. If you bring a crowd, reserve a suite to seat 60 with wet bars and buffet dining. Half of the Speedway's suites are leased by famous fans like Ross Perot Jr., Dale Earnhardt, and Dallas Cowboys quarterback Troy Aikman. The 10-story Lone Star Tower's living-room windows overlook the track's second turn. A second tower above the first turn will be built to house speedway offices. Racing teams in 18-wheelers, as well as racing fans in motor homes and campers, can go under the racetrack and enter the infield through tunnels at each end of the racing oval. They can park and sleep in the middle of the action. From the Dallas/Fort Worth Airport, take State Highway 114 west to State Highway 170, then head west to Interstate 35W, and north to the Speedway. For more information about race events scheduled and lodging, call Fort Worth Convention and Visitors Bureau at 800-433-5747, or to purchase tickets or to reserve infield camping spots, call Texas Motor Speedway at 817-215-8500.

If you want excitement without the roaring sound of high-speed races, try the dog races. At Gulf Greyhound Park the action runs all year long, and millions of dollars are paid to winners every week. Watching the greyhounds' graceful strides round the track in pursuit of the rabbit thrills spectators. The pace quickly jumps from race to race with no lulls in the action. There's time to look at the lean contenders before each race. Dogs sit just a few yards away so you can get a close look before handlers lead them onto the track for introductions. Seasoned gamblers look for particular personalities before betting, or consult free programs with a breakdown of dog weights, ages, and past performances. Checking the times, figuring the odds, and placing a few dollars on your best guess fuels the thrill of the race. Once bitten, veterans find their own method for picking the champ. While taking a gamble on a surefire winner or a wild card can be exhilarating, watching the greyhounds race is fun for those who don't gamble, too. Children can get a close-up view of the track in outdoor seating on the sidelines. The Horizon Clubhouse, reportedly the largest restaurant in Texas, has a table waiting for you equipped with a color television monitor. Teller windows for wagering and three gift shops are in the Clubhouse. The Player's Lounge seats 500 people with private or semiprivate rooms and a mutuel line.

Greyhounds almost identical to those sprinting around Gulf Greyhound Park existed more than 3,500 years ago. Revered in ancient Middle Eastern, Egyptian, Roman, Persian, and Greek cultures, the dogs held positions of honor and esteem in households. The "Sport of Queens," otherwise known as dog racing, originated nearly a thousand years ago in England. At that time, the Royal decree was that only citizens of noble blood could raise and race the elegant, lightning-quick dogs. Today, you don't have to be nobility to raise a racer or place a bet. At Gulf Greyhound Park, races are under a mile long with the traditional Win, Place, and Show wagers. A guide available at the track explains how to bet Quiniela, Exacta, Trifecta, Superfecta, Daily Double, Pick Three, Twin-Tri, and Tri-Super wagers. The low risk $2.00 bet is fun for beginners.

The $55 million Gulf Greyhound Park is the world's largest greyhound racing operation. Since opening day in 1992, more than five million fans have passed through the gates. About 14,000 can fit in the park to take advantage of the more than 300 teller windows, 70 self-service machines, and 850 closed-circuit television sets broadcasting action on the Gulf Greyhound track. The park is located one block west of Interstate 45 South at Exit 15, just 30 miles south of Houston and 15 miles north of Galveston in La Marque. Call 800-ASK-2WIN for information.

Have you ever seen nearly two tons of pure horsepower thundering down a track? At Sam Houston Race Park you can discover the meaning of horsepower. More than four years ago, the $90 million Sam Houston Race Park opened its doors with hundreds of betting machines, and more than 1,000 television monitors focused on the seven-eighths-mile oval track. The track averaged close to $1 million in bets during the first 14 days of quarter horse racing in 1998. Country and western entertainers Glen Campbell and Rhett Akins performed at Sam Houston. Concerts are scheduled throughout racing seasons. The track made its Hollywood debut; a portion of the movie *Makeover* with Crystal Bernard was shot at Sam Houston Race Park.

Jockeys begin their day bright and early in the stable area. Each horse in the evening's races is exercised. Jockeys try to get used to a horse's running style and temperament in a short period of time. After a race you can meet jockeys as they walk through the building on their way back to the Saddling Paddock. There are more than a thousand horse stalls with veterinarians on staff to care for the horses. Texas is the number one state for quarter horse breeding and fourth for thoroughbred breeding. Horses at Sam Houston are walked or ridden daily. Horses have their hooves trimmed and new horseshoes put on every four weeks by a blacksmith. It takes about a half hour to do all four shoes.

Located on Beltway 8 in Houston between U.S. Highway 290 and Interstate 45, the Race Park covers 320 acres of land. For information, call the Greater Houston Convention and Visitors Bureau at 713-227-3100.

38

City by the Sea

CORPUS CHRISTI

THE COMBINATION OF STRONG WINDS AND WAVES MAKES Corpus Christi the ideal port of call for windsurfers and sailing enthusiasts. The city annually hosts the U.S. Open Windsurfing Regatta at Oleander Point, the southern end of Cole Park. Sailboat regattas are also held each Wednesday evening on Corpus Christi Bay, which can be viewed from the marina. For beginners and experienced windsurfers, rentals and lessons are available.

Whether you sail into Corpus Christi for the weekend or pull a boat on a trailer to launch from the Bayfront, boaters will find ample space and great facilities. The Corpus Christi Marina has more than 500 wet slips available, four new floating piers, fuel dock and pump out station, trailer and board boat storage, a boat repair facility with travel lift, free launching ramps, and bait stand. Slip rentals for visiting boats are available at daily, weekly, and monthly rates. For additional information call 512-882-7333.

Concrete T-heads and L-heads form marina protection for boats in slips. Sightseeing boat cruises and bay fishing trips take off from this area. Rentals of paddleboats, jet skis, aqua trikes, and small sailboats are available. Watch shrimpers come in with their daily catch. Take a moonlight cruise, or take sightseeing boat with a narrated tour of Corpus Christi

Bay, the Port of Corpus Christi, and along North Corpus Christi shore where you will see the USS *Lexington* and the Texas State Aquarium. Charters of all kinds are available in the marina area. You will find signs posted indicating what is offered by different companies and individuals.

Located on the Gulf of Mexico, Corpus Christi is best described as the sparkling city by the sea. Two distinct features of the city are the harbor bridge and the seawall. The harbor bridge rises above the Port of Corpus Christi and is the only way for cars to travel between downtown and North Corpus Christi. The seawall, designed by Mt. Rushmore sculptor Gutzon Borghum, is a two-mile walkway along the Corpus Christi bayfront with steps leading down to the water. A popular activity along the seawall and convenient way to see attractions is to roller-blade.

On skates or on foot, be sure to see Miradores del Mar, eight gazebo-style bayfront overlooks along Shoreline Boulevard designed for resting or viewing Corpus Christi Bay. Inside each Miradores is a plaque depicting a different phase of Corpus Christi's history. The design and structure of the Miradores are based on similar white-on-white waterfront structures in Tangier, Manzanillo, and the Costa del Sol of Spain.

Port of Corpus Christi, the sixth largest port in the nation, is a place to view the shipping industry and massive cargo vessels from around the world. You can get a close and personal view of a huge ship as it docks. The James C. Storm Pavilion, formerly known as Cargo Deck One, is located on the south side of the channel and is home to a bronze statue of Christopher Columbus by Roberto Garcia.

Two other interesting ways to get around Corpus Christi are provided by the Regional Transportation Authority. The Trolley Ride covers the scenic route on the bayfront and downtown area or over the Harbor Bridge to Corpus Christi Beach and other attractions on the shore of North Corpus

Christi. The Water Taxi is a passenger transport ferry that can take you from the barge dock on Shoreline Boulevard across the ship channel to Corpus Christi Beach. Call the RTA for seasonal schedules at 512-289-2600.

Replicas of Christopher Columbus's famous ships, the *Nina*, *Pinta* and *Santa Maria*, from his 1492 trip to America, are docked in the bayfront area. The deckhands aboard the vessels are knowledgeable about how life was aboard these tiny ships for passengers making the historic voyage. These reproductions provide a look at the legend. Explore a working shipyard and watch the master shipwright and his journeymen as they restore the *Pinta* and *Santa Maria*. See Columbus's quarters, go below the decks on the *Santa Maria*, watch sailors at work, or try tying knots and splicing rope yourself.

Afterward, go by the Corpus Christi Museum of Science and History for more about the fleet, plus exhibits of treasures from a sunken galleon. Young and old can see, touch, and explore interactive exhibits. Be sure to check out the shell collection, one of the largest in the state. Xeriscape Learning Center and Design Garden is an outdoor educational area with winding pathways, native plants, and tropical gazebos designed to teach water and energy conservation in landscaping. It is located near the museum.

The Art Center of Corpus Christi at 100 N. Shoreline Boulevard was built in 1942 for the USO Club. The Art Center showcases both amateur and professional artists of the area and beyond. The Center houses four individual studios where you can to see artists at work. Demonstrations and workshops by artists are regularly scheduled. Call 512-884-6406 for more information.

Art Museum of South Texas, 1902 N. Shoreline Boulevard, offers a continuous program of films, lectures, art classes, and changing exhibits, in addition to a permanent collection. The building was designed by architect Philip

Johnson. Don't miss Kidcade, a children's activity area including an architecture computer software program for children.

Other city sights you might want to see include the Water Street Market with restaurants and shops. For beach-goers, the nearby beaches at the Holiday Inn are clean and convenient. Also McGee Beach, a public beach at the south end of the seawall, is recommended.

On Corpus Christi's north shores, the Texas State Aquarium and the battleship *Lexington* can be viewed on a combination ticket. Many visitors come to see the Texas State Aquarium's displays of the sea environment in the Gulf of Mexico, the Flower Gardens Coral Reef, and an artificial reef similar to those growing around the Gulf's many offshore oil rigs. The aquarium's exhibits include a 350,000-gallon seawater display, an artificial reef, and 250 sea creatures. Pet a shark, watch divers feed manta eel, and see otters play. Texas river otters, the endangered Kemp's ridley sea turtle, and hands-on exhibits can be found outdoors. The aquarium's living displays are designed to give the sensation of gradually immersing deeper and deeper into Gulf waters. New exhibits include "The Wonderful World of Sherman's Lagoon" featuring the quirky stars of Jim Toomey's popular cartoon strip. These characters guide you through the exhibit and explain lagoons, barrier reefs, and the animals that inhabit them. Call 512-881-1200 or 800-477-GULF for more information.

Within walking distance of the aquarium is the USS *Lexington*, a retired aircraft carrier permanently moored by North Corpus Christi shore. The *Lexington,* also known as the "Blue Ghost," is an acclaimed naval aircraft carrier that was decommissioned on November 26, 1991. Take a self-guided tour with a choice of five tour routes. The educational exhibits, restored aircraft, and a collection of historical memorabilia give you a better understanding of life and work on the carrier. Squeeze through the ship's narrow hallways and climb steep stairs just as the crew did during the years of service. Tours include the Hangar Deck, Flight Deck and Bridge, the Admiral's Quarters, the Engine Room, and Sick Bay. Be sure to stop by the "Above and Beyond" Kamikaze Exhibit and the high-tech Flight Simulator. Call 512-888-4873 or 1-800-LADY LEX for more information.

Other Sites in Corpus Christi

- Corpus Christi Beach, which has picnic tables, restrooms, and playground equipment, is located near the aquarium and Lexington. It's a beautiful stretch of beach with a great view of Corpus Christi Bay.

- At the Corpus Christi Botanical Gardens, 8510 South Staples, you will find almost 300 acres with 1,000 native plants in displays, greenhouses, wetlands, and a mile-long "Mesquite Trail" nature walk. It is a great for bird-watching and picnicking.

- Corpus Christi Greyhound Racetrack is located at 5302 Leopard Street, 512-289-9333. You can enjoy races there and watch simulcasts from Galveston and Miami. A club-house area has a restaurant featuring an excellent view of the track.

- For local theater, Harbor Playhouse, 512-888-7469, is the oldest continually performing community playhouse in Texas. The Harbor Playhouse has been in operation since 1925 and presents 15 plays annually.

- Heritage Park, 512-883-0639, is a collection of restored turn-of-the-century homes. Heritage Park sheds light on the lives of Corpus Christi's early settlers. All homes have

City by the Sea

been restored by nonprofit organizations, except the Galvan House, which is home to the City of Corpus Christi's Multicultural Center.

- The International Kite Museum, 3200 Surfside, is inside the Best Western Sandy Shores Hotel. The museum traces the history of kites as they have been used in the Orient, Europe, and the United States in science and warfare. A kite shop gives you a chance to try your hand at a popular Corpus Christi pastime.

- The Asian Cultures Museum and Educational Center is located at 1809 N. Chaparral, 512-882-2641. You can meet ancient Japanese warriors, gaze at the artistry of the Chinese, or admire the beauty of India. You will see permanent displays which include a 200-year-old, five-foot Amida Buddha. Also displayed are pieces of ancient bronzeware, lacquerware, porcelains, and fine Hakata figures, with more than 3,000 Japanese Hakata "dolls." Paintings, examples of kimonos, utensils, games, and toys from China, Japan, India, the Philippines, Taiwan, and other Asian countries are included in the museum. The museum is located in a new Asian-designed building with a traditional Zen-type garden.

- Artesian Park and Sulphur Well are located at Chaparral at Twigg Street. In 1845, General Zachary Taylor brought 4,000 men of the U.S. 3rd Infantry to Corpus Christi and remained in the city for eight months. Among his troops were three future presidents: Taylor, Franklin Pierce, and Ulysses S. Grant. A landmark of Taylor's stay was a sulphur-rich artesian well he drilled by the camp. You will see a Texas Historical Marker on the spot.

- Old Bayview Cemetery on Ramirez at Waco Street is the oldest Federal Military cemetery in Texas. It was laid out by U.S. Army engineers while General Zachary was encamped in Corpus Christi in 1815. Seven of Taylor's soldiers are buried there, as are many pioneer settlers and veterans of the War for Independence, the Mexican War, Indian campaigns, and the Civil War.

- Centennial House, 411 Upper N. Broadway, is the oldest existing structure in Corpus Christi. The Centennial House was finished in 1850. It served as a Confederate hospital, a hospital and officers' mess for the Federal army, and a citizen's refuge during desperado and Indian raids of the 1870s.

- Hans A. Suter Wildlife Park is at the intersection of Ennis Joslin Road and Nile Drive. As part of St. Andrews Park, it is one of the best bird-watching locations in Texas. This 72-acre park is a haven for birds and nature lovers alike. Stroll along the 800-foot-long boardwalk spanning the marshy flats of Oso Bay and watch the birds from the viewing tower. Hiking trails offer glimpses of ducks, geese, and other shore birds. For more information, contact the Corpus Christi Parks and Recreation Department at 512-880-3460. Another bird-watching spot is the Nueces River Park, which can be reached when you take Exit 16 off Interstate 37 north. Facilities include a soccer field, camping sites, picnic area, covered shelter, boat ramp, fishing pier, and birding area.

City by the Sea

39

Butterfly Beginnings

GRAPEVINE

FOR AN UPLIFTING EXPERIENCE DON'T MISS THE FIRST FLIGHT of thousands of monarch butterflies in the annual Grapevine Butterfly Flutterby festival in mid-October. The event celebrates the migration of the monarch butterfly from Mexico to Canada. The spectacular orange and black winged airlift could just be the beginning of a weekend that will make your heart flutter. In a short life, the monarch will travel some distance. But you don't have to travel so far to reach Grapevine, which is just north of the Dallas/Fort Worth Airport.

Few moments in nature are as magical as watching a butterfly emerge from its chrysalis. During the months of October and November, millions migrate from their summer homes of eastern North America to their winter homes in the mountains of Michoacan, Mexico. A migratory animal, the monarch is shared by Canada, the United States, and Mexico. The Popolucas of Mexico believed butterflies represent the spirits of the dead. At least two deities of the Aztecs, who dominated the Central Valley of Mexico between 1300 and 1523, were personifications of butterflies. In the Aztec and other cultures, butterfly motifs appear not only in pure form but in many highly stylized renditions,

243

some so abstract that they were frequently mis-interpreted by archaeologists. The butterfly symbol has been found in ceramics, stone carvings, mural paintings, featherwork, wood carvings, and gold ornaments.

You can lift your spirits at La Buena Vida Vineyards, a family-owned winery in a charming limestone building in Grapevine's Historic District. It features native Texas gardens, fountains, an herb garden, and a winery museum. Also, there is Delany Winery and Vineyards, a 10-acre vineyard in southern Grapevine, planted in 1992 by Jerry Delany. It features the Barrel Room. Learn firsthand about the winemaker's craft while touring this working vineyard before sampling matured wines in the outdoor gardens. If you come a month earlier, in September, you can take part in the Grapefest, with the popular People's Choice Wine Tasting Classic, a gourmet black-tie gala with live entertainment, tasty food, arts, and crafts.

At any time of the year, after tasting the fruit of the Texas sun, you can satisfy almost any craving for Italian, Tex-Mex, down-home southern cooking, Chinese, or barbecue at one of a hundred different restaurants in Grapevine. Tour the offerings on foot while viewing some of more than 50 restored homes and buildings erected by Grapevine's earlier settlers. In 1843, General Sam Houston camped by Grape Vine Springs and laid the groundwork for a treaty of peace and friendship between the Texas Republic and Native American tribes. This opened the land to settlers, who started with cotton as their first crop. Today the wine industry leads.

While you are strolling down Main Street, you will discover a community of artists and gallery owners. Native American art is shown at the Pueblo Connection. Original watercolors, oils, pottery, woodworking, sculpture, jewelry, and photographs can be found at Beaux Art Galleries and the Main Street Market and Coffee House. Custom leather-work at Aubry Mauldon's and blacksmithing at Jim White's also can be found on Main Street. Air Nostalgia, on Main Street, deals exclusively with commercial aviation art, books, models, toys, and memorabilia. On South Barton Street you will find stained glass art at Grapevine Art Glass and at Barton Street Stained Glass of Grapevine. East Hudgins Street is home to the Grapevine Heritage Complex, a living history center, where you can watch artists at work blacksmithing, sculpting, woodcarving, quilting, basket weaving, and rug hooking.

Step back in time onto the Tarantula, a restored 1896 steam train with turn-of-the-century Victorian coaches and open-air patio cars. Tickets can be purchased daily at the 1901 Cotton Belt Depot in Grapevine, or the historic Stockyards Station in Fort Worth. The train follows a 21-mile track between Grapevine and the Fort Worth Stockyards where you can purchase authentic Western wear and go two-stepping at Billy Bob's Texas with live music nightly, indoor bull riding, two dance floors, and 40 bar stations. Also, the White Elephant Saloon, an authentic Old West saloon, has live music nightly.

Once in Fort Worth you can rest awhile as the Rodeo and Wild West Show at the Cowtown Coliseum provides entertainment. The Coliseum has hosted rodeos since 1908, and the action still takes place there on Friday and Saturday nights year-round. You can call Fort Worth Convention and Visitors Center at 817-624-4741 for more information.

The history of Fort Worth is centered around cowboys, cattle drives, railroads, packing houses, and Western music, clothes, art, and architecture. With the help of cowboys, railroaders, wildcatters, and entrepreneurs, Fort Worth has grown up from the wild frontier days of a century and a half ago. Downtown Fort Worth is a blend of historic structures and glass high-rises, but the Fort Worth Stockyards is much the same as it was in the days of the Old West. Don't miss the Livestock Exchange Building, built in 1904 as offices for livestock traders. It was once considered the "Wall Street of the West." The Stockyards Collection Museum, also located in the Exchange, chronicles the importance of the Stockyards to the development of Fort Worth. Stockyards Station has about 30 shops and restaurants in old hog and sheep pens. The young can enjoy the Western theme amusement park. Saddle up at the Cowtown Corrals, which provides horseback riding along the Trinity River and the old Chisholm Trail.

Fort Worth was once the biggest, busiest hog and sheep marketing center in the Southwest, where more than 83 million head of hog and sheep were sold. Stockyards Station today is busy entertaining tourists. Call the Stockyards Visitor Center at 817-625-9715 for information. While you are walking, catch the Texas Trail of Fame honoring men and women who have made a significant contribution to the Western way of life. Sidewalk markers are patterned after a frontier marshal's badge. Honorees include Will Rogers, Quanah Parker, Bill Pickett, Roy Rogers, and Dale Evans.

To top off the day of Old West adventure with a feel for more recent history, don't miss the 1934 Bed and Breakfast, an old red-brick home in Grapevine's Historical District that has been restored to its original condition. You can relax on an outdoor deck nestled among pecan and walnut trees. Located at 322 E. College Street in Grapevine, call 817-251-1934 for information and reservations. Some of the highlights of your stay at this bed-and-breakfast include a five-course gourmet breakfast served each morning in the dining room. Choose between the Main Street Room, the Rose Room, or the Sun Room Suite. Grapevine's historic Main Street is only one block away.

Summer

Close by is the ideal chance to cool down on a hot summer day, the NRH$_2$O. The park is equipped with a wave pool, water slides, and picnic grounds. Just go to 9001 Grapevine Highway, North Richland Hills, and splash down. Call 817-656-6500 for more information about the water park.

Butterfly Beginnings

Fall

40

Reviving the Wild West

GUADALUPE MOUNTAINS

IF YOU ARE IN SEARCH OF THE GREAT WEST AND THE COWBOY of bygone days, re-create the feeling by hitting the Texas trails on your own horse. The best location to sample what the Wild West would have been like in the 1800s is the Guadalupe Mountains National Park. The park is on the Pecos Trail that cowboys traveled north to market cattle, and bandits traveled to run from trouble after a few wild days in the Fort Worth red district. Many banditos passed through Guadalupe National Park area to hide gold in caves. Apaches reported seeing golden bars as thick as their arms, but feared going mad like the white man if they touched them. Instead, the Apaches found their riches in the land as you can still do today.

If you don't own a horse and can't find one to borrow for a weekend, most mountain trails would be just as enjoyable on a good mountain bike or on foot. Call for advice if you are uncertain about the safety of biking on trails. There are some trails better left to the horse traffic. All trails in Guadalupe are open for hikers if you don't have a good mountain bike or horse. The national park is primitive, not as developed as Texas state parks.

Guadalupe is horse friendly with 80 miles of hiking and horse trails in its acres of reserved land. The park also has the state's highest mountain, Guadalupe Peak, with an elevation of 8,749 feet. El Capitan with an elevation of 8,085 feet is the most photographed mountain in the Southwest. El Capitan's rock formation resembles a huge face keeping watch for enemies coming from the east during the rough days of the Old West. Today, it keeps a lookout for tourists heading up the long, flat highway leading to the park gates.

Other features of the park are wildlife, such as bats, elk, mountain lions, and on a rare occasion, a black bear. Bats spring from caves forming black clouds at sundown. Wildlife in Guadalupe today cannot compare to a hundred years ago, but some of the native species close to extinction have been saved and are increasing in numbers. Deer and elk roamed in abundance at one time, but hunting and trapping almost eradicated the population. Elk were reintroduced to the area around 1930.

Riders can begin at one of two places in the park for all trails, but Williams Ranch Road is the best. Start at the corrals on Frijole Ranch Road off State Highway 180. Trails can be rugged and difficult to ride. The Tejas Trail is especially dangerous and should not be taken if you or your horse can't handle it.

Call ahead to make reservations for your riding party and horses to camp because space is limited. Discuss plans with the rangers ahead of time. There is no food or lodging available in the park. You cannot build a wood or charcoal fire, so you need to bring a stove for cooking. The area is dry and windy, a bad combination when it comes to forest fires.

There is no water on the trail, so plan ahead and bring plenty for yourself. When planning your ride keep in mind you will need to return to your starting point to water your horse. Always turn around when your personal water supply is about half gone. El Capitan may be a good trail to start with, but if you need some experience riding on the terrain, take the road to Williams Ranch first. The 18-mile road, which is off State Highway 180, is gated and locked. Get a key from the ranger's station. Along that route you will see some remnants of the days when Williams Ranch was a town. The front porch of the Williams Ranch house faces Salt Lake with Bone Canyon behind it. The house was built by Robert Belcher for his new bride, who only lasted one day in her new home. The town was named for Dolph Williams, who took over the Belcher ranch in 1917 to raise goats.

The Butterfield Stage Line made its cross-country treks through the Guadalupe Peak Pass. It was the only way through the mountains for the stagecoach line that lasted one year and preceded the Pony Express. The 2,800-mile route took 25 days at a 5-mile-per-hour pace. About 50 employees were killed and many horses stolen during the year Butterfield made deliveries. Remnants of the stagecoach line are preserved in the park. Standing next to the stone ruins, you can take in an awesome view of the mountain range. Be sure to purchase enough film if you like to take pictures because the nearest shopping center of any size is more than 100 miles from the Guadalupe Mountains. On the way to the park keep in mind you are driving at today's speed limits to an old stagecoach stop that used to be reached only by horseback. The drive in a car seems long and the mountains are visible for many miles before you reach them. Harsh weather is minimized by heating and air conditioning. Ground temperature during the summer months in the desert in front of the mountains can easily reach triple digits.

What makes Guadalupe ideal is its still rugged 1800s exterior; both mountains and desert have remained unchanged. The mountains are part of an ancient reef known as Captain Reef. The Bowl is a forest that makes its way through the mountain highlands. Keep your eyes open as you drive to Guadalupe Mountains as you can easily spot deer on your way. You may get a chance to see elk, mule deer, cougar, and even black bear along this drive.

McKittrick Canyon is where desert, canyon woodlands, and highlands merge. A hike along this rugged terrain may prove too difficult for some. Stop by the visitors center as you reach the park and ask for a trail guide. There are hiking trails ranging from one hour to six hours, with varying difficulty. Rangers are happy to explain what you will encounter. You can hike to a mountaintop campsite for a night in the clouds, or take a round-trip hike for a day full of sights.

Other parks can be just as exciting for horse riders and other adventurers. Other horse friendly parks include Angelina National Forest, Big Bend National Park, Caddo National Grasslands, Caprock Canyons State Park, Cooper Breaks State Park, Davy Crockett National Forest, Dinosaur Valley State Park, Lake Mineral Wells State Park, Sabine National Forest, and Sam Houston National Forest.

In the national forest parks riders are restricted to undeveloped areas, which offer primitive campsites in most cases. You may encounter situations where there is inadequate or no water. It is a good idea to bring your own water no matter where you travel with horses. In the national grasslands no permit is required for small parties. If you have more than 25, you'll need a recreational permit. Call ahead to find out what conditions are like at the time you want to visit. Many areas of the state can encounter special problems during drought or heavy rainfall.

Fall

41

Canoe Bayou City

HOUSTON AREA

IF YOU ASK MOST PEOPLE WHO LIVE IN HOUSTON WHY THE city is called "Bayou City" they might tell you it is because of Buffalo Bayou. But Buffalo Bayou is only the tip of the iceberg when it comes to waterways running through Houston. The city has more than 2,000 miles of bayous and streams traversing it. The number of waterways also contributes to Houston's tendency to flood during a good rain. The bayous are also why so many highways are built high above the other streets.

The San Jacinto, San Jacinto-Brazos, or Trinity basins are the source of these waterways. Some of these bayous have been named after famous Houstonians who contributed to the city's growth. Some names sound good enough to eat. Most Houstonians can name Buffalo Bayou or Sims Bayou. The more knowledgeable residents can tell you of Brays Bayou or Green Bayou. And those who live beyond the city limits can tell you about Armand Bayou or Chocolate Bayou.

While Chocolate Bayou sounds delicious, you wouldn't want to taste it. But you might want to drop a canoe in and have a great adventure seeing the city from a different angle. You won't see just the usual city life of concrete, asphalt, brick, steel, and workers dressed in three-piece suits, scurrying between traffic lights. You will actually see wildlife, of the naturally occurring sort. On some parts of the water-ways in Houston, you may think you have traveled south to the Amazon since plants are thick and tropical, and the normal humidity of Houston accentuates the jungle experience. If you are lucky, you may see an alligator, bobcat, or deer along with many species of birds.

In Clear Lake, on the southeast side of Houston city limits, you will find a 2,500-acre wilderness. The Armand Bayou Nature Center is one of the most popular places for canoe lovers. At times, you will have to wait in line to drop in and pull out of the water. But the bayou stretches so far into the wilderness that you will lose others and find a place to paddle alone. This urban escape has choices in scenery. You can take a less populated route or one that goes through neighborhoods part of the way.

In Armand Bayou salt water and fresh water meet to form a brackish estuary. Fish found in Armand Bayou include gulf menhaden, stripped mullet, red drum, black drum, speckled trout, golden croaker, and alligator gar, along with blue crabs and brown shrimp. A variety of birds come to fish the waters, such as the yellow crowned or black crowned night heron, osprey, and egrets. Egrets fishing for a snack may be wading in shallow waters as you pass. Or you may see the white birds with outstretched wings glide over water in search of mullets.

You can put in at the nearby Bay Area Park on NASA Road 1, or at the park on Bay Area Boulevard. Only human powered motors, or paddlers, are allowed on the bayou. Public access and the use of motors are restricted to ensure the purpose of the nature center is carried out. The abundance of plant life and wildlife is evidence the nature center works.

The nature center also preserves the environment. Only 1 percent of original prairie land in North America still exists. You can see what the prairie land along the Texas coast used to look like when you paddle through the park. New plants not native to prairies have moved in and taken over, killing the existing plants. Chinese tallow trees have taken over Texas prairies, and that invasion included the nature center at one time. Many of these trees have been cut down to restore the prairie. Armand Bayou Nature Center also preserves marshland, another vanishing natural resource.

The center has a number of events for families and education programs. The center is run and maintained by four full-time staff members, a handful of part-time employees, and more than 200 volunteers. For more information about the Armand Bayou Nature Center, call 281-474-2551.

When canoeing in the Houston area, the experience you have depends a lot on the amount of rainfall during the year. Canoeing isn't the best right after a heavy rain, especially if the rain increases the number of mosquitoes. A long drought can leave the water dirty and too low for canoeing. The best family place to canoe is Armand Bayou, but if you're looking for an urban adventure, Buffalo Bayou runs through the heart of the city.

You can paddle through downtown Houston on this waterway and park the canoe on a landing area by Brown Theater. If there are no theater events to stop for, then you might try taking the bayou to the Houston Ship Channel. But beware of other water traffic; a good-sized barge could take you under. The bayou enters the channel that goes all the way to Galveston Bay and the Gulf of Mexico.

The path starts in the posh neighborhood of River Oaks on the west side of the city. Of course, you would be looking at the backyards of some of the best houses in Houston. If the water level is up, you might find rapids Class 1 or better. A well-used spot to drop your canoe in the bayou is at San Felipe Road just west of its intersection with Voss Road.

Canoe Bayou City

You might want to take it out in the Memorial Park area. If you want to see the heart of the city, take the canoe down to Allen's Park Landing, which is the section by Brown Theater. You will see street people along this route. Those familiar with canoe routes in Houston advise pulling out before going on down through the ship channel.

If you brave the channel, or are foolish enough to venture in and make it out alive, then you will find Battleship State Park and the San Jacinto Monument Park past Interstate Loop 610. You can start in the Battleship State Park if you just want to explore the east side of Houston. Get an up close view of the battleship from the water by paddling around the base or check out the other bays in the area. Enjoy watching the ship channel traffic or birds in the park.

The uss *Texas* was one of the first generation of dreadnought class battleships. These warships ranked among the most powerful military weapons in the early 1900s. Newport News Shipbuilding and Drydock Company began work on the battleship *Texas* in 1911. At the time the uss *Texas* was commissioned in 1914, it was the most powerful battleship around. It is the only surviving U.S. naval vessel to have served in both World Wars. The ship was named after another ship commissioned in 1895, which served in the Spanish-American War.

While sitting in the park and taking in the view, you might also remember the Alamo. Before you will stand the tallest monument column in the *Guinness Book of World Records*—the San Jacinto Monument. The 570-foot tower dedicated to the heroes of the infamous battle at the Alamo was built 100 years ago. The monument stands on the same prairie where General Sam Houston stood when he used the now famous phrase "Remember the Alamo" before his men commenced to do battle and win the war.

Fall

The state of Texas is a big place, so if you prefer an out-of-city experience, then try Palmetto State Park near Gonzalez. The San Marcos River runs through the park. You can put your canoe in the river at Luling City Park and travel 14 miles to Palmetto, portaging around one dam along the way. If you would like a shorter trip, then put in at Palmetto and take out at Slayden bridge, 7.5 miles downriver.

Canoe Bayou City

42

Trade Days

CANTON

IF YOU ARE LOOKING FOR THE ULTIMATE FLEA MARKET EXPERI-ence, look no further than Canton Trade Days, in north Texas, about an hour east of Dallas. Due to the sweltering heat of summer, November would be a good time to hit the trade days. The cooler weather will be worth it. The time of year will also give you a chance to pick up Christmas gifts. Plan to spend many hours outside walking the miles of makeshift shops and searching tables for bargains and trea-sures. Collectibles and new stuff are there, as well as plenty of food. Be sure to visit the First Monday Pavilion 1, a newer section in the market.

In Pavilion 1 you can look for some regular shops like Hearts in the Country, which sells hand-crafted ceramics. The Family Affair sells a variety of wood items, including tables, shelves, bread boxes, and trunks. While the addition of the pavilion is celebrated among buyers as an opportunity to see more vendors, the trade days did lose a longtime ven-dor named Geneva Pittmon, who was called the Blue Lady for her amazing offerings of blue dinnerware and china. But Canton has collectibles and crafts at stores in town, too. The Blue Lady's wares can still be found in the Timeless Trea-sures shop.

You can find Victorian porcelain dolls, appliqued T-shirts, wood art, Czech imports, cedar pole beds, and antiques. Taste a bit of Texas in some picante sauce, hot pepper relish, jalapeno jelly, or sweet hot pickle chips. You can also find many practical items to purchase. Horse and dog supplies or tools for work can be found. And if you are in search of a new pet, you can probably find one waiting for a new home. Check Dog Alley. Besides dogs, you may find goats, chickens, horses, and mules.

If you are wondering how all this fits into one location, trade days are held on 100 city-owned acres with more than 5,000 registered vendors and many more unregistered just off the city property. While Canton's big event is called "First Monday Trade Days" it really occurs the weekend before the first Monday of the month. By Monday morning, most vendors and patrons are packing up their goodies and heading out.

In 1973, the trade days celebrated its centennial. The trading days began when ranchers gathered around the courthouse during the circuit judge's monthly visit. In order not to waste the time between court hearings, ranchers spent their time trading horses and other items. The town tired of the rowdiness involved when trading began and the mess left behind. Moves were made to outlaw the event, but those participating outnumbered those opposed. If you can't beat them, join them, the town decided. The town set aside about six acres. The acreage increased with the years. Electricity, showers, and restrooms were added. The event has grown so much it really pays off to use a map to find your way around.

The rent paid by vendors has benefited the locals by subsidizing their taxes. Local businesses have also benefited from the additional customers lured by improvement and expansion. These tired shoppers need somewhere to sleep, supplies to keep up the shopping pace, and a nice place to sit down for a meal.

Two days may be the minimum needed to make it through the entire area and see it all. The First Monday Trade Days has more than one area to shop. You can start with the original grounds called Olde Town Canton or you can shop the relatively newer sections. The newer area is divided up into different indoor and outdoor marketplaces. You can shop the Mountain, The Village Pavilions, or the Old Mill Marketplace Pavilions. The Village Pavilions have air conditioning, which might make shopping in July and August much more bearable. When you are juggling your hours during a Canton weekend, make sure to add in a little extra time for bargaining. Prices marked may say firm, but bargaining with the vendors is accepted and expected. The atmosphere is family oriented and profanity is prohibited. You won't find nude art, alcohol, gambling, or loud music. A friendly place to shop may be the best way to describe Canton.

Considering the number of people attending the monthly event, making reservations ahead of time to stay in Canton is a must. To end the day in a relaxing homestyle atmosphere, choose from some of the best bed-and-breakfasts Texas has to offer.

- Baili Teal Farm in Grand Saline can be reached by calling 800-875-4874. If you are not too tired, you can take advantage of recreation on the premises, such as hiking trails, a fishing pond, and a volleyball court. You can enjoy refreshments and evening desserts.

- Heavenly Acres Bed and Breakfast in Mabank can be reached at 800-283-0341 or 903-887-3016. It has kitchen facilities and wagon or hay rides. You can go fishing in

Trade Days

three private lakes, take the little ones to the petting zoo, or go for a ride on paddleboats. For those who enjoy mountain bike trails, bring your bike along if you are staying at Heavenly Acres. Call ahead for reservations and if you have children staying with you.

- Saline Creek Farm Bed and Breakfast in Grand Saline can be reached at 800-308-2242 or 903-829-2709. You will find recreation on the premises and a private fishing lake, but there are no children allowed here.

- Texas Star Bed and Breakfast near Canton can be reached at 903-896-4277. There are kitchen facilities, 10 acres, and farm animals.

Fall

- The Wind Sock Inn in Canton can be reached at 800-476-2038. Facilities for disabled, workout facilities, outdoor pool, and cottages with kitchens are some of the features you will appreciate here. Call ahead to book a cottage or room as the fall flea market days are reserved sometimes as much as a year in advance. Other times of the year, call two months in advance to make reservations.

- Willow Pond Bed and Breakfast, eight minutes from Canton, is a Victorian farmhouse with antique furnishings and a casual atmosphere. Call Bob and Pattye Parker at 800-830-5822.

More Texas Trade Days

There are other trade days around the state worth checking out, but small enough to tackle in less than a day.

Near Canton you can find Lake Tawakoni Trade Days every Saturday and Sunday. In the same location for 25 years, Tawakoni has covered stalls filled with a variety of items. Call 903-356-2520 for more information. Tawakoni also has a lake where you can fish and boat.

Larry's Old Time Trade Days at Larry's Antique Mall is located at Interstate 10 and Highway 1663, take Exit 829, in Winnie between Beaumont and Houston. Call 409-892-4000 for more information about the event, which is the weekend following the first Monday of the month from 9:00 A.M. to 6:00 P.M.

Old Time Trade Days on the Square is sponsored by Belleville Chamber of Commerce, 409-865-3407, on the first Saturday of every month, April through November from 9:00 A.M. to 4:00 P.M.

Fourth Saturday Trade Day is held in the Coldspring Courthouse Square and sponsored by the San Jacinto County Heritage Society. Call the Coldspring Chamber of Commerce at 409-653-2184 for more information about this event, which is the fourth Saturday of each month, March through November.

Old Gruene Market Days, Gruene, pronounced like the color green, is four miles north of New Braunfels. Texas Homegrown at 830-629-3176 can tell you more about the event held on the third Saturday and Sunday of each month, every month except January, from 10:00 A.M. to 6:00 P.M.

Medina Valley Market Trail Day, Hondo Chamber of Commerce, 830-426-3037, can be found on the second Saturday of every month, 9:00 A.M. to 4:00 P.M.

Nacogdoches Trade Days, 1304 Northwest Stallings Drive on Loop 224, is across from Foretravel; call 409-564-2150 for information. It takes place on the third Saturday week-

Trade Days

ends of every month. You will find more than 700 booths open, plus showers and restrooms.

First Monday Trade Days on Santa Fe Drive in Weatherford is held the first weekend of every month, 7:00 A.M. to sundown. You can call the city of Weatherford offices during regular business hours at 817-598-4000 for more information.

Traders Village, located in the heart of the Dallas/Fort Worth Metroplex, is in Grand Prairie. It's a Texas-size marketplace with a little bit of everything, and is open Saturday and Sunday, 8:00 A.M. to dusk. More than 1,600 dealers are present every weekend. More than two million people visit this market each year. There is an RV park and campground with over 212 sites. From Interstate 20 take State Highway 360 north, exit Mayfield Road. From Interstate 30 take State Highway 360, exit south for five miles to Mayfield Road Exit, 2602 Mayfield Road, Grand Prairie. For more information, call 972-647-2331.

Also in the Dallas area shop the Atrium Antique Mall and Restaurant with 450 dealer spaces. Open seven days a week, you can find the Atrium at 3404 Beltline Road in Farmers Branch. Call 972-243-2406 for more information.

For a large flea market near Austin and San Antonio, try the Austin Country Flea Mart at 9500 U.S. Highway 290, 512-928-2795, and Flea Mart San Antonio at 12280 State Highway 16 at Zarzamora, 210-624-2666. Each has more than 500 booths open every weekend.

Fall

43

Discover Days of the Dinosaur

GLEN ROSE

SOME EXPERTS WILL TELL YOU THAT DINOSAURS ARE STILL LIV-
ing today. They say dinosaurs have left living descendants
in the form of cockatoos and cassowaries. But for those
interested in the fantastic creatures featured in *Jurassic Park*,
find evidence of the extinct dinosaurs of this larger variety
in Dinosaur Valley State Park, San Angelo State Park, or
Austin's Zilker Park, the Blanco River Trackway.

Dinosaur Valley

Dinosaur Valley State Park is located a few miles west of
Glen Rose, Texas, where the Paluxy River, a tributary of the
Brazos River, flows across Cretaceous rocks. Dinosaur footprints were first discovered on rock layers in the bed of the
Paluxy River early this century. The Paluxy River contains
some of the best preserved tracks in Texas. The Glen Rose
Trackway, as it is known, is a series of fossilized dinosaur
footprints left about 107 million years ago at the edge of a
lagoon.

The small prints are the three-toed impressions of a theropod, a meat-eating 12-foot dinosaur that walked on its hind feet. The large prints are so well defined you can see the detail of the dinosaur's toes. These were probably left by a plant-eating sauropod dinosaur, like the apatosaurus, which was 60 feet long and weighed 30 tons. The hind feet of these dinosaurs measured one yard in length and three-quarters of a yard in width. This particular trail gave scientists a better idea how dinosaurs stood and moved.

In 1938, Roland T. Bird was in Texas looking for dinosaurs and other fossils when he discovered the Glen Rose Trackway. The trackway was partially underground and underwater. It was excavated in three sections. You can see part of it at Dinosaur Valley, but the others are at the University of Texas and the Smithsonian Institution.

There are two fiberglass models in the state park, a 70-foot apatosaurus and a 45-foot Tyrannosaurus Rex. Both were built under the commission of the Sinclair Oil Company for the New York World's Fair Dinosaur Exhibit of 1964–1965. Also in the park is a portion of the Texas longhorn herd—living, of course.

Dinosaur Valley State Park is on Park Road 59, off Farm to Market 205. Call 800-792-1112 for park information and 512-389-8900 for camping reservations. Because of the tracks' locations, call about water levels before you visit the park. There are seven miles of trails you can take on foot, bike, or horse, with 22 backpacking campsites nearly six miles into the wilderness. Campsites equipped with water and electricity are available.

A nearby spot to see is the Creation Evidence Museum, which includes artifacts and fossil displays, acrocanthosaurus bones, dinosaur footprint casts, and more. From Dinosaur Valley State Park, go four miles west on U.S. Highway 67, then take Farm to Market 205. Call 254-897-3200 for more information. There is a video presentation every hour and monthly lectures.

San Angelo

Take a look at San Angelo State Park where you can see another track location in Texas. The park has dinosaur tracks and Indian petroglyphs. It is located on the shores of O. C. Fisher Reservoir, next to the city of San Angelo, in an area of West Texas known as Concho Country because of the Concho River. Mostly an undeveloped park, archaeological findings there indicate 18,000 years ago Native Americans occupied the area. Traces of Indian civilizations start with the Paleo-American hunters of giant Ice Age mammals and end with the defeat of the Comanches in 1874. Spanish exploration in the 1500s and the establishment of missions in the 1600s, were followed by German immigrants in the 1800s.

Camping and picnicking are some other favorite things to do in the park. Or try hiking, mountain biking, and horseback riding on the multi-use trails. Swim, fish, or boat in the lake. Gem hunting is another popular activity. The name *Concho* means "shell" in Spanish, and it comes from the plentiful freshwater mussels that inhabit the area's rivers. The mussels produce beautiful gems of all sizes and colors, especially purple ones called "Concho pearls" by Spanish explorers. Also in the park, you can find 350 species of birds and about 50 species of mammals.

To reach the park from San Angelo, take U.S. Highway 67 south to Farm to Market 2288 to the south shore park entrance or U.S. Highway 87 north to Farm to Market 2288 south to the

Discover Days of the Dinosaur

north shore entrance. Nearby is Fort Concho, a restored historic fort. For park reservations, call 512-389-8900.

Austin's Zilker Park

Austin's Zilker Park has crisscrossing theropod trackways. The tracks were made by dinosaurs smaller than the ones at Dinosaur Valley State Park. The area in the park where the trackways are located is easy to find. After entering the park from Barton Springs Road, park at the visitors center, and follow the signs through the rose garden to the chain link fence. Follow the dirt path along the fence to the gate. This is the old quarry area. The trackways are on the bedding planes of the limestone that forms the floor of the quarry.

Access to the trackways is by guided tour only, with tours given by local amateur paleontologists on Saturday mornings. The maker of the tracks has not been identified. You can see a great number of individual claws marks and foot pads. Zilker Park may have been a popular spot for dinosaurs 100 million years ago. Ask your guide to point out the rumored evidence of a theropod attacking a turtle. A turtle skeleton was found when the trackways were being excavated. The actual bones have been removed and a cast occupies their place in the quarry. There isn't a telephone number specifically for Zilker Park. Try the Austin Parks and Recreation Department at 512-477-7273 if you need more information.

Fall

44

Enchanted Rock

EL PASO AREA

ROCK CLIMBERS CAN FIND QUITE A FEW AREAS IN TEXAS TO
challenge their thirst for excitement. One of the more beau-
tiful climbs may be in Enchanted Rock State Natural Area
where the Indians claim to have seen ghost fires at night.
Hueco Tanks State Historical Park and Franklin Mountains
State Park are good places for climbing in the El Paso area.
Other parks climbers might want to try including Caprock
Canyon and Mineral Wells Lake State Park.

Enchanted Rock State Natural Area on Big Sandy Creek,
north of Fredericksburg, is a huge, pink granite boulder that
rises 425 feet above ground and covers 640 acres. It is the
second largest "batholith," an underground rock formation
uncovered by erosion, in the United States. The park is open
to technical and rock climbing, as well as geological study.
Rock climbers must check in at headquarters where you can
pick up route maps and climbing rules.

The park's name was given by the Tonkawa Indians who
believed the rock was enchanted. The Tonkawa believed
ghost fires flickered at the top. Indians also heard strange
creaking and groaning, which geologists now say resulted
from the rock's heating by day and contracting in the cool
night. In the early 1700s, the Spanish began exploring the
Hill Country area where Enchanted Rock is located. A

Spanish conquistador contributed to legends Indians held about the rock. Captured by the Tonkawa, the conquistador escaped by hiding in the rock area, leading the Indians to believe he was swallowed by a rock. The conquistador himself felt he joined the spirits of Enchanted Rock when he spent his night in hiding.

You can join the spirit of Enchanted Rock as you climb. The park has a hiker's campground and there are places for vehicles. Around the rock you will find oak woodland and mesquite grassland. In the spring, bluebonnets, Indian paintbrush, yellow coreopsis, bladderpod, and basin bellflower bloom. Like most areas of Texas, you can see armadillos, squirrels, and white-tailed deer. The park is 18 miles north of Fredericksburg on Ranch Road 965. Mild fall and spring temperatures make it a popular place at those times of the year. The summer highs are just below 100 degrees.

To climbers, the Franklin Mountains are more than a scenic backdrop to the city of El Paso. The range is a well-preserved mountain climbing region open to the adventurous. The Franklin Mountains were saved from development after investors proposed building roads through the range 20 years ago. The state legislature swiftly stopped any road construction when they passed legislation to protect the range. It is the largest city park in the nation, covering 37 square miles. Even though the entire park lies within city limits, wildlife flourishes there. Golden eagles, hawks, and falcons rule the skies by day, with bats and owls taking over at night. The Franklin Mountains, which overlook the Rio Grande, are at the northern end of the Pass del Norte, a pass between what is now Mexico and America. The mountains were also home for Indians, who left pictographs on boulders in rock shelters.

In the future, the park plans to include more than a hundred miles of hiking trails with half also open to mountain bike traffic, and more than 20 miles for horseback riders. Rock climbing is new to the park, which has a limited number of tent sites for campers. There are no ground fires allowed, and no water or electricity in the park. No motorized vehicles are allowed on any dirt roads or trails. The Franklins are the largest mountain range in Texas with the summit of North Franklin Peak rising to an elevation of 7,192 feet above sea level, with 3,000 feet of the peak rising above the city below. On the eastern flank of The Franklin Mountains are the remnants of the only tin mining, milling, and smelting operation in America. The mining operation was open from 1910 to 1915. The area is in the northern Chihuahuan Desert with lechuguilla, sotol, ocotillo, yucca, and cactus common in the landscape.

To get there take Interstate 10 west to the Canutillo/Trans-Mountain Exit, turn toward the mountains, and the park is located about four miles east of Interstate 10. The temperature during winter months is fairly mild, ranging from 32 to 60 degrees. Summer temperatures range from 68 to 95 degrees. Spring and fall are the busiest times for the park. For more details, call the park's office at 915-566-6441.

Rock climbing at Hueco Tanks State Historical Park has been popular for years. Located 32 miles northeast of El Paso, the park is named for the large natural rock basins, or "huecos," that collected rainwater for people in this West Texas desert. Thirsty riders and horses on the Butterfield Overland Mail Route took advantage of this water source. You can see the ruins of an old stagecoach station in the park.

Climbers at Hueco Tanks also can see rock art—from archaic hunters and foragers of thousands of years ago, to the more recent Mescalero Apaches and other Native Amer-

Enchanted Rock

icans. Strange mythological designs with human and animal figures are dominant in this ancient art. Guided tours are given in the park on weekends. The lowest point in the park is 4,500 feet and the highest point is 4,800 feet. You can camp in the park, but no fires are allowed. Much of this region is so dry it could easily catch fire. You will find the climate, terrain, and wildlife similar to the Franklin Mountains area.

At Caprock Canyon State Park the trails range from very difficult with rugged terrain to easier trails with less than 1 percent grade. However, many of the trails include cliffs and drop-offs with steep climbs and descents. Heading down into the canyon includes many steep grades. The trails and rocks in Caprock Canyons are the big attraction. The view from the top of the canyon is breathtaking, but the hike there may be agonizing to the young ones. If they complain, just let them know there are almost 90 miles of hiking, biking, and equestrian trails, including a 64-mile trail that used to have railroad tracks. That trail stretches from the park through Floyd, Briscoe, and Hall counties. The trail runs through Clarity tunnel, the last active railroad tunnel in Texas. Caprock Canyons camp sites on the canyon floor do not have facilities, but the Honey Flat camping area on the canyon rim has facilities. This may be an incentive for the young ones to walk back up after running down.

Caprock Canyon State Park is geologically similar to Palo Duro State Park with canyons etched into the caprock by seasonal streams. The canyons expose red sandstone, siltstones, and shale that are about 200 million years old. The bright red sediments are also laced with white gypsum. The canyons were home for Indians, including the Folsum culture of more than 10,000 years ago. African aoudad sheep, deer, raccoons, coyotes, bobcats, opossums, porcupines, and foxes all live in the canyon. A herd of pronghorn antelope, the largest herd of buffalo in the state park system, and the rarely seen golden eagles also live in Caprock Canyons.

There is a group lodge with a kitchen, a rustic bunkhouse with 10 beds, a stove, a refrigerator, heating and air-conditioning, restrooms, showers, a picnic table, and a barbecue grill. The lodge is in a shaded area on a cliff overlooking Lake Theo. The park is three and a half miles north of State Highway 86 in Quitaque, a spot in the road with a population of about 500, on Farm to Market 1065. Caprock Canyon is about an hour and a half south of Palo Duro Canyon. You could see both canyons in the same weekend, but Palo Duro is not a place to go rock climbing.

Lake Mineral Wells State Park and Trailway is located four miles east of Mineral Wells on U.S. Highway 180. Rock climbers and rappellers must check in at headquarters. The terrain consists of hilly, varied soils broken by Brazos and Trinity tributaries. Wildlife there includes white-tailed deer, turkeys, raccoons, ducks, birds, and squirrels.

For reservations at all state parks, call 512-389-8900. For more details, call the state park information at 800-792-1112.

Enchanted Rock

45

Safari on Texas Terrain

North Central Ranches

EVER DREAM OF GOING ON A HUNTING SAFARI IN THE WILD country of Africa? You can fulfill that dream without ever leaving American soil. Try it Texas style in areas that could be the wilds of Africa. Texans are hunting experts with hunting as one of the state's biggest recreational activities.

Hunting leases are advertised in every Texas newspaper, for all kinds of wild game to hunt on thousands of acres. But for a unique hunting experience try one of Texas' exotic ranches with free ranging herds and a chance to take some very unique trophies.

Most ranches are under a game management program and breed high quality exotic or native wildlife. Game animals from other continents can be found with a great chance of trophy quality. Ranches do charge for the type of animal you take and prices vary. Taxidermy services and butchering are provided by some ranches. Most ranches also have freezer space for you to use. And if you don't hunt for the meat, ranchers will make sure the meat goes to one of the many Texas agencies that distribute it to the needy.

Hunt blackbuck antelope along with your white-tailed deer in the fall, or try your hand at turkey hunting in the fall or spring. Try hunting on more than 11,000 acres with free-ranging herds to chase. Mountainous, rugged, or open country can be found with ready facilities and guides. You can conquer valleys, grassy meadows, and forests or the oak-covered hills of North Central Texas. You can hunt with rifle, bow, black powder, or handgun on most ranches. A valid hunting license can be purchased at most convenience stores. A license is necessary for whatever you are hunting, including varmint. Check Texas State Guidelines available at all stores that sell licenses.

Have you ever wanted to hunt an American bison, a Marchor goat, or a big bull elk? Whatever you are after, you will see more game on these ranches than any other place in Texas. Watch and listen as an experienced guide calls in the elk. Hunting on these ranches isn't easy, but exciting fair chase hunts on foot, safari style, or in a stand await you. A combination of open pasture and thick brush offers escape cover for animals and a challenge for hunters.

If you go away empty-handed, some ranches will only charge for the guides and lodging. Lodging can range from first class with all the comforts to very rough with only the bare essentials. Lodging can range from cabins for groups to single rooms for one or two. Most ranches require 50 percent down with reservations and it may be nonrefundable.

Texas is famous for its lineup of varmints. While you are hunting at your stand you may see bobcat, coyote, mountain lion, ringtail cat, raccoon, fox, skunk, and jackrabbit. You can hunt varmints any time of the year. Ask those running the ranch if there is any reason why you can't try your luck at catching one. Most places should let you take these with little or no charge.

This sport has become very popular as hunters try exotic game ranches in Llano, Burnet, and Blanco Counties. You can see exotic deer, antelope, elk, and zebra from the road on many of these ranches. But in Texas there may be 5 million white-tailed deer and Llano County is called "The Deer Capital of Texas." You can spot herds of deer in open fields as you drive down the road. Hunting leases are available, but if you want a deer lease, be sure to reserve well in advance of hunting season.

For more information, contact Texas Outfitters LTD., P.O. Box 180, Christoval, TX 76935. The Outfitters owns and leases ranches in North Central Texas and is located approximately 60 miles northwest of Fort Worth, Texas; North Texas Outfitters with Craig A. Wood, 940-683-5174, or Paul Cantrell, 940-644-5356; Ryno Hunting Service in Kerrville welcomes the family even if not all of the family wants to hunt, 830-792-3385; for a southern location try Southern Safaris in Ingram, 800-488-GAME.

Other exotic ranches include Total Outdoors Adventures, contact Dave Fulson in Fort Worth, 817-461-6129; Hill Country Adventures, contact Roger Dillard in Boerne, 830-816-1763; or La Media Sportsman's Ranch, contact Kris Kallina, Linn, 956-845-6600. La Media is close to Mexico and South Padre Island. The Lodge overlooks a 10-acre lake and a natural, free-flowing hot tub in the front yard is fed by an artesian spring steady year-round at 80 degrees. The Cantina located on the ranch overlooks the lake and has become famous for its "Glacier Margaritas."

If you are looking for a chance to view exotics but are not a hunter, there are places you need to visit. You can learn more about the endangered cheetahs or zebras while touring Fossil Rim Wildlife Center in your own car. Or you can go behind the scenes on a guided tour to see what the center is doing to help endangered species.

More than 1,100 animals roam free across 2,700 acres of hills and Africanlike savannas. Home to 14 endangered species, the center participates in breeding programs for animals such as cheetahs, black rhinos, and Mexican wolves. You can feed and photograph animals that are roaming freely along the nine-mile drive.

Overnight accommodations are available. There is a chance to pet animals in the petting pasture. Take a walk on a nature trail, learn more in the education center, or enjoy horseback trail rides and an overnight camp. The Foothills Safari Camp is a three-day, two-night safari you can take part in, but you must make reservations. Fossil Rim is located off U.S. Highway 67, just three and a half miles west. Call 254-897-2960 for more information.

Natural Bridge Wildlife Ranch, another good place to view exotic and native wildlife, is divided into four pastures and a walking safari area. The Ranch is a sanctuary where a variety of native, exotic, and endangered animals thrive and reproduce. The ranch is populated with 65 different species from six continents and the numbers are constantly growing and diversifying. Feed and photograph animals from the endangered addax antelope to zebras, and llamas to ostriches. You might see horn-to-horn combat, births, and mating rituals.

The climate and terrain of the Hill Country are similar to the native habitat for many of these animals. At Natural Bridge Wildlife Ranch animals roam freely, live on specially formulated diets, and are constantly monitored. The endangered and threatened species include white rhino, reticulated giraffe, dama gazelle, scarlet macaws, ruffed lemurs, ring-tailed lemurs, addax antelope, jaguar, aoudad sheep, and scimitar horned oryx.

The ranch is located at 26515 Natural Bridge Caverns Road, midway between San Antonio and New Braunfels off Interstate 35. Take Exit 175 to Natural Bridge Caverns Road. Call 830-438-7400 for more information.

46

Riding the Rails

FREIGHT AND FUN

WHEN THE RAILS WERE LAID ACROSS TEXAS much of the state's future was laid with it. Cities grew up around the railroad stops, settlers hastened the job of taming the Wild West, and Indians were pushed from their land. This new means for transporting goods depended on a booming economy to grow. Throwing track down in West Texas where land is flat was fairly quick. Crews saw the remains of abandoned homes where settlers had been forced out by Indian attacks, but crews were not attacked.

Before the Civil War, construction of railroads proved essential to cross the vast spaces around Texas, but the beginning of railroad development was slow. The first line built in Texas covered 20 miles from Harrisburg to Stafford's Point in 1853. Less than 500 miles of track were down by the start of the Civil War. After the war ended, expansion began with an additional 2,500 miles laid down by 1880. The 1880s proved to be a good decade for the railroads and total Texas miles tripled. In 1881, track gangs laid down more than 1,500 miles. Rail miles peaked at the height of the Great Depression with just over 17,000. The number of miles has dwindled over the years to around 12,000 today.

While you still have to stop to wait for passing trains at railroad crossings and can count the number of commercial cars attached, trains also serve another more pleasurable purpose. Many like to plan vacations around using rail transportation or take the train for the sheer pleasure of the ride and the passing view.

One of Texas' best pleasure runs is the Hill Country Flyer's trek through the hills for which it was named. You begin the trip at Austin's Cedar Park at the corner of Highway 183 and Farm to Market 1431. This restored steam locomotive and cars of the Austin & Texas Central Railroad will take you on a 66-mile round-trip through some of Texas' prettiest countryside. The rough and rocky land has been home to hunters and ranchers for a century and a half. It is a source of granite, limestone, and marble, which in the early 1880s lured the railroad to locate the route you can take today.

The Austin & Northwestern line was built from Austin to Burnet in the 1880s. It branched out to include Marble Falls, Llano, and Lampass in its reach. Passenger trains served these towns until the 1930s, but these lines most frequently paved the way to Hill Country pink granite, used in the construction of the state capitol. The rails are currently owned by the City of Austin and Capital Metro.

The Hill Country Flyer runs every weekend to Burnet. Get to the train station at least 20 minutes before departure. The train takes two hours to get to Burnet where there is a three-hour layover before the two-hour return trip. There are several places to eat, but packing a picnic lunch may be a good idea. There is an open air theater just a few blocks from the train station in Burnet. About an hour before the train departs town the local theater group puts on an Old Western style shoot-out re-creating the last days of Billy the Kid.

You can travel first class or coach class on the Flyer and prices vary between the two. First-class riders sit in newer, air-conditioned cars while the coach-class passengers ride in vintage cars and get to feel a breeze. With the windows open to let in the sounds of the train you may find yourself transported back in time. If you are looking for a shorter ride, you can take a two-hour excursion to Liberty Hill and back with hors d'oeuvres, musical entertainment, and drinks. Sometimes the Flyer runs a Twilight Flyer, a short evening trip complete with wine and cheese. Some runs include a murder mystery, but you need to call for the schedule of events. In 1997, the Austin & Texas Central RR kicked off a new downtown, weekday charter service. For information, call 512-477-8468.

The Flyer's steam engine, Southern Pacific #786, hauled passengers and freight in Texas and Louisiana for 40 years before retirement in 1956. For nearly 40 years afterward it was displayed in an Austin park. The Austin Steam Train Association began a two-year restoration effort in 1989. The 143-ton Mikado type engine was built by the American Locomotive Company in 1916. It was one of 57 locomotives of its class, and one of 5 that survived the scrap pile in the 1950s. Three stayed in the Texas cities of Victoria, San Antonio, and Austin while two went to Louisiana.

In 1986, the City of Austin acquired 163 miles of railroad line being abandoned by the Southern Pacific. While the Hill Country Flyer runs down these lines, the line also is in daily use by the Longhorn Railway for diesel-powered freight service. When the city obtained control of the track, it was easy to put together the dream of a pleasure cruise across miles of undeveloped land with rough hills, wildlife, and wildflowers in the spring. The Hill Country route begins at Cedar Park. The track runs up the cedar and oak wooded valley of the South San Gabriel River. The train crosses that stream on a spectacular trestle. The train climbs 500 feet to the top of the valley before dropping down a steep grade into the town of Burnet. Townspeople got together to provide the depot there.

Riding the Rails

The Flyer's heavyweight coaches, typical of the steam engine era, were built for the Pennsylvania Railroad in the 1920s. The train may have one or more special parlor cars of various vintages, leased to the line by ASTA members. In the food coach there is a souvenir section where you can purchase train whistles, T-shirts, and even a video about the restoration of the #786 steam locomotive.

The passenger cars on the Hill Country Flyer reflect passenger railroading of various types, time periods, and parts of the country. The first acquisition, after the locomotive, was a set of seven Pennsylvania Railroad commuter coaches. One had already been transformed into a concession car and five others were fixed up for service.

Next, three sleeper lounge cars came available for lease, each one with four to five bedrooms and lounge or diner area. First, the Eagle Cliff once ran through Austin on the MoPac Texas Eagle. Second, the renamed Red Rock is a Santa Fe car that originally had a barbershop in one compartment. Third, and the farthest from home, is the Nickel Plate City of Chicago, which is probably the only Nickel Plate passenger car still in regularly scheduled service. Last but not least, there is a Santa Fe caboose.

In May 1997, the Flyer weathered a tornado, which lifted its 57,000-pound tender off the ground and turned it upside down. Based on a survey of the damage, the tornado must have made a direct hit on the steam locomotive. The tender had been disconnected from the engine to allow for quarterly inspection of the drawbar. The curtains in the cab of the locomotive were shredded, the smokestack was bent out of shape, and some piping was struck by debris. Workers saw the tornado approaching and fled by car. No one was injured.

Passenger service by train through Texas is also provided by Amtrak. You can take Amtrak trains to reach destinations around Texas. The Texas Eagle takes you to many

Texas cities and beyond the state's borders. The Texas Eagle's route is a 1,300-mile journey from start to finish beginning in Illinois and ending in Texas. You can travel very comfortably with room service provided or go economy class. While all accommodations have windows, you can get a better view of the passing scenery from the Sightseer Lounge car with panoramic windows. There's a children's hour during the day and first-run movies at night, plus full-service dining cars.

Along with the Texas Eagle, you can take the Sunset Limited through Texas as it makes its way between the coasts. In Texas alone, your itinerary includes Houston, San Antonio, and the high country of the Del Norte Mountains where pronghorn antelope, mule deer, and jackrabbits are part of the scenery. For more information on Amtrak's scenic rail routes, call 800-USA-RAIL.

Riding the Rails

47

Ancient Cultures

CADDOAN MOUNDS

WEST OF NACOGDOCHES IN THE PINEY WOODS OF EAST Texas, some mysterious mounds were discovered. These mounds were built by the Caddo Indians beginning in A.D. 800. Caddoan Mounds State Historical Park was established to protect these mounds. In the park are exhibits and interpretive trails through reconstructed Caddoan dwellings. You can see a full-size replica of a Caddoan house built with the type of tools used in their culture. Two temple mounds, a burial mound, a village, and a museum are open to the public on weekends.

The Caddo Indians lived in East Texas for almost 1,000 years before they were driven to Indian Territory in Oklahoma. Today, about 2,000 descendants live in the Anadarko, Oklahoma area. These last links to the ancestors who populated a large part of the country connect the people with their lost culture. The Caddo Indians were one of many tribes who lived in East Texas during the past 12,000 years. Learning to live off the land and adapt to the environment helped these people thrive in Neches Valley.

Before settling down into a village, the early Caddos were wandering hunters and gatherers. Learning how to farm helped the Caddos who settled in East Texas and parts of the Mississippi Valley. After the Caddos moved into Neches

Valley in East Texas, the people took on their own customs. But a peaceful existence was interrupted by the French and Spanish explorers. Later the American settlers pushed the Caddos out of the valley.

The East Texas Caddoan mound builders' customs reflected those of older mound building cultures dating as far back as 1000 B.C. Mound building developed because of the elaborate burial ceremonies of these people. Ceremonial centers have been found along rivers from Georgia to Oklahoma. The largest known ceremonial center is at Cahokia, Illinois, on the Mississippi River across from St. Louis.

While archaeologists are uncertain as to the ancestry of the Caddos, there is evidence to show the culture was influenced by others. A sharp increase in population about 800 A.D. is linked to the introduction of eight-rowed corn, a more nutritious variety. The pressure of population growth and the need for more extensive trade probably led to the expansion of Caddoan culture.

The Caddos were peaceful people leaving no signs of fortifications or weapons. In a social setting however, the community was divided. The inner circle of the village found in East Texas had two temple mounds and a burial mound. An elite ruling class lived and conducted the ceremonial functions of government and religion there. The outer circle of the village had scattered dwellings, shaded work areas, and farming plots for the common class. The Caddos lived in round houses between 25 and 45 feet in diameter. These houses, which looked like beehives, were thatched structures that stayed warm in winter and cool in summer. Fire played a major role in rituals. One inner village structure may have held a perpetual fire.

The Caddos slowly built the mounds we see today, starting with the burial of four to five individuals and building up with ceremonial events during the 400 to 500 years they occupied the area. The size and number of mounds shows

Fall

the wealth of the tribe; building took place when extra labor and resources were available. By the time the village in the state historical park was abandoned, the mound rose to 20 feet and was more than 90 feet in diameter. When the Caddos destroyed a temple they covered the area with dirt. The new temple was built on the same sacred ground. Soil for mound construction was carried in about 40-pound basket loads from pits around the outer circle of the village.

East Texas provided the Caddos with plenty of wild game for food, pelts for clothing, and bones for tools. Trees abundant in the area were used for building homes and temples. Clay was used in pottery pieces found by archaeologists. Stone artifacts reveal some use of tools. The early Caddos probably left the area when buffalo were no longer in East Texas. Evidence shows the early Caddos left in a very orderly manner as they sealed the mounds.

Although gone from the scene, these early Caddos left some of their cultural heritage in East Texas. Much of this heritage remained with the late Caddos until Indians sold their land to new American settlers moving into Texas. However, the late Caddos didn't know what the mounds were used for and did not build mounds. Many Indian cultures are called Caddoan. The Caddos lived in a large region of the United States and had a strong influence on many cultures as their trade networks reached across the nation. But the Caddoan culture preserved in East Texas sheds light on the life of the mound builders.

Even after the early Caddos left their mounds as a lasting reminder, other Caddos continued to farm the area. The late Caddos lived in beehive houses and retained the pottery vessel forms of the earlier culture, but did not have designs as fine as their predecessors. Ceremonial traditions were not as elaborate as the early Caddos'. Most of what is known about Caddos was found in writings of French and Spanish explorers and missionaries. Caddos underwent tremendous change as Europeans arrived in the 1540s. The French and the Spanish fought over the area in the late 17th century. Robert Cavelier Sieur de la Salle failed to establish French control over the Mississippi Valley and died among the Caddos of East Texas in 1686. Three years later, Spain began establishing missions there. The first was Mission San Francisco de los Tejas, located near the Neches River. Spain won the right to the territory in 1763. One group of Caddos were also called Tejas by the Spanish, and from *Tejas* came the name of Texas.

In Spanish documents the Caddos are described as good looking, tall, and friendly. The Spanish did not like the way Caddos tattooed their faces and bodies. The Caddos traded with the French and Spanish, especially for red and blue clothing, jewelry, and liquor. In 1803, the United States purchased Louisiana, and change came quickly. By 1835 Americans wanted more land, so the Caddo groups in Louisiana sold their lands to the United States government and moved to Texas. The next year Texas won its independence from Mexico, and Americans began to settle East Texas in droves. Then the Caddos made their move from East Texas.

In 1834, Amos Andrew Parker, an American traveling along the old Camino Real, paused to investigate Caddoan mounds. Parker wrote in his journal: "I have seen no satisfactory explanation given of the origin and use of these mounds . . . and, at this late stage of the world, their origin and use may never be fully and satisfactorily explained." Many questions about the mounds and the people who built them are unanswerable.

The first archaeologist to investigate the mounds came as early as 1919, but work didn't begin until 1939. Work on the site abruptly ended in 1941 as World War II began. The Uni-

Fall

versity of Texas at Austin archaeological schools, Texas A&M University, and a private archaeological contractor have worked on the site for the past 20 years. Their work revealed concentrations of artifacts and surface cultural features that suggest the village was much larger than originally determined. Those working on the site believe it extends north beyond the old Camino Real.

The volume of information gathered from all investigations at the Caddoan mounds has made an important contribution to the understanding of prehistoric life in East Texas. However, many questions remain unresolved and excavations continue sporadically. To see the park, take State Highway 21 six miles southwest of Alto. For more details, call Park Information at 800-792-1112. Nearby you will find Mission Tejas and the Texas State Railroad State Historical Park. Mission Tejas has a small wooded camping area.

Alto, also near the mounds and home to a couple of bed-and-breakfasts, was established as a stop on the Old San Antonio Road. Located in the redland belt, Alto is a tomato growing center. The town's name comes from the Spanish word for "high." Alto is the highest point between Angelina and Neches Rivers.

Ancient Cultures

48

Take a Trip on Route 66

AMARILLO

WHEN YOU FEEL LIKE RAMBLING, START DOWN A ROAD FROM the past with a colorful history, sleep in an elegant room, and end the trip in the state's second largest canyon. Famed Texas State Highway Route 66 is an attraction for many travelers. Combine Route 66 with some sites between Texola and Amarillo for an interesting excursion. And don't forget one of Texas' most unusual sites: Cadillac Ranch.

From the town of Texola, planted in both Oklahoma and Texas, the way to Shamrock is 14 miles. The trip takes you on parts of Route 66. Once in Shamrock, use the south frontage road, which becomes Business Loop 40 when entering the city, to continue the Route 66 journey. Continue through the city until you reach the U-DROP-INN Restaurant and service station with a tower. It is located at the point where Business Loop 40 intersects U.S. Highway 831. Built in 1936, the U-DROP-INN is an example of art deco and a good place to have a snack.

From Shamrock, you follow Route 66/Business Loop 40 west. When you come up to the Interstate 40 West sign, stay left to continue on Route 66. You will come to a stop sign and be forced to make a left onto the south frontage road of Interstate 40. This is the original concrete pavement of

Route 66. Continue westward, passing through Lela, and check out the infamous Rattlesnake Zoo.

In McLean, follow the curve around the ramp at Exit 143, turn right at Kingsley Street and Route 66. Established in 1901, McLean grew from being just a water well and switch on the Choctaw, Oklahoma, and Texas Railroad to the city it is today. McLean was once called the "uplift city" because of a ladies undergarment factory located there. You should find the Devil's Rope Museum after taking Exit 143 to the right—admission is free. The museum has a large collection of barbed wire artifacts. Also, a collection of old Route 66 memorabilia, including maps, old "66" cafe items, and tourist court re-creations are there. It is open April through October. A restored 1930s Phillips 66 station sits on old westbound Route 66 in McLean and is one of the attractions re-created by the Old Route 66 Association.

The Alanreed-McLean Area Museum has mementos of early settlers of the Texas Panhandle, including the original record book of births from 1901 to 1920 in McLean. Several rooms are furnished in pioneer style. Here you will find community history, as well as the history and records of a German prisoner of war camp of World War II. The museum is located at 117 N. Main Street, 806-779-2731. Murals along Main Street depict the history of McLean. Don't miss the Cactus Inn on the west side of your route.

From McLean, you go to Alanreed next. If you follow the south service road in Alanreed, you can see the state's oldest cemetery and the oldest Baptist church in Alanreed on Route 66. You should pass by a 66 Super Service station and the remains of the Reptile Ranch. West of Alanreed, beyond the Interstate 40 exit ramp, Route 66 becomes unpaved for about one mile. This is part of the infamous 18-mile "Jericho Gap," which was not bypassed until the late 1930s. At times the Gap had mud deep enough to trap a car. If the weather is wet, avoid this remaining piece of the Gap.

There is an interesting piece of Route 66 along rock ledge. Take Exit 124 off Interstate 40 at Jericho, then cross Interstate 40 to the south side and follow the frontage road. From that point Route 66 zigzagged south during the late 1920s. To follow the same route today, you would need to take several different highways and streets. Look for signs.

Your next stop is Amarillo, with Palo Duro Canyon south of Route 66. Information about Palo Duro Canyon is included in Chapter 13.

On South 6th Street in Amarillo, old Route 66 features include the Golden Light Bar and Grill, and the Broncho Lodge at Bell and Route 66. Many antique shops on 6th Street are trying to recapture the old Route 66 days. You may want to find a place to eat dinner after a day of driving or you may want to check into a comfortable place and relax.

A Place to Stay

In historic downtown Amarillo you may want to book a night or two at Auntie's House, a bed-and-breakfast that is a favorite romantic hideaway for residents as well as visitors. Skip and Corliss Burroughs take pride in their home. You will not have too many nights like one in this romantic cottage. The 800-square-foot room has a 16-foot ceiling and a four-poster bed with 10-foot posts. You will have no problem relaxing in the jacuzzi inside the room. Who has to fight over the shower when there are two shower heads and plenty of room? Skip says they worked hard to create a garden surrounding the lodge, which has been chosen as "Yard of the Month" in Amarillo. To top off your stay, Skip suggests flying into Palo Duro Canyon to watch the sunset produce fire on the canyon's red rock walls. Skip, who has a private pilot's license, can make it happen for you. Give Skip and Corliss a call at 806-371-8054. Auntie's House is at 1712 S. Polk Street.

If you are looking for another romantic country setting, try the Country Home in Canyon, 800-664-7636. Ask for Tammy when you call the Country Home, which can be compared to the Waltons' house on the popular 1970s television series. Surrounded by 200 acres, the secluded getaway is a popular spot for weddings, honeymoons, and anniversaries. Party facilities include a barn equipped with a dance floor. Tammy says she hosts 100 weddings a year at her place.

If you aren't getting married and you aren't looking for romance but would prefer a place for the whole family, Tammy's mother, Jonell, has just what you are looking for at Mom's Place Bed and Breakfast. Right across the street, you can find Mom's two acres equipped with a playground for the little ones. Between the two, they can accommodate up to 10.

The historic Hudspeth House Inn at 1905 Fourth Avenue in Canyon was rated one of the 10 best inns in Texas by *Southern Living Magazine.* Owners Mark and Mary Clark can be reached at 800-655-9809. Hudspeth House, built in 1909, was where artist Georgia O'Keeffe took her meals when working on her paintings of Palo Duro Canyon.

Dubbed "the Hood Ornament of Route 66" by one of its creators, Cadillac Ranch gained the nation's attention when first built in 1974. It has continued to be a favorite stop along the road for many tourists. Ten Cadillacs buried nose-down in concrete, at the angle of Cheops' pyramid, break the monotony of ranch land. The models are from 1948 to 1964, representing the Golden Age. The creation was a collaboration between Amarillo's eccentric emeritus Stanley Marsh and a San Francisco–based designers' collective called the

Fall

Ant Farm. Together they created this American icon, Cadillac Ranch, with its tail fins silhouetted against the Panhandle sky. It is 24 years old and starting to rust severely. Cadillac Ranch became a national symbol practically from the moment of its birth in a wheat field, which was its inspiration. Ant Farm designers watched the wheat form waves in the wind and thought of dolphin fins, which turned into Cadillac fins.

In 1970, Marsh had undertaken his first major pop art project, building what he called "the world's largest soft pool table" on a farm outside Amarillo. The Ant Farm constructed its "house of the century" in Houston, which resembled a "praying mantis eating a Volkswagen," according to Marsh.

The location of Cadillac Ranch was just off Route 66 at that time. Today it is on Interstate 40. Marsh provided the land, food, and accommodations for Ant Farm designers. Marsh said the car is what makes America great because it represents freedom. Photographer Wyatt McSpadden and the late Don Reynolds captured the creation of the Cadillac Ranch. Austinite McSpadden repeatedly photographed the Cadillac Ranch since its birth. Stop by and shoot your own photograph; you won't be the only one.

Some unusual facts about Amarillo are (1) it is the world's leading helium producer, and (2) the city's first settlement in 1887 was a buffalo-hide-tent camp of railroad construction workers. Today, it has much more to offer. Check out some of the following sites during your visit.

- The Helium Monument at 1200 Steit Drive is a six-story stainless steel Time Column erected in 1968 to commemorate the unusual natural element found near Amarillo.

- The Amarillo Art Center is a complex of three buildings that were designed by Edward Stone, who also designed

Take a Trip on Route 66

the Kennedy Center in Washington, D.C. Devoted to fine arts, music, and drama, the Art Center combines exhibition space with teaching areas. The Center has permanent collections of paintings and sculpture, plus regular performing arts. It is located at 2200 Van Buren Street.

- The American Quarter Horse Association is the headquarters for the world's largest equine registry with more than 2.6 million horses registered. The quarter horse was the first American horse breed and is still the cowboy's favorite. You will find the Association on Interstate 40 at Nelson Street Exit.

- The Cowboy Morning Dinner is in operation from April to October. You can join groups for an Old West style chuckwagon breakfast on the open range. Feast on scrambled eggs, ranch sausage, sourdough biscuits, brown gravy, and campfire coffee. Or you can have a dinner of steak or hamburgers with all the trimmings. Enjoy a wagon ride, and watch real cowboys roping and branding. Make reservations at the city visitors center, 1000 Polk Street. For information you can call the Amarillo Convention and Visitor Council at 806-374-1497.

- The Don Harrington Discovery Center at 1200 Steit Drive has plenty to offer everyone in the family. In the center of a 51-acre park with lake and picnic area, this museum is full of hands-on activities. "Aquariums of the World" features fish from exotic waters. There's the Black Hole and Giant Kaleidoscope, and the planetarium has star shows.

- The Harrington House, a 1914 Neoclassical house at 1600 S. Polk Street, has fine French and English furniture, porcelain, crystal, silver, carpets, and paintings.

- Old San Jacinto, situated in Amarillo's first downtown, along the route of old U.S. 66, is a cluster of shops with antiques, art, restaurants, crafts, small theaters, and boutiques. The area is on Sixth Street between Georgia and McMasters.

- Storyland Zoo is a playground and zoo with themes from children's stories. The zoo's animals are those that appeal to youngsters. Open daily in Thompson Park at NE 24th Street and U.S. Highway 287.

- Wonderland Park is Texas' fourth largest amusement park with 21 rides, miniature golf, arcades, bumper cars, Big Splash log flume, Fantastic Journey spook house, Raging Rapids water slide, Texas Tornado double loop roller coaster, and food concessions. Open daily Memorial Day to Labor Day, and weekends from April to May, it is located off U.S. Highway 287 North, on NE 24th Street.

Amarillo is headquarters for an immense ranch and cattle feed-lot area. Each year more than 600,000 cattle move through the auction ring at Western Stockyards at 100 S. Manhattan. For a look at everyday Amarillo life, stop by the stockyards to see what Texans do for a living.

Take a Trip on Route 66

49

The Big Thicket

BEAUMONT

TUCKED IN PINEY WOODS ON THE NECHES RIVER, BEAUMONT was first discovered by French and Spanish explorers. The town started with the lumber industry in 1837, but boomed with the discovery of oil in 1901. Just 30 miles upstream from the Gulf of Mexico, location and warm weather are two reasons to visit Beaumont.

A fair-sized city of more than 100,000 people, Beaumont has 19 museums within city limits and has been dubbed the Museum Capital of Texas. Besides indoor attractions, you can still enjoy the woods surrounding the city in the Big Thicket. If you like to picnic outdoors, Beaumont has 35 parks. The largest is Tyrrell Park, located just off Fannett Road, with an extensive garden center and nature trail with native plants. In downtown, you can visit Riverfront Park for a panoramic view of the Neches River and the Port of Beaumont. If picnics aren't what you want, Beaumont has 200 restaurants with the local Cajun flavor and fresh seafood on the menu along with traditional Texan items such as barbecue and steaks.

While Beaumont is a great getaway, it is easy to find at the crossroads of Interstate 10 and several state highways, 90 miles east of Houston and 25 miles from the Louisiana border. Beaumont is not exactly a sleepy little river city. To take in a panoramic view of harbor action, try surveying the sights from the Harbor Island Transit Warehouse observation deck. Beaumont has many malls to shop in or you can try the Old Town District where there are specialty shops with fashions, antiques, decorative interiors, jewelry, and more.

The Beaumont Civic Center and Julie Rogers Theatre for the Performing Arts are sites of many downtown cultural activities. The Julie Rogers Theatre, a 1,700-seat performing arts center, is the home of Beaumont's opera, symphony, and ballet. The Jefferson Theatre, a restored movie and vaudeville house, plays host to the Beaumont Community Players. You can listen to the sounds of the Beaumont Symphony Orchestra from September to May or see a performance by Beaumont Civic Opera, Beaumont Civic Ballet, or Beaumont Ballet Theatre.

A boat ride on the Neches River can take you winding through the city's east end and through the Big Thicket National Preserve. The Gulf of Mexico and miles of beach are less than an hour's drive away. If you are a hunter, then you will appreciate the wet climate that attracts duck and other wild game. If you are going to Beaumont for a weekend, you should plan to reserve half your time for the Big Thicket.

Exploring the Big Thicket can be done with a canoe or on foot. You can easily find river rides, swamp tours, canoe expeditions, and camping. Plan on wearing comfortable shoes for walking, so you can experience the area up close. The 86,000-acre preserve is where eight ecosystems converge to make up what scientists refer to as a biological crossroads, with thousands of animal and plant life forms, from alligators to zygospores. The eastern hardwood

Fall

forests, the southern coastal wetlands, the western prairies, and the arid terrain of the Southwest converge in the preserve.

Rain averages 55 inches a year, combined with temperatures up to 95 degrees in the summer. High humidity is a typical weather condition. Considering the weather, September through May is the best time to see the preserve. A visitors center has information about the park. There are nine trails ranging in length from a quarter mile to 18 miles, with bicycles and horses only allowed on the Big Sandy Trail. Allow one mile per hour hiking time on most trails; heavy rain can cause floods. Wildflowers can be seen from March to October, but bird-watching is best from mid-April to mid-May. The best time for boating, fishing, and canoeing is April to October. Hunting is by permit only from October to mid-January. You can take tours of the Big Thicket in swamp buggies or on a miniature railroad.

A vast expanse of swamp, conifers, palmettos, and abundant wildlife, this lush primordial forest extends through Southeast Texas from the area around Beaumont in the south to the edge of the Pineywoods in the north. Although hiking is good, camping is not pleasant because of marshy ground and mosquitoes. Heavy releases of water from Steinhagen Reservoir can flood sandbars, which are used as campsites along the Neches River. Also, watch out for three poisonous snakes making their home in the preserve—cottonmouth, copperhead, and coral.

One feature of the preserve you should not miss is the carnivorous plants like pitcher, sundew, bladderwort, and butterwort. You can watch pitcher plants devour wasps. Another attraction in the park is the Alabama-Coushatta Indian Reservation on the western edge of the Thicket. Open to visitors, the reservation has a museum, tribal ceremonies, camping, fishing, swimming, and restaurant with

The Big Thicket

traditional Native American foods on the menu. For more information about the Big Thicket and the reservation, call 409-246-2337.

The Museum Capital of the World

Check out these great museums. Each has something unique to offer.

- Art Museum of Southeast Texas at 500 Main in Beaumont, 409-832-3432. Texas artists are featured in a permanent collection of mostly paintings and sculptures.

- Babe Didrikson Zaharias Museum is at 1750 Interstate 10, or Exit 854; call 409-833-4622. The life and times of the world's greatest female athlete, Mildred "Babe" Didrikson Zaharias, are chronicled in this museum. Exhibits include awards and medals from her athletic career.

- The Fire Museum of Texas is at 400 Walnut; call 409-880-3927. This museum devoted to the history of firefighting is housed in an early 20th-century fire hall. The museum displays firefighting equipment, machinery, and fire department memorabilia to show advances in firefighting techniques from 1779 to the present.

- The John Jay French Museum is at 2975 French Road. This restored 1845 home serves as an example of the simple Greek Revival style prevalent in Beaumont at the time. While telling the story of the French family who originally lived in the home, it also documents the history of East Texas settlers.

- The McFaddin-Ward House at 1906 McFaddin Avenue, 409-832-2134, is an example of Beaux Arts Colonial-style architecture. The 1906 home exhibits the lifestyle of one of the wealthiest families in Southeast Texas. The house has original furnishings, including elegant porcelain, fine Oriental rugs, and antique furniture. Reservations are recommended and no children under eight are allowed.

- Spindletop and Gladys City Boomtown Museum, University Drive at U.S. Highway 69, is on the Lamar University campus; call 409-835-0823. This is the town that sprang up overnight when the Spindletop well started gushing in January 1901. The town, which disappeared just as quickly, is re-created using structures that are representative of the era, including a post office, blacksmith shop, saloon, photographer's studio, and wooden oil derricks. Also, you can see a 58-foot granite monument dedicated to the Lucas Gusher.

- Texas Energy Museum at 600 Main, 409-833-5100, has earned high regards from the Smithsonian Institution because of its comprehensive collections that trace the evolution of the petroleum industry from Spindletop to modern times. Its exhibits are enhanced by multimedia, so you can see and hear rig sounds, motion, and light. The museum brings the history of the oil industry to life by full-size, authentic looking, moving, and talking mechanical figures of historical characters.

- Anthony Lucas, a main character in the building of Beaumont, was Austrian-born and had been educated at the Polytechnic Institute in Graz. He theorized that some elevated mounds of the Gulf Coast region were natural reservoirs of petroleum. On January 10, 1901, when the

The Big Thicket

Spindletop oil field stunned onlookers as oil shot 200 feet into the air, Lucas was the proud creator of a well that could produce up to 100,000 barrels a day. The Spindletop wells could produce more oil in one day than the rest of the fields in the world combined at the time.

- The Edison Plaza Museum lays claim to the largest collection of Thomas Edison artifacts west of the Mississippi. Art museums include the Art Museum of Southeast Texas; the Art Studio, Inc.; the Beaumont Art League; Brown and Scurlock Galleries; and the Dishman Art Gallery. Another site of historical interest is the Tyrrell Historical Library with its vast archives and genealogical records.

- The Beaumont Police Department Museum has a collection of guns and unusual weapons that were used to commit crimes, along with law enforcement memorabilia dating back to the turn of the century. The Eye of the World Museum houses a unique display of hundreds of separate wood carvings depicting scenes from the Bible and Ancient Greece. For more information about these sites and others, contact the Beaumont Convention and Visitors Bureau at 801 Main, Suite 100, or call 800-392-4401.

50

Down-Home Country

TEXARKANA

FROM SCOTT JOPLIN'S RAGTIME TO JANICE JOPLIN'S SOUL-
screeching blues, from barbecue beef to Cajun style seafood,
from Pineywood forests to sandy beaches, East Texas is
down-home country you can relax in. Start at the northern
end of the state with the city of Texarkana, which has a foot
in two states, Arkansas and Texas. End the East Texas journey in Port Arthur or somewhere between.

Texarkana was home to Scott Joplin, the ragtime piano
player and composer who supplied background music for
the movie *The Sting* starring Robert Redford and Paul Newman. Joplin was born in 1868 near Texarkana to a poor family. Joplin's father was a former slave, and his mother made
sure he studied classical piano as a young boy. In his late
teens, Joplin worked as a dance musician and pianist, traveling throughout the Midwest.

In 1894 Joplin found himself at the Maple Leaf Club, playing for patrons in Sedalia, Missouri. He studied at the
George R. Smith College for Negroes. With the help of a
local merchant, he published his first composition, "Please
Say You Will."

A few years later, the Maple Leaf Club contributed its
name to Joplin's most well-known composition, the "Maple

Leaf Rag." Joplin published some 60 compositions, of which 41 are piano ragtime pieces. He was never acknowledged as a serious composer during his lifetime because he was a black man. Today, Joplin's Texarkana is proud to acknowledge his achievement in a mural on the side of a building at 3rd and Main streets in downtown.

Texarkana also has a claim to another Texas celebrity, billionaire and independent presidential candidate Ross Perot. Attractions to see in Texarkana include the historic Perot Theatre. Ross Perot backed the effort to save the historic theater, which now bears his name. You can see the theater's royal blue interior, chandeliers, and mirrored checkerboard marble lobby. Find out what's on the schedule and enjoy the symphony or a play. It is located at Third and Main Streets.

An unusual attraction in Texarkana is the Draughn-Moore "Ace of Clubs" house. Locally, people say James Draughn won a huge pot in a poker game by playing the ace of clubs. The house, located at 420 Pine Street, is built in the shape of that card. You will see how elegantly the 1884 Italianate-Victorian house is furnished. Opened as a museum, the house underwent extensive restoration to uncover original wall coverings. The coverings, which were not able to be restored, were reproduced. Mahogany treatment on paneling embellished with gold leaf brings back the house's original style. Call 903-793-4831 for additional information.

Texarkana's Regional Art Center is located in the former U.S. District Courthouse at Fourth Street and Texas Boulevard downtown. Built in 1909, the courthouse features ornate plaster, a copper cage elevator, and a 26-foot ceiling in the grand hall. The Texarkana Historical Society Museum is located at 219 State Line Avenue. It has displays with archaeological, pioneer, early medical, and farm tools. The museum's building, built in 1879, was the first brick structure in the city. Union Station at 101 West Front Street was built in 1929, but no longer serves as a train station. The restored building houses a restaurant.

One of Texarkana's big events is the Four States Fair and Rodeo in October. For the photo album, you can take a picture of the family while they are standing in two states at the city's post office. One side of State Line Avenue is in Texas, the other is in Arkansas. Near Texarkana is Crystal Springs Beach, a theme park with rope swings and water slides. As you are leaving Texarkana, you will find one of the state's Travel Information centers located on Interstate 30, west of U.S. Highway 59. These centers are located at a few key entrances to the state. You can find maps and travel guides to the state's attractions there.

Traveling south on U.S. Highway 59, you will pass many small towns before reaching Marshall. You pass the Caddo Lake area near Jefferson on your way. At Marshall, head west on Interstate 20 to Tyler, a favorite for many travelers. Stop by for the Texas Rose Festival held in the middle of October and see the Municipal Rose Garden for an atmosphere guaranteed to rekindle romance. To further the pursuit of a romantic time in Tyler, book a night or two at the Woldort-Spence Manor Bed and Breakfast. Parts of the house were built in 1859. The elegant structure is placed in beautiful surroundings. Small children and pets are not allowed at the Woldert-Spence Manor. For more information, call 800-WOLDERT.

Down-Home Country

Continuing from Tyler, take U.S. Highway 69 south to the Davy Crockett National Forest. Close to the forest is Mission Tejas State Historic Park. You will be surrounded by forested hills and streams as you drive along U.S. Highway 69 and State Highway 21, which take you to Nacogdoches. You can also see Angelina National Forest on Farm to Market 420, off U.S. Highway 69. But don't hike on your own. Guides are necessary to see the forest up close.

Nacogdoches is north of Angelina National Forest on U.S. Highway 59. People there claim to live in the oldest town in Texas. You can see a

Caddoan Mound in the 500 block of Mound Street. The Sterne-Hoya House, 211 S. Lanana Street, is the town's oldest surviving home that has not been reconstructed. It is open to the public. Stop by the park next to Stephen F. Austin State University for a scenic walk on a forested trail along a stream. Stop by the Chamber of Commerce at 513 North Street or call 409-560-5533 for more information about Nacogdoches.

If you continue south on U.S. Highway 59, you will find Houston before the highway turns west and heads for Victoria. If you continue south on U.S. Highway 69 you will find Beaumont, just north of Port Arthur. Port Arthur sprang up in the 1890s with the railroad. Port Arthur has grown from the oil industry and has managed to develop many attractions. The French and Dutch influence are evident in the food and architecture of Port Arthur. The Museum of the Gulf Coast, 700 Procter Street, has exhibits dedicated to rock and roll legends, including Port Arthur's Janis Joplin. It is in a Renaissance-style building originally constructed as a library by the John Gates family.

There are many other places to see, including

- La Maison Acadienne and Dutch Windmill Museum at 1500 Boston Avenue, five blocks west of Twin City Highway in Nederland. The park is dedicated to country music legend Tex Ritter. Among the structures is a 40-foot reproduction of a Dutch windmill housing the star's memorabilia and tracing the history of Dutch settlers in the area.

- Pleasure Island at 520 Pleasure Pier Boulevard, 409-982-4675, is located on an island where pirate Jean La Fitte liked to hide out. It is a 10-acre concert park, marina, beach club, and yacht club. It is a great place to fish, launch a boat, or have a picnic.

- The Pompeiian Villa, 1953 Lakeshore Drive, is an authentic reproduction of a Pompeiian home built by merchant Isaac Ellwood in 1900. The house is furnished with antiques, including a Louis XVI parlor set, Baccarat crystal, a Sheffield candelabra, and a George Hepplewhite dresser from the late 1700s.

- The Queen of Vietnam Church, 801 Ninth Avenue, is a *hoa-binh*, or shrine, built by Vietnamese Catholics in gratitude for their escape from Vietnam, and dedicated to the city that welcomed them. Beautiful gardens and a large statue of the Virgin Mary contribute to the center's dedication to peace.

- Sabine Pass Battleground State Historical Park is in Sabine Pass and can be reached from Port Arthur by taking State Highway 87 south about 14 miles. The park is located in the spot where a small band of Confederate soldiers took on 20 Union vessels with 5,000 men. The one-hour battle ended with an amazing Confederate victory. The park includes a statue of Dowling, a picnic area, and a boat ramp. Sea Rim State Park, also in Sabine Pass, is located on State Highway 87, about 10 miles southwest of Sabine Pass. It is the only marshland park in the state. Also along State Highway 87 is the McFadden National Wildlife Refuge.

51

The Wonder of Whooping Cranes

ROCKPORT

WITH THEIR LONG SLENDER NECKS POINTING THE WAY AND large white wings spanning the sky, the whooping crane takes several weeks to make a 2,500-mile journey annually from Canada to the shores of Texas at Rockport. The Aransas National Wildlife Refuge is the sanctuary on the southern Gulf Coast that attracts the endangered whooping crane and nearly 400 other types of birds. The best way to view these creatures is on a whooping crane tour boat. Many tours leave from the harbors in and around the town of Rockport.

The whooping cranes' story testifies to how delicate nature's balance can be and how tragic the consequences are when it is disrupted. In the 1940s, there were just over a dozen whooping cranes counted by conservationists. A move was afoot to protect the great bird before its existence was completely extinguished. The whooping crane, although a large bird, can be frightened into flying into wires or other obstacles. It needed space to survive and thrive.

In 1937, the refuge north of Rockport was established as a winter home, and their nesting grounds were found in Canada. Sightings were made on nearby St. Joseph Island

and on Welder Flats, which is north of the 55,000-acre refuge. With the seclusion of the refuge and the care provided by the whooping cranes' protectors, the flock has grown to 133. There were 47 pairs of whooping cranes and 25 young in the 1997 stopover. The number was expected to increase to 150 in 1998.

Wildlife officials hope those who see migrating whooping cranes will report the time, place, and other details of the sighting to local officials. This will help them track the migration, health, and numbers of whooping cranes. If you haven't seen one before, the adult is white with black wingtips and a red forehead. Their young have white and rusty brown feathers with black wingtips.

If you spot one in flight, you should see its long neck held straight forward with long black legs extending beyond the tail. Listen for the trumpeting sound that is their distinctive call. Migrating during the day, whooping cranes make regular stops to eat and rest away from people. Sometimes a whooping crane will travel alone. Sometimes you will see them in pairs or in a family. But if whooping cranes are in a flock, look for the common V-shaped flight formation between 2,000 to almost 5,000 feet up. At times, whooping cranes join with sandhill cranes for part of their migration. When the day is done, cranes roost in the shallow water of lakes, ponds, or rivers.

The birds are usually first spotted in the Texas coastal area in November, but the full flock arrives by December. They start their journey back to Canada sometime around March. Aransas National Wildlife Refuge has observation towers for a great view of the birds. You can get a map at the interpretive center. There is a self-guided driving tour with places to stop to walk the trails around some of the ponds. Watch out for another local, the alligator. Generally, it is a good idea to leave alligators alone since there are no fences. Other wildlife to see are deer, javelina, armadillos, sandhill cranes, egrets, and herons. As with most wildlife, the best time to see any of these is in the early morning or near sunset.

The park is 25 miles north of Rockport on State Highway 35. Turn right on Farm to Market 774, then go seven miles to Farm to Market 2040. Follow the signs to the headquarters. For a birder's guide, contact the Rockport-Fulton Area Chamber of Commerce at 404 Broadway in Rockport or call 800-826-6441. Birding assistance can be provided by guides available through the Corpus Christi Guides Association.

South Texas draws thousands of migrants along the Central Flyway. Tropical species from Mexico frequently cross the Rio Grande into the area. The scene changes with the seasons. In the winter you can see birds from as far away as the Arctic staying warm in South Texas. For young and old who love to watch birds, you can earn your official Aransas Pass Birding Patch by finding 15 species on the designated seasonal list.

If you come in November to see the whooping cranes as they arrive, look for 15 from this list: white pelican, northern harrier, white-tailed hawk, red-winged blackbird, eared grebe, pied-billed grebe, double crested cormorant, tricolored heron, white ibis, blue-winged teal, green-winged teal, cinnamon teal, northern shoveler, ruddy duck, osprey, American kestral, sora, greater yellowlegs, sanderling, western sandpiper, long-billed dowitcher, herring gull, laggerhead shrike, savannah sparrow, and black-bellied plover.

If you prefer to wait until March, closer to the end of the whooping cranes' stay, look for birds from the spring list: mockingbird, brown pelican, scissor-tailed flycatcher, roseate spoonbill, cattle egret, barn swallow, yellow-rumped warbler, indigo bunting, northern oriole, red knot, blue-gray gnatcatcher, blue grosbeak, snowy egret, American coot, green heron, willet, western kingbird, cliff swallow, reddish egret, killdeer, ruby-throated hummingbird, Swainson's thrush, Tennessee warbler, great egret, and eastern meadowlark.

To pick up your award patch, bring your list to the Aransas Pass Chamber of Commerce at 452 West Cleveland during business hours. A nominal fee is charged for your checklist and patch. After a day in the great outdoors, you can enjoy some fresh seafood in the town of Rockport. You can even watch the catch of the day being transferred from boat to dock. You can tour the Fulton Mansion, built in 1875, if you knock off bird-watching early enough. The house was a showcase for several inventions like hot and cold running water, toilets, and central heating and air-conditioning. Rockport is also known for a selection of art galleries in the bayfront area. There is the Military Museum with an extensive account of maritime history for the coast, including details of sunken Spanish ships and lost treasure.

Fall

Other Wildlife Viewing Areas

- Goose Island State Park, just off State Highway 35, north of Copano Bay Causeway. You will find good birding in an oak habitat and along the water's edge. Call Goose Island State Park at 512-729-2858 for more information.

- The Audubon Outdoor Club of Corpus Christi celebrates the spring migration with bird walks in Blucher Park in Corpus Christi every Saturday and Sunday morning during April and May.

- Boat trips from Rockport and Port Aransas to see the whooping cranes and other birds are available during the winter; or boat from Rockport to observe rookery islands in the breeding season.

- A 12-mile loop drive on the Santa Gertrudis Division of the King Ranch is open to the public daily, with free maps available at the ranch entrance on State Highway 141 at Kingsville.

- Welder Wildlife Refuge near Corpus Christi offers free tours on Thursday afternoons.

- Other bird activity can be found on bayside marshes between Gregory and Refugio. From State Highway 35 turn onto Farm to Market 136, and go 10 miles to the extensive marshes and mud flats of Copano Bay.

- Hazel Bazemore County Park is a brushy, wooded park on the Nueces River. The entrance from State Highway 624 is a half mile west of State Highway 77 South. You may have a hard time seeing the sign on the right at County Road 69 that marks the way. The photographers' blind at Nature Pond is to the west, and Nature Trail to the east. There are resident, migrating, and wintering birds. You can see bluebirds during the winter and owls, paraque, warblers and other passerines, hummingbirds, and shorebirds. You will find good viewing of spring and fall hawk migrations.

- Choke Canyon State Park is north on Interstate 37, take Exit 69, turn left onto Farm to Market 72, and follow the signs to the entrance. You will find nesting swallows, turkey, caracara, titmice, thrashers, and rock wrens. For more information, call 512-786-3538.

If you sight any whooping cranes during your visit, call the Aransas National Wildlife Refuge at 512-286-3559. You can also call 800-344-WILD to report sightings.

The Wonder of Whooping Cranes

52

Christmas on the River Walk

SAN ANTONIO

THE STATE'S MOST ROMANTIC SPOT HAS TO BE THE RIVER Walk in San Antonio. You can stroll along the water below street level, stop at a restaurant for a meal, shop, or hear live music and dance in any of the nightclubs along the way. Some people compare the River Walk to New Orleans, but you won't find the offensive aspect of New Orleans in San Antonio. You will find an escape from everyday life.

The easiest direction to approach the River Walk is from Interstate 37 to Commerce Street. Commerce Street is a one-way street that will take you to the parking garages of the Marriott and the River Center Mall, which anchor one end of the river. You can sit on the patio surrounding the river and listen to a band comprised of traditional Mexican instruments, or get in line for a boat ride. You can find modern places like Planet Hollywood and the Hard Rock Cafe, as well as places unique to San Antonio like Dick's, a restaurant where waitstaff insults customers for fun, and the Kangaroo Court, an old English pub.

The boat ride takes you on a tour of the most developed part of the river, and guides tell you river trivia on the trip— some interesting facts, and some embellished stories of San Antonio's past. If you believe everything the guides tell you, then you will find bullet holes from 1836 when Texans fought for independence from Mexico. You can take a photograph of an optical illusion that will boggle friends' minds. At just the right angle from the boat one triangular-shaped building along the River Walk appears to be flat.

Guides on boat tours point out the significant landmarks of the River Walk, such as the statue of St. Francis and the small island where many wedding ceremonies have been performed. You can learn the development of the River Walk from its humble beginnings as a tree-lined walkway along the river with one Mexican restaurant, to the maze of shops and restaurants it is today. You will find out the name of the church overlooking the River Walk—the San Fernando Cathedral, a Catholic church started in 1738. Visitors are welcome inside the cathedral to see the beautifully sculpted statutes, ornate stained glass, and Stations of the Cross. San Antonio's beginnings are attributed to the Catholic priests who established missions in the area; the influence of the Catholic church continues.

From the River Center Mall on Commerce you can take Bowie Street to Market Street and see the Tower of the Americas, the Convention Center, Beethoven Hall, and Hemisphere Park. The Tower of the Americas is the most recognizable structure in San Antonio. As you drive on Interstate 37 in San Antonio, you know Commerce Street is near when you see the tower getting closer. Exit left on Commerce and buy an elevator ticket to the observation deck on top of the Tower of the Americas for a great view. There is a revolving restaurant on top, which is a great way to enjoy lunch or dinner.

San Antonio grew up around Spanish missions established along the San Antonio River in the 1700s. The Mission San Antonio de Valero, known as the Alamo, was central to growth in the area. San Antonio has significant sights for a look at history, but it is also full of new sights, such as Planet Hollywood, Hard Rock Cafe, and Six Flags

Fiesta Texas. San Antonio is the tenth largest city in the nation.

The missions established before 1731 are under the care of the National Park Service. You can visit Mission Concepcion, San Francisco de la Espada, San Jose, and San Juan Capistrano. Every Sunday at Mission San Jose a mariachi Mass is celebrated. If you stay only in the River Walk area during your visit, stop by the Alamo. The humble mission was the location of the battle in which a meager force of less than 200 men gallantly fought 7,000 Mexican troops in the Texas War for Independence.

The Spanish and Indian influence of the past has combined with the current Mexican influence from south of the border, and has blended with small pockets of other cultures. The majority of San Antonio's residents are Hispanic and their influence on the city's culture makes dining, shopping, and sight-seeing a rich experience.

El Mercado is known by most shoppers as a great place to find Mexican crafts, clothing, and art at a great price. The atmosphere and prices are comparable to the markets of Mexico. While at El Mercado, stop by Meteaires for a lunch or dinner you won't forget. El Mercado, or Market Square, is close to Interstate 35. Take Commerce Street from the River Center Mall until you run into the square. Turn right, and then left, and look for parking. You will also find handcrafted items and clothing from other countries around the world.

The Institute of Texan Cultures houses exhibits on the ethnic groups that have settled in Texas. The institute is in Hemisfair Park, site of a 1968 World's Fair. Special events sponsored by the Institute include the Texas Folklife Festival. The Institute appeals to both tourists and serious researchers, and was created as the Texas Pavilion during HemisFair '68, but is now part of the University of Texas at San Antonio.

If you haven't figured out what is so special about Texas, you might find the answer in the Institute. You can learn about famous Texans there, at the corner of Bowie Street and Durango Boulevard on HemisFair Park, next to the Tower of the Americas. Call 210-458-2291 to book tours.

The city has a German flavor that might suit your taste buds, quench your thirst, or offer an aesthetically pleasing view. Germans settled in the area in the 1800s, contributing to the city's development. Their impact can be seen in everything from architectural styles to breweries. The King William District has restored historic homes of German immigrants. If you prefer an English-style pub when it's time to relax, the Kangaroo Court on the River Walk is a fun place to eat lunch or dinner outside while listening to live entertainment. It is located in the section where the river forks. It is a great riverside seat for people-watching. Riders in boats will yell and wave to you.

While you are touring breweries, don't forget to stop by the Lone Star Brewery. One of the strangest museums is the Buckhorn Hall of Horns. Hunters will enjoy looking at the Hall's collection of hunting trophies of every imaginable horned creature. Bizarre exhibits, such as fleas dressed in miniature human clothing, are to be found in the Hall of Horns. If you have a good time, include the Hall of Fins and the Hall of Feathers. After those three, you should be ready for the Hertzberg Circus Collection, which documents the development of the Big Top circus. Be sure to see the miniature circus.

Stop by the Chamber of Commerce location on the River Walk and get a map of the Texas Star Trail, a 2.6-mile walking route where you can see 80 historic sites. Then stop in some of San Antonio's more serious museums, such as the Witte Memorial Museum of Natural History and Science.

Fall

The San Antonio Botanical Gardens, including the Lucile Halsell Conservatory, can give you glimpses of living exhibits.

Arts and Crafts

If El Mercado isn't enough to satisfy your craving for crafts, here are some other great places to visit.

Old Ursuline Academy A former convent that houses the Southwest Crafts Center

La Villita An accumulation of quaint adobe buildings that house artisans' workshops, restaurants, and gift shops; located close to the Arneson River Theater by the River Walk

McNay Art Museum Primarily post-Impressionist art, as well as some examples of Diego Rivera, El Greco, and New Mexican Native American art

San Antonio Museum of Art Mexican folk art, mostly from Nelson Rockefeller's private collection

The Instituto Cultural Mexicano Another fun stop, located at HemisFair Park

Guadalupe Cultural Arts Center Works by Chicano artists; a good stop for art enthusiasts

You might prefer live performances instead of wall hangings. Book a seat for the San Antonio Symphony at the grand old Majestic Theater. Be sure to look up at the ceiling, which resembles an indoor mission skyline, complete with peacocks. Another architectural attraction is the Spanish Governor's Palace, a restored 240-year-old structure, built to house the captain of the presidio.

Christmas on the River Walk

If you want to keep on the theme of looking at what is "living" in San Antonio, you should stop at the beautifully landscaped San Antonio Zoo in Brackenridge Park. The zoo has a large collection of snow leopards, and monkeys on Monkey Island. Also in Brackenridge Park is a Japanese garden, theater, aerial skyride, bridle paths, and miniature train ride.

Save the best attraction for last and allow a whole day and night to see it: Sea World of Texas, one of the world's largest marine parks. A walk within the park gardens provides a look at native Texas plants and 16 life-size bronze statues of famous Texans. But you may prefer to see Shamu the killer whale or penguins in their artificial subantarctic home. An addition to the park includes the Lost Lagoon with a wave pool, water slides, a walk-through aviary, and an alligator habitat.

Christmas Along the River Walk is a special ongoing event featuring the candlelit Fiesta de las Luminarias. During the Christmas season, the River Walk is decorated with lights and wreaths. Large trees lining the walkways are covered with multicolored lights. It is easy to get into the Christmas spirit in the evenings on the River Walk in December. The close proximity of shops make it a great place to find gifts. Mass at Cathedral San Fernando or Mission San Jose gives time for reflection on the meaning of Christmas, the year past, and the new year ahead.

Fall

Index

Notes

Notes